Communication and
Social Action Research

Communication and Social Organization
Gary L. Kreps, series editor

Communication and Social Action Research
Joseph Pilotta

Organizational Communication and Change
Philip Salem (ed.)

Ethics and Organizational Communication
Matthew W. Seeger

Conflict and Diversity
*Claire Damken Brown, Charlotte C. Snedeker, and
Beate D. Sykes (eds.)*

Communicating with Customers
Service Approaches, Ethics, and Impact
Wendy S. Zabava Ford

forthcoming

Community at Work: Creating and Celebrating Community
in Organizational Life
Patricia Kay Felkins

Building Divese Communities: Applications of
Communication Research
Trevy A. McDonald, Mark Orbe, and T. Ford-Ahmed (eds.)

Communication and Social Action Research

Joseph Pilotta
The Ohio State University

Jill A. McCaughan
Susan Jasko
John Murphy
Tricia Jones
Liz Wilson
Tim Widmon
Kristin Endress

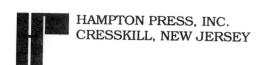

HAMPTON PRESS, INC.
CRESSKILL, NEW JERSEY

Printed in the United States of America

Library of Congress Cataloging-in-Publication Data

Pilotta, Joseph J.
    Communication and social action research / Joseph Pilotta
       p. cm. -- (The Hampton Press communication series)
    Includes bibliographical references and index.
    ISBN 1-57203-305-5 -- ISBN 1-57273-306-3
       1. Community power. 2. Action research. 3. Communication
in politics. I. Title. II. Series

HM776.P56 2000
361.2'072--dc21

                          00-046126

Hampton Press, Inc.
23 Broadway
Cresskill, NJ 07626

Contents

Preface

The purpose of this book is to outline the basic methodological, theoretical, and technical issues in the development and practice of community social action research.

The development of the methodology and the studies were set in the context of attempting to create a program in the Department of Communication at The Ohio State University, *Communication in the Public Interest*, 1981. As the name implies, we believe that Communication Research can serve the public through pedagogy and research with policy payoff.

However, there were few studies and fewer methodologies which were consistent with public interest and truly addressed the political domain of our society. While my orientation was theoretically oriented from the phenomenology of Husserl and Merleau-Ponty, the hermeneutics of Gadamer, the critical theory of Habermas and Marcuse, and the cynicism of the 1970s, that an a priori methodology must efface itself in favor of the subject matter is critical (see *Science of Communication*, 1990, and *Democracy and Technocracy: Some Issues in Political Communication*, 1997, Pilotta & Mickunas).

The concretization of the public interest program as well as our search for a method was created by the Driving Park Project (Chapter 4), which formulated our thematic of *community justice* and set in motion the ongoing "inner" dialectic between methodology/method/and public concern, while there have been several community social action research projects, some 25 in all, we have selected three exemplars demonstrating pertinent issues and practical recommendations. They are pivotal studies for our own development and reflection on developing social action research. The Driving Park Project was our initiation in the world of political research contestation. The Legal Education Project Through Cultural Dialogue with the Case of the New Americans facilitated

ix

the development of our methodological principles, and the Windsor Terrace Profile focused us more clearly in communication and policy issues, thematically reflecting on system and organization issues *qua* communication, and the politics of difference and otherness.

The three studies thematically point up the role community social action research can have, as our orientation was, upon reflection, communication as politics which is founded upon the political covenant of democracy. Like democracy, community social action is not set once and for all, but must be consistently re-won prior to any social contract to make civil sense.

I would like to thank and am indebted to all the co-authors, however they are really to-authorial; so all I can say is thanks for making it through and always being there for the count.

We are indebted to Khari Enaharo, President of the Driving Park, who posed the challenge, or otherwise told us university types, "Put up or shut up." Khari also formed the Urban Consortium at OSU, housed in the Department of Communication, in order to work with 25 other civic associations in Columbus when Khari was Director of Human Services for the City of Columbus, and for spearheading with Dennis Guest, Director of Columbus Metropolitan Housing Association. The Windsor Terrace Project, through a grant from the Department of Housing and Urban Development, backed us all the way through the politics of dealing with vested interest.

Also, the Department of Communication, including Chair James Golden, William Brown, Joe Foley and Brenda Dervin, supported us through turbulent times during the research as we had to manage competing interests and turfdom of several human service agencies, city officials, and university administrators who did not seem to understand the rights of citizens and research to openly engage the political.

Engaging the political now has been referred to as the justice gap or the rethinking of the welfare state under capitalism. In light of globalization, our civil rights to health, education, and employment are placed under the sign of scarcity economics, creating zero-sum solutions, which means our basic civil institutions are in trouble, particularly the political. It appears that another right is placed under the sign of scarcity—the right to communicate. The very civic/political virtues of access and understanding, cornerstones of the political institution, have been placed under the sign of scarcity by academic administrators caught in the rhetoric of marketization of global rankings, and economic "hard choices." Equality of freedom, fairness of efficiency, global rankings, or communication are up for grabs in the administration of public education. Perhaps the academic administration of public education should consult the political in the public.

ONE

Introduction

Many institutions have well-established histories of avoiding public education programs that teach citizens how to act in order to collectively reduce or solve social problems. In doing so, they maintain the illusion of authority in the community and enhance funding opportunities on the basis of numbers of persons served by keeping people returning to obtain services and information over which the institution asserts private ownership. Institutionalized authority becomes, from the perspective of the community, an abstract one, having little to do with community social realities. At the same time, it engenders citizen dependency.

In their experiences with community groups, research associates of the Urban Consortium for Human Services Development (UCHSD) found that citizens are looking for greater responsiveness from public institutions, including concrete community-based assistance for implementing social action plans. What is in question among the citizenry is not the proper scope of public education, but rather the proper role that service institutions and agencies should take in relationship to communities. Increasingly, citizens are seeking to take control of circumstances generating social stress. There are various reasons for this, including the inability of service institutions to provide equitable, effective solutions. In the search for self-sufficiency, however, lack of necessary knowledge and skills often stands as a barrier to community action. This is one point at which public education finds a proper social role: teaching commu-

1

nity organizations methodology and strategies, and a philosophy in some cases, for developing social action plans. The UCHSD is a research group that takes this role. Here we explicate the objectives of this group, outline its approach to social research, and illustrate, through case studies of community enablement projects, the role it plays in the urban communities of Columbus, Ohio.

COMMUNITY ENABLEMENT

The UCHSD is an interdisciplinary group of faculty and graduate students at The Ohio State University, Columbus. Although research associates come from all areas of the social and behavioral sciences, the project itself is part of the Department of Communication, and the Public Interest program. Having conducted community-based research since 1981, starting with the Driving Park Project, the UCHSD was "officially" established in September 1984, when its community enablement activities were funded by Community Development Block Grant monies through a contract with the Columbus Department of Human Services. Criteria for research and technical assistance are, principally, that the community organization (a) serves a low to moderate income constituency, (b) is working on social rather than physical improvement projects, (c) has formal organizational status (including a charter, by-laws, election of officers, and some fiscal responsibility), and (d) is a not-for-profit organization.

In all projects undertaken by the UCHSD, community enablement is the ultimate goal. Some of the organizations with which UCHSD works are neighborhood civic associations, and, therefore, are geographically defined by residents. The UCHSD works with the idea of a community as a network of interpersonal relationships characterized by concern for common interests and problems (e.g., drugs, crime, police). Sometimes, communities are geographically proscribed; sometimes they are not.

Community enablement is a process by which members of community groups develop knowledge, skills, methods, and strategies necessary to formulate social action plans sensitive to citizen-identified problems, which can then be implemented and sustained by the community group. Objectives of community enablement are to broaden the base of participation for addressing common concerns, expand community self-reliance, and promote self-advocacy.

A problem with many community groups is that the same individuals do all the work. This is often due to the tendency of these individuals to be self-selected. Consequently, there is no guarantee that they can garner support for their activities because they may not articulate and negotiate their perceptions of drug addiction, for example, in a given community. Similar methods also allow them to negotiate divergent perspectives, in light of common concerns, for the purpose of coordinating action such as intervention. From the point of view of public education, qualitative methods have yet another practical application for community development. Community members can learn them and may employ them to sustain existing projects and to implement future ones.

Although the strategic details of community enablement projects are negotiated on a case-by-case basis, UCHSD associates follow a general project model. This model consists of the following components:

1. *Gaining an Historical Understanding*: This refers to the starting point for all community-based projects. The researchers want to know the goals and purposes of the community groups and their understanding of the problem for which they are seeking assistance. It also includes research into the ways social scientific communities have sought to explain the problem, and how relevant social service providers typically treat the problem relative to the given community and its cultural composition.

    To gain an adequate historical understanding, UCHSD researchers must also adopt and maintain a reflexive/critical posture toward their own presuppositions relative to community, culture, causes of social problems, theory, methodology, and so on. As O'Neill (1982) notes, reflexivity is, additionally, the means by which "social science knowledge . . . recognizes its ties to individual values and community interest" (p. 111), at the same time guarding against bias.

2. *Solidifying Project Objectives and Rationale*: Working with representatives of the community group, research associates must be clear on what the project seeks to accomplish both immediately and long term. Involved parties must also articulate why they want to achieve specific objectives (this relates back to historical understanding), and pay particular attention to barriers to achieving objectives (lack of human resources, budget concerns, attitudes in the larger community, etc.).

3. *Negotiating an Action Plan*: UCHSD research associates make and give reasons for specific recommendations as to methods and strategies for achieving objectives. At this point, representatives of the community group may express reservations about the efficacy of the plan.

Together researchers and community representatives modify the proposal as is determined necessary.

4. *Conducting Preimplementation Strategies*: Research associates work with the community group's members to develop needed instruments (questionnaires, training materials, etc.).

5. *Conducting Implementation/Evaluation Strategies*: When the community enablement process reaches the point of implementing the action plan, researchers remain involved as observers and/or participant observers in order to evaluate the process. Process evaluation possesses definite advantages over the typical evaluation of a product or ultimate outcome. Locating problems before it is too late is the obvious advantage. Furthermore, in utilizing quasi-evaluation methods, the evaluator serves as an "instrument" possessing important characteristics not found in those such as paper-and-pencil tests and performance measures. These include responsiveness to people and situations and adaptability to the myriad interpersonal and environmental cues, as well as to emergent needs of the data collection process.

6. *Submitting a Project Report*: Once implementation of the action plan has been completed, UCHSD research associates conduct a final compilation and analysis of data. These are written up in a formal report, along with a history and description of the entire project. Recommendations for policy and planning are also included for all relevant parties—the community group and the service provider whose interests converge on the particular social problem(s) addressed by the project.

   Submission of the project report also signals the exit of the research associates. Having served as the primary project implementors, community members possess skills and knowledge to maintain programs created through the enablement process, and they also possess a methodology for creating new programs.

It must be noted that this research model is far from a recipe for the perfect community enablement project. Although the components are ones the UCHSD has found necessary to its activities, sufficiency depends on the addition of "everyday" resources: commitment, time, and funding sources. Furthermore, the model should not be viewed as linear. With the exception of the beginning and ending points, it is in practice reflexive, with each new activity turning back to confront the assumptions of those preceding it.

THE ECOLOGY OF PRODUCING INFLUENCE

The apparatus for knowledge acquisition in science is not necessarily the same as the apparatus for knowledge acquisition in society. Scientific truth and falsehood are not the everyday truth and falsehood of social life, nor should these be apprehended as equivalent. The difference between scientific truths and everyday truths is commonly described as a problem of *application*. But this is a limited and relativistic way to approach the problem. A dubious motive for research is established where social science proceeds as the accumulation of knowledge. Eventually, the question must be asked "Knowledge for what?" In as much as it keeps social truth at a distance, scientific truth is only a self-legitimizing super-perspective on society.

Clearly, the dilemma of the truth of science versus the truth of the everyday poses for us the key methodological question: "How is social science knowledge related to the social world?" This question also constitutes the foundation for the critical self-reflection of social scientific research practices. The methodology of phenomenological social action research proposes a particular configuration of *accountability* as a basis for the social legitimation of social scientific research. Typical scientific standards efface themselves in favor of the meaning structures of the lifeworld, such that social scientific knowledge is oriented to contributing to the self-understanding of social actors rather than only to the interest structures of social science. Social action research practice seeks to open up the field of possible social action in relation to the actual situations viewed as problematic by a community of social subjects. It additionally utilizes this activity as the field of orientation for its theoretic. In this manner, social action research practice is a scientific one. It proposes an analytic as well as a description of social phenomena. Here, however, we will limit discussion primarily to methodological issues.

Researchers working from a social action perspective acknowledge the premises that (a) a socially legitimate social science must respond to the interests of the community of the researched, (b) a valid response can only emerge from an active engagement of the researcher in the community, (c) a responsive and engaged research program increases the probability of developing a social scientific knowledge that does not reify social experience.

Our objective here is to elaborate the bases for these premises through a discussion of the concepts central to the methodology of social action research and to their implications for social influence, trust, and accountability. Subsequently, a discussion of how this methodology augments qualitative methods of data collection generally is undertaken.

In the communication literatures, *dialogue* is typically concerned with the notion of speaking "with" rather than speaking "to" or "at." Presumably, speaking "with" signifies a concern for the other, whether that other be an audience, a research respondent, or a conversational partner. From the perspective of a social action methodology, dialogue is expressive of the hermeneutic principle of interpretive understanding configured in the part–whole relationship, and it additionally signifies a particular point of view on the social.

In light of the hermeneutic principle, social science necessarily speaks from the pre-interpreted, pre-reflective, pre-theoretical ground of the lifeworld. In other words, the taken-for-granted fund of meaning that constitutes everyday social and cultural experience is the condition for the possibility of theoretical knowledge about the experience. Social scientific knowledge, then, is necessarily reflexive—it is dependent on a pre-understanding of tradition that is not first its object of understanding or interpretation but its condition of existence. This circumstance is not, however, the be-all and end-all of debates regarding the relationship between social science and the social world. The "speaking from" only reflects the foundational experience that makes social science possible. It does not reflect the founding activity by which social science creates a different social world. Intervention and transformation are unavoidable components of research activities; thus it is critical that the interests of social scientists be aligned with those of the communities of the researched. In keeping with this critical mandate, social action research acknowledges the possibility that *accountable enactments of social scientific research can enable social action for positive change.*

Explicit in the conception of dialogue formalized in a community-based methodology is the elaboration of social experience as a relationship between self, other, and world. The dialogical character of interpretation is not simply looking *at* an *other*, rather it is a looking *with* an other at some *thing* which the other seeks to communicate. For the community-based researcher, speaking to the social world is dependent on the interobjectivity of the social relationship—self and other oriented toward a thing held in common. This is where the role of interpretive understanding comes into play in community-based methodology. Language is the ontological condition for understanding.

The notion of interpretive understanding further points to the inanity of a "presuppositionless" social science. Were it even possible to purge oneself of one's presuppositions, understanding could not be accomplished. It is only on the basis of one's own presuppositions that the point of view of another person can be understood. In the research activity, the point of critical self-reflection is to determine which of one's presuppositions are appropriate and which are inappropriate given a particular situation. Understanding is understanding *something.* In this case, interpretive understanding is the grasping of the way in which a community defines its own (situated) interest. In social action research, social issues become the common object of orientation for researcher and researched, and it is in terms of the community's definition of those issues that the interest structures of social science and social action can be aligned. But in order for this to happen, researchers must effectively gain community access.

The practice of social action research requires that we develop general influence in the community, and it demands that we create public trust and public accountability. In other words, in critical social action research, the role of the researcher-who-produces-research is replaced by research activities that define the *public* characteristics of the researchers. In this, the history of the research generates a motivational basis, a public history establishing a place for the researcher in the organization of the social setting. It is presupposed that it is the reality of a viewpoint that provides a working necessity, not that of an inaccessible viewer. This premise operates to generalize the social code of authority beyond the private sphere of researcher-dominated contingencies.

One must focus on the creation of places where the explicitness of the research activity can become impressed on the researched. It must be kept in mind that research activity is thematically oriented on a problem of reference. Hence, in effect, the explicitness of the research activity diminishes the personal characteristic of the researcher. It is these personal, privately established life-histories that form the basis of the researcher's *anonymous authority,* namely, those things that cannot be "checked out" by the researched, either because the relevant information is unavailable or simply uninterpretable or meaningless to the research population. A different style of authority must be established for social action research to be operative, one that makes sense within the social context.

This style of anonymization is one that effaces locally irrelevant characteristics of the researcher and at the same time permits, even requires, the demonstration of the researcher's abilities. The researcher thus becomes a "public" person, with the relevant dimensions of "public" being established within the research setting. Nameless authorities, even and perhaps most especially the authority of "science," do not in a social research setting give motivation for the researched population to answer questions enabling it to be understood.

It is a cliché to suggest that *entrée* is a continual process throughout the research that constantly requires the attention of the researcher. Yet, entrée is a continuous activity of building reputational linkages for the purposes of establishing social validity and enticing relevant persons to cooperate in the research process. It is a process of finding points of access through which to bring to bear the general power of social scientific research in a form that is generalizable both from the point of view of professional researchers and from that of the community of subjects who provide the setting for the research.

The social action researcher must build networks. Without the networking of the community of the researched, it will not be possible to establish the relevant parameters of the community *or* to conduct the research in a fashion that the community will perceive to be valuable. In some cases, merely finding the community poses a problem, especially when we keep in mind that this is not an exercise in demography or geography, but rather in identifying nodal points of *interests* and *concerns*. The parameters of the *community of concern* of course include community members, but they can also include social service agencies, police officers, public officials, and even local funding agencies.

"Truth" of the research is a function of the viewpoints of the community of concern; if one is not known and one's credentials not established to relevant persons, then the assumption is that one has not done anything worthwhile, and that is a good enough reason not to cooperate with the researcher. It is virtually impossible to obtain adequate information as well as to work with relevant individuals if one is perceived as a stranger who has nothing to offer. The more one's name is heard, the more involved one is viewed as being, and the more power is attributed to one in obtaining reliable information, which is precisely what one needs in order to get access to that information.

It is also imperative to establish contacts within the community in order that different community members will be able to check out one's credibility. One contact leads to the next, and crossing networks enables the comparison of perceptions about the researcher. These networks are also valuable for the purpose of the researcher being able to identify ways in which information is being screened for her or his benefit. It is also important to learn about any other research activity that may be going on or that has recently been conducted in the community. Past encounters with researchers may have adverse consequences that must be attended to. All of this involves a process of making the rounds sufficiently in order that one's name, in terms of level and degree of involvement, precedes one in the community.

Social reality is much too complex for research to set abstract ethical maxims for decisions in how to go about establishing trust. Trust is not a set of principles to which the researcher conforms or behavioral signposts for specific situations. Rather, trust is acquired through sharing various research practices and through formulating the research in such a way that the populace will be able to perceive in it the potential for increasing their own individual or community potential for action. Trust is indispensable for getting beyond the momentary interpersonal rituals. Yet, for trust to be built and sustained, there are required auxiliary mechanisms of learning, symbolizing, controlling, and even institutionalizing distrust. Trust can be built and diffused if credible institutionalized supervisors are built into the research process (e.g., community leaders). On the other hand, where properly managed, trust can actually be increased where distrust has been institutionalized, particularly in minority communities. In such a situation, one needs to appear "different" by standards of some local code, thereby employing a history as a means to gaining a forum.

The reason for networking, trust building, and allowing oneself to be evaluated by community members, generally of staking out the research agenda within the community, is that many communities are social-science-wise. That social research and social researchers in truth are objects of distrust is a conviction in which many community members sincerely trust. At this stage in the history of social science, many communities view social science as either producing social disenfranchisements or as being simply irrelevant. Because of this broad tendency, one must be prepared at the very first encounter to answer thematic questions like "Who is doing the research?", "Who is this good for?", "Will it be of value to us?", and "When will we see results?" The researcher who has worked to develop a generalized influence in the community will be able to respond effectively to these concerns.

Social influence ultimately derives from successful research involvement in the community. "Success," however, is not an end product; it is more or less descriptive of the high points of any specific project and can be anything from creating a public uproar beneficial to the project, to identifying and meaningfully addressing community significances. In order to create conditions for maximizing the possibility of attaining such high points, products generated by the research must receive endorsement from relevant, recognizable community leaders, and media resources must be utilized to make the project and its objectives known. Publicity, in its most general sense, institutionalizes the public character of the research. We will focus briefly on utilization of media resources.

Media coverage can be employed to open up a project to the possibility of influencing agencies and, indirectly, for drawing other public institutions into the project at key points. In addition, the community will begin to "see" itself and develop ways of placing the face and the activity within the structure of overall community activity. Media coverage is important for other reasons. First, the community at large will be able to monitor the project over time. Second, it will be viewed as pragmatically effective in a way that is open for all to see for themselves. Community participants, especially leaders, will be less likely to have to constantly justify the effectiveness of the project. Because it tends to "enshrine" what is significant, media coverage also helps to secure cooperation and interest from public institutions and their officials. Eagerness to avoid public embarrassment, or its possibility, is motive enough for many public institutions.

Community newsletters, newspapers, and public forums offer important channels for informing the community, expanding its contacts, and for providing a general thematic into which individuals can be attracted according to dimensions of their personal interests. In addition, events become pragmatic accomplishments symbolizing the project. Moreover, these events eventually become decontextualized points of reference whose meaning is not time-bound but instead an enduring "fact" or rationale for the project. Project participation can be intensified by involving community organizations at levels that grant them access to institutional power, thereby solidifying the roles of the organizations within the community. Every fact of a project needs to take on the character of publicness. Such facts are not only information but also function as reasons for the project. Whether in the form of significant information or of activities, every fact provides a justificatory structure for the project and a way of creating its history.

All of these elements create a generalized influence establishing a superstructure of public meaning and involvement within which the research activity can proceed. But at the research level proper, the generalized condition is that the research itself establish distinctive expectations having a centered meaning-structure that has reference to specific themes, concerns, or purposes. At each point, the influence the researcher expects and assumes must be connected with something that can be specified in the social environment.

For influence to occur, the circumstances must be linked up with local imperatives. The activity must be able to be located within the social system. Clearly, social action research creates thematics, but these cannot provide *a priori* the full specification of the research process to the community, the media, or the scientific community. Rigid specification of the research process will limit the flexibility—and so its power—to pursue variation of the thematic in response to the contingencies of the environment. Eventually, the selection and generalization process come full circle; the research activity is justified not by interpersonal arrangements about expectations, but on the basis of community thematics. These thematics in turn are related to the influence of the research activity on the thematics, which refer to the activities of the researcher in establishing thematic orientations. Thus, even research "authorities" are tied into and must appeal to generalized communication structures.

The issues we have discussed thus far—trust, influence, and accountability—also have particular relevance to the actual conduct of social action research; that is, to the methodical procedures utilized to accomplish particular community projects. As methods for accessing information about the social, both qualitative and quantitative techniques can be subjected to the criticism that is typically leveled exclusively at quantitative methods; they fail to reflect the orientations of social actors and thus result in inaccurate, irrelevant social scientific portrayals (knowledges) which reify the social. Implicit in qualitative methods, on the other hand, is an element of "personalization." Around this notion of personalization has arisen an ideology of qualitative research, one that seems to make qualitative methods impervious to challenges that they do not reflect the interests of social actors. Much irrelevant knowledge has been compiled by social researchers whose technical (methodical) stock in trade ostensibly confers on them the status of "swell human beings." "Being ethnographic," "checking with people," and "face-to-face interaction" are pandered as ways of being more *human* in our approach to *science*, of capturing that human quality and essence in our respondents that is somehow supposed to erect a better social science.

In fact, such a perspective seems frequently to be a cover-up for a thorough lack of theoretical knowledge and methodological acumen. Neither sentiment nor technique have ever been appropriate substitutes for insight. Furthermore, the ideology of qualitative methods serves as a mask to its own duplicity. All methods are techniques for accessing data, and it is a fundamental fact of social scientific life that data collection is a voyeuristic and exploitative activity. And this aspect of the social scientific endeavor is exaggerated in the utilization of qualitative methods. Survey research, opinion polling, and so forth, at least do not instill the expectation in their responding publics that "something will come of" the research that will "do something relevant" for those publics in relation to some problem situation. Although this certainly does not minimize the voyeurism and exploitation present in the contexts in which quantitative methods frequently are used, it does point out that "personalization," "concern for," "face-to-face interaction," and such will quickly be the objects of hostility for the social actors when the activity of data collection fails to bring anything of relevance to the community. When ethnographic exoticism poses as social science, the life of the community devolves into subject matter for a game of Trivial Pursuit. No technique of data collection can guarantee *social relevance*.

Social action methodology does, however, suggest that there are ways in which the voyeuristic and exploitative tendencies of our social scientific methods can be offset. This is most critical in terms of qualitative methods, not only because, as was noted previously, these tendencies become more pronounced when the style introduced by qualitative methods implies a measure of social responsibility that is not always actualized through the research, but also because qualitative methods are better suited to the practice of social action research. Although the statistical regularities introduced by quantitative measures may establish some basic parameters for community self-understanding, these do not contribute much to explicating the meaning of the social experience that, for example, income and race have for social actors. Participant observation, field research, unstructured interviewing, and the like are better suited to that task.

Social action research acknowledges a fundamental responsibility to the researched community, as well as to the research activity. Something of value must be returned to the community that provides the researcher with her or his data. Social action research operationalizes this responsibility by means of the concept of enablement. Enablement is related to an accountable methodology in as much as the research activity serves community self-determination. In order for the research activity to contribute to self-determination, it must be prefigured by participation. Rather than merely reflecting a positive sentiment or value, participation refers to drawing the community into the research activity and immersing the researcher in the goings-on of the community. The researcher's task is to transform the typically anonymous social experience into a thematic interest and public agenda for action, or if you will, into a participatory sociality.

Finally, an accountable methodology does not engender dependency. Self-sufficiency cannot be achieved if the researcher operates in such a way as to make her- or himself a community necessity. Social action researchers teach skills, provide information, impart knowledge, and so forth, which can be generalized to other situations. In the next chapter, we will introduce community organization research as a relevant form of social science that is interest-laden. This in turn, makes it relevant to the community with whom it is engaged.

In closing, it will be recalled that Weber (1970) sought to defuse the problem of human interests or value in social science by confining its influence to the formulation of research questions of interest to the researcher. This move was critical, Weber believed, if social science was to be anything other than a science of values. Social action research, as it has been here discussed, clearly demonstrates that a *socially relevant* social science practice resonates interest. Thus, if social science is to be socially relevant, it must be a science of values. The ability of social science to articulate social truth depends on its being a pragmatically oriented activity that contributes to the self-understanding of social actors. The very activity is value relevant.

TWO

Community Organization Research

In the late 1950s and early 1960s, the work of Elizabeth Bott, Hylan Lewis, Richard Cloward, and Lloyd Ohlin cast serious doubt on the "culture" and "historical continuity" constructs as useful for dealing with lower-class behavior. "It is probably more fruitful to think of lower-class families as reacting in various ways to the facts of their position and to relative isolation, rather than to the imperatives of a lower-class culture" (Lewis, 1967, p. 43). Additionally, according to Cloward and Ohlin (1960), "the historical continuity theory of lower-class values reports the extent to which lower-class and delinquent cultures are predictable responses to conditions in our society, rather than persisting problems" (p. 75). In 1957, Bott directly challenged the use of the culture concept, saying "I do not believe it is sufficient to explain variations . . . as cultural or sub-cultural differences. To say that people behave differently or have different expectations because they belong to different cultures amounts to no more than saying they behave differently" (p. 18). And it was Liebow's (1967) classic work, *Talley's Corner: A Study of Negro Streetcorner Men*, that finally put these theses to rest. At least within the intellectual community, "an attempt was made to see the man as he sees himself, to compare what he says with what he does, and to explain his behavior as a direct response to the conditions of lower-class Negro life rather than mute compliance with historical or cultural imperative" (p. 208).

15

Persistent poverty is not necessarily the result of bad luck or bad candidates at the federal level. This condition, instead, is the product of both the New Deal and Reaganomics. The vision imparted by Franklin Roosevelt in the New Deal contained the following three tenets:

1. Increases in expenditures or tax cuts, inspired by Keynes, would be used to prevent depressions or deep recessions.
2. A social safety net in the form of social security, unemployment insurance, health insurance, and so on, should be established to help the poor. But, even more important, these same programs should reduce economic uncertainties for the middle class. The middle class would not have to worry about falling into poverty due to illness, unemployment, or old age.
3. A commitment to equal access to education and training would open up economic opportunities for everyone, especially for victims of race discrimination.

In light of these commitments, the New Deal democrats can be said to have created the American middle class. Lyndon Johnson's Great Society programs can be viewed as the telos of the New Deal. With the Great Society programs in place, "more of the same" no longer made sense. It was not that social welfare policies failed; rather, they succeeded but came to rest at their rational limits. Take, for instance, the drive for equal opportunity in education. The percentage of the population with a high school diploma has doubled since the 1930s and currently is approaching 90%. Since the 1930s, a college education has become no longer an opportunity only for the rich, but is now something half of all high school graduates begin and one quarter finish. Americans have become aware that education needs to be greatly improved, but that is a problem quite different from simple expansion.

It can be demonstrated statistically that an equal opportunity society has not yet been created. After correcting for education and experience, the average African American, Hispanic, or female is still paid less than a comparable White male. But the gross visible abuses have vanished, as these groups have gained new employment opportunities, and because no one is explicitly denied the right to vote. Although affirmative action programs are necessary to achieve equal access in areas where individual discrimination cannot be proved, this strategy does not necessarily increase economic opportunities. A much broader and novel policy is necessary to expand the economy.

As a result, affirmative action programs are not viewed as beneficial, even by those who may benefit from this policy. Former President Ronald Reagan dismantled the Equal Employment Opportunity Commission, but won the majority of the female vote. The answer is not to abandon the goal of real equality, but to develop these programs in an economy where the negative side effects on innocent bystanders are minimized. Affirmative action in a no-growth economy is very different from inaugurating this practice in a rapidly growing economy.

But Americans are uncomfortable talking about equity or economic fairness. They are willing to help people in need, but they do not think about economic justice in the larger context. Public housing is constantly viewed as a welfare program, whereas the tenants are believed to be the recipients of federal "giveaway" projects. The rising incidence of poverty is not caused by transfer payment programs that work to encourage people to become poor in order to be eligible for benefits. Rather, an economy that did not perform in the late 1970s and the early 1980s is to be blamed (Gottschalk, 1984). Job training programs failed to train people because they were too small to make any significant impact and because there were no jobs to be filled in the period between 1979 and1982 (Burtless, 1984).

Nonetheless, one would think there would be less political resistance to job programs than to welfare programs, and this is true. To the general public, however, the opposite is true when it comes to special interest groups. Special interest groups are generally producer groups, and are generally more willing to see tax revenues spent to expand welfare programs than they are to see the government actively working to alter the distribution of earnings. Producer groups pay only a part of the higher taxes to finance welfare payments, but any restructuring of the economy to produce jobs or a more equitable distribution of earnings is perceived as a threat to the status quo.

During the Nixon administration, an implicit compromise was reached. Programs would be expanded to help the poor. These would be welfare programs, not programs that would fundamentally restructure the economy. After correcting for inflation, income transfer payments to persons rose 156% in the 8 Nixon–Ford years. This rise was more than twice that which occurred in the 8 years of the Kennedy and Johnson administrations (Economic Report of the President, 1984).

Reagan was not willing to extend the implicit compromise made by Nixon and Ford. Indeed, he included as one of his campaign themes an attack on the "welfare mentality." Essentially, if one believes that welfare programs have failed, one need not feel guilty about people being hurt by cutting back on welfare expenditures and eliminating certain programs. The fundamental belief of the Reagan administration was that social institutions and structured arrangements either do not matter or they take care of themselves (i.e., "Get the government out of the economy and off the backs of the people"). Underlying this political battle cry is the belief that competition fosters the best possible institutional arrangements. The logic expressed is "if it were not efficient, it would not exist. Since it exists, it must be efficient. If there is a better way to do things, that way will surface to drive inferior methods out of existence." Therefore, as the argument goes, societies do not have to make deliberate changes in order to improve institutional arrangements and social organization. Change for the "good" will occur naturally. Americans merely need to stand aside and "let free enterprise, self-help, do its thing." In this manner, the culture of poverty thesis is recycled, not as a new set of problems, but to legitimize the zero-sum solution proposed by Reagan. What is needed, in short, is a policy that fosters both growth and fairness. But such a proposal has never materialized.

The emphasis in this chapter is on the organizational implications of bonding. The choice of this emphasis has allowed us to dispense with the obsolete conceptual residue bequeathed to social scientific reflection by reason of its naive reliance on one of the available (and we should recognize *never* the only) natural scientific systems of axioms. That power enables some individuals to "do things" to other individuals presupposes a more fundamental behavioral/perceptual commitment. Even the slave must acknowledge his or her prior interpersonal obligation, however perverse, as the prior condition for his or her enslavement. The analysis has sought to suggest that power can be conceptualized at least from the communication standpoint as a function of position and perception framed by an action-dominated interpersonal network.

Piven and Cloward (1971) persuasively argued that societies have expanded relief programs, not in altruistic response to hard times, but to ward off social unrest. Not need but demand, not the deserving but the unruly poor, not misery but the unwillingness to put up with it any longer—historically these have been the motivating forces in liberalizing welfare benefits. When stability has been restored, the relief system, typically in contracted form, remains in place but is administered in adherence to the principle of "less eligibility." Relief is made to be so onerous and demeaning that any and all other resources will be resorted to before the state's grudging bounty is tested.

During the 1970s, in the absence of disruptive social unrest, there were gradual—and in the early 1980s, abrupt—reductions in the levels of benefits and numbers of beneficiaries in many social programs. This occurred in tandem with the worst unemployment levels since the 1930s, reaching depression dimensions in certain industries and sectors of the population. Under these circumstances, the main effect of contracting assistance programs was not to channel people into the workforce, for there were few jobs to be had, but to lower real wages and living standards for those working and to diminish the power of unions.

It is not surprising, then, to find that even before the Reagan administration's assault on welfare benefits, there had been a steady erosion. The number of families receiving Aid to Families with Dependent Children (AFDC) benefits tripled in the 1960s and continued to rise steadily until 1976, then leveled off for the rest of the decade. But the real value of AFDC benefits declined by 29% between 1970 and 1980 (U.S. Bureau of the Census, 1982e, pp. 340, 361).

More than half the states do not make AFDC payments to families when both parents are present in the home. These families—along with single adults who are not eligible for the Supplemental Security Income (SSI) program for the blind, the disabled, and the aged—find themselves relegated to locally funded General Assistance (GA, also known as Home Relief)—assuming they live in states and counties where it is available. Compared with other income-maintenance payments, GA benefits are invariably lower, sometimes woefully so. Moreover, the real value of these benefits fell 32% during the 1970s (U.S. Bureau of the Census, 1982e, pp. 340, 361).

Early in the 1970s, the first reports surfaced of the failure of a "bold new reform" in community psychiatry launched in 1963 with the Community Mental Health Act. Actually, the policy of emptying out the state hospitals had begun in the mid-1950s, when asylum populations and costs were at record levels. It accelerated in the 1960s, prodded by a raft of patient's-rights lawsuits, mounting evidence of the deleterious effects of hospitalization on long-term patients, widespread use of "antipsychotic" medication to quell the more disturbing overt symptoms of psychiatric disorders, and the lure of cost savings that community-based treatment promised (Rose, 1979; Scull, 1977).

It should be stressed that deinstitutionalization was not, at its inception, a bad idea—quite the contrary. Its architects were thoroughly acquainted with the hazards of the hospital and were well-versed in the humane rhetoric of community-based care. But the reality bore little resemblance to the ideal. The depopulation of mental hospitals—from 559,000 patients in 1956 to 13,550 by 1980 (U.S. Bureau of the Census, 1984f, p. 120)—was never complemented by the mobilization of the resources needed to make community placement a workable reality. Specifically, the network of appropriate housing and support services failed to materialize

(Baxter & Hopper, 1980). In most instances, the route from hospital to homelessness was a circuitous one. Although direct discharges from the hospitals to the streets or shelters were not unknown, they were by no means typical. Most ex-patients were transferred to nursing homes (where the chronic mentally disabled now constitute the majority of the resident population), or returned to their families.

The argument that public housing should not interfere with the private market logically led to the view that public housing should be clearly differentiated. This had important implications, for example, for its physical design; public housing, with its austere appearance, is usually easily distinguished from the overall housing stock. But not all low-income people were eligible for public housing units. From the program's inception, it was aimed at providing housing only for the deserving, temporarily poor—the "submerged middle class" (Frieden, 1968).

The country's first major subsidized housing program was not enacted until the need for better housing could be coupled with another national objective—the need to reduce unemployment resulting from the Great Depression. Section 1 of the U.S. Housing Act of 1937 made clear the dual objectives of the legislation: "to alleviate present and recurring unemployment and to remedy the unsafe and unsanitary housing conditions and the acute shortage of decent, safe, and sanitary dwellings for families of low income. . . ." Although the need to stimulate the economy was key to creation of the program, other forces determined its shape.

Probably the major factor that contributed to the form of the public housing program was the extent of the opposition to it. Although the 1937 Housing Act held out the promise of jobs and apartments for the deserving poor, there were still many dissenters. President Roosevelt himself had to be coaxed; a large-scale public housing program had not been part of the first phase of the New Deal (Frieden, 1968). Organized opposition came from several interest groups, such as the U.S. Chamber of Commerce and the U.S. Savings and Loan League. Also in the forefront of the opposition was the National Association of Real Estate Boards.

The right of local communities not to participate in the public housing program guaranteed that, within metropolitan areas, public housing would be most prevalent in large cities. As a result, low-income people, already lacking housing options, were to be restricted still further; the choice to move to the suburbs usually was not available to them. Thus, local control over the program meant that little or no public housing was built in more affluent areas.

As the program evolved, accommodating increasing numbers of African Americans and other minorities, local control over public housing contributed to patterns of racial segregation, with White areas effectively keeping out Blacks. Large cities, with large minority populations, also served a high percentage of minorities in their public housing developments. As of 1976, 83% of public housing tenants in 20 large cities were members of minorities, compared to 61% for the overall public housing population (Kolodny, 1979).

The Reagan administration sought to shut off the public housing spigot altogether. Housing starts for all Housing and Urban Development (HUD) lower income housing programs (public housing, Section 8 new construction and substantial rehabilitation, 235 homeownership program) had dropped steadily in this decade: from 183,000 units in 1980, to 119,000 in 1983, to 42,000 in 1984, to an estimated 28,000 in 1985. ("Starts" reflect the rather long pipeline period for authorization and planning, and so it takes several years before the effects of turning off the spigot show up at the other end.) The administration's proposed 1986 budget (released in early 1985) called for a 2-year moratorium on all HUD assistance for additional lower-income housing, and for wiping out completely the rural housing programs of the Farmers Home Administration (Low Income Housing Information Service, 1985).

Other significant Reagan administration cutbacks, attempted and implemented, are worth noting:

- Community Development Block Grant (CDBG) outlays at the time of this study, about 30% of which in the past have gone to rehabilitate substandard housing, not only have not been increased to keep up with inflation but have been steadily cut—from $3.7 billion in 1981, to an estimated $3.5 billion in 1985, to a proposed $3.1 billion for 1986. And programs that formerly were subsidized separately have been folded into the CDBG pot, increasing competition for these monies. Furthermore, the administration has attempted to weaken the congressional requirement that CDBG funds primarily benefit low- and moderate-income households.
- Neighborhood Self-Help Development grants were terminated, which once provided the kind of help that increases communities' ability to resist displacement pressures, thus forcing 2.5 million Americans from their homes and neighborhoods each year.
- Comprehensive Employment and Training Act (CETA) public service jobs have been cut; among other effects, this results in higher home-heating bills for low-income households, mainly the elderly, as the various home-weatherization programs largely depended on CETA labor.

- The Legal Services program was under severe attack, with attempts to limit its effectiveness, cut back on its scope and budget, and perhaps eliminate it altogether. In areas of displacement, tenants' rights, and housing program benefits, the Legal Services program was a key force, both in providing gains for individual clients and in reforming the law.

In October 1984, the UCHSD began work on a project initiated by the director of the Hilltop Council. This neighborhood civic association operated a community health center; a Women, Infants, and Children Food program (WIC); a youth counseling center; and a variety of other human service programs. Included in the Hilltop Health Center's catchment area are approximately 90% of Columbus' 1,000-plus Indochinese (Cambodian, Laotian, and Vietnamese) refugee families. The council's director initiated the project with the UCHSD in order to begin development of programs to meet the basic needs of these people, and, in this manner, to facilitate social learning necessary to achieving self-determination.

After UCHSD research associates met several times with the Hilltop Council's director and some staff members from its various programs, two project objectives became clear. Enablement of "New American" communities would be dependent on: (a) determining the needs of these communities so that effective programs could be developed, and (b) educating other citizens and service providers about the cultural and social practices of Indochinese peoples so that social learning might take place without the often attendant destruction of cultural tradition.

Initially, the action plan developed to meet these objectives consisted of the following components:

- Design a needs assessment intake mechanism.
- Develop an interview training packet for Hilltop staff members.
- Conduct a process evaluation of the intake mechanism.
- Hold community forums.

We focus here on the first two components, which make up the first level of needs assessment strategies. The last two components form both a second-level needs assessment and a public education mechanism.

The first level of needs assessment strategies (the intake interview) was implemented after the May 10, 1985, opening of the Hilltop Refugee Social Service Center—a house owned and renovated by the Hilltop Council, located next to the health clinic. Two multilingual persons, both Cambodian, were hired to conduct interviews at the Refugee Center. The UCHSD research associates work-ing with this project did not act as observers in this case, because interviews were conducted in the languages of the Indochinese clients. In the place of direct observation, we functioned as project evaluators by means of debriefing/discussion sessions with the pri-mary links to the communities: the interviewers.

It was quickly discovered that the intake mechanism was not working well for the interviewers, and in some respects it was not working for the clients. The research associates, in designing the intake mechanism, had been concerned that the interview process embody principles of "cultural sensitivity." That is, *cate-gories* of questions should reflect the real needs of the community; therefore, they should be constructed from primary, rather than secondary, source information. Due to the language barrier, we could not access the "in need" communities directly, but relied instead on information regarding categories of need given by Hilltop personnel (some of whom are Indochinese refugees, but who are no longer "in need"). We took care, also, that the interview *questions* did not tacitly assume Western cultural concepts. Questions about family structure and concerns about the children, for example, were constructed to admit the structure and concerns of extended, rather than nuclear, families.

In addition to concerns about the cultural sensitivity of the intake mechanism itself, there was a need for an interview *tech-nique* that would facilitate a true dialogue between interviewer and client. As such, the interviewers were trained in the technique of "directed conversation." This method allows the interviewer to begin with a general question ("What can we help you with today?"), and, depending on the interviewer's thorough knowledge of the categories of needs, to "talk through" the intake mechanism with the client without relying on the interview form as a script. This method should be contrasted with the too frequently employed method of an interviewer doggedly pressing on—one, two, three, four—with a series of questions, to which all of the answers are yes or no, agree or disagree, and the like. Although that may be a time-saving procedure, it does not allow to surface the full meaning and significance of the client's experiences nor does it help build trust between interviewer and client. Directed conversation, on the other hand, can accomplish both; thus, as a method of gathering needs information, it is to be preferred.

Although these issues of cultural sensitivity and questions of method had been researched and discussed in the pre-imple-mentation phase of the project, in practice there were several prob-lems. After about 20 interviews had been conducted, the research associates met with the interviewers to discuss whether the intake mechanism was working for them. The first evident problem was that some of the questions were perceived as "silly." For example, under the category of transportation appeared the question, "Do you know how to use public transportation?" Laughter was the most frequent response. As the interviewers expressed it, "everyone can use the bus"—they have to because most lack automobiles. The question actually should have been one concerning the client's ability to use public transportation to accomplish a goal. Imagine carrying bags of groceries onto a crowded bus, for example.

Another problem confronting interviewers and clients was the length of the intake mechanism. Interviews were often not completed because clients needed to leave to catch a bus to go home, or a neighbor who had driven them to the clinic was waiting, or a sick child took precedence. The length was also prohibitive to the interviewers who, in addition to functioning in that capacity, also transported people to the hospital, served as translators for other staff members, made hospital visits, and so forth. This problem, in fact, revealed its origin in an inadequate understanding on the part of the interviewers that could, in turn, be traced to a faulty assumption on the part of the researchers.

The intake mechanism had been divided into two levels. The first was a "screening" interview designed to cover all of the needs categories, but in a superficial manner. On the basis of results of this interview, the interviewers were to prioritize client needs and then to recommend conducting in-depth, supplementary interviews on subsequent visits. As it was, the interviewers were attempting to ask some 60 questions at the first contact, rather than the intended 20. The researchers felt that this misunderstanding could have been avoided had they been culturally sensitive to the interviewers during training. Questioning, especially questioning those perceived to be authorities or experts, is not part of Cambodian culture. We knew this prior to the training session, yet we still assumed they would answer "honestly" when asked whether they had questions about or problems with the intake mechanism.

Problems with "silly" questions and interview length were easily corrected with rewriting and retraining. The next series of problems discussed were not to be solved as easily. After several more meetings with the interviewers, it became apparent that: (a) people were not coming to the Refugee Social Service Center in the expected numbers; (b) Indochinese refugees, having endured squalor and terror in their own countries, were not responsive to queries about life in the United States couched, either implicitly or explicitly, in terms of problems; and (c) the interviewers were frustrated at their lack of personal resources for helping take care of urgent client problems. Taken together, these facts necessitated a redirection of the action plan designed to achieve the needs assessment objective. Following a discussion of the aforementioned problems, the new strategies are outlined here.

With the continuing resettlement of refugees in Columbus and the opening of the Refugee Center, Hilltop staff members anticipated seeing 8 to 10 families per week at either the clinic or at the Center. Actual visits numbered half of those expected. There appeared to be two reasons for this. First, there was, as pointed out previously, a lack of adequate transportation. Second, contacting the center directly was contrary to cultural norms. When the center was opened, Hilltop staff members sent out approximately 800 notices/invitations to refugee families. These were written in the languages of the families and included a list of services available at the center, along with its location and phone number.

Staff members hoped that knowledge of services would compel people to contact the center, but that was not the case. In the event of an urgent problem, individuals first contacted their sponsors, an action consistent with practices in rural areas, especially those in Cambodia, where one or a few elders are consulted to provide solutions to problems such as family disputes. This same capacity may be bestowed on the American sponsor who is responsible for the family's or individual's initial resettlement, and who therefore may be cast in the role of the authority who will take care of problems. If the sponsor did not know about the center, he or she could not make referrals.

In addition to the small number of families utilizing Hilltop services, when people did go there, it was normally because they had an urgent problem or emergency. On the surface, this may not appear to be of great consequence. It is, however, one result of a deeper problem which was revealed in the first group of 20 interviews conducted at the center. Negative responses were often given to questions that implied some type of problem. Two of these were, "Is there anything about your house/apartment that you need help with?" and, "Is there anything about the adjustment of the children in your family to life in this country that worries you?" When asked in-depth questions on categories of "housing" and "children," however, individuals often reported that their dwellings were bug-infested, cold, wet, and so forth, and that the children were doing poorly in school and that they (the parents) could not help them with schoolwork.

We (the researchers) could not understand the inconsistency. The multilingual interviewers explained to us that, after experiencing life in the refugee camps, there *are* no problems with life in the United States. The only things that are *problematic* are the immediate circumstances that bring the individual or family to the center—"the baby needs milk."

Regarding the gathering of needs data, one seeks to overcome problems with inconsistencies through changes in intake questions. The long-term goal of self-sufficiency is seriously impeded by the lack of problem recognition and an attendant lack of future vision. The interviewers believed, and they are experts in the area, that an infusion of future orientation would be the key to facilitating social learning among many Indochinese.

Finally, evaluation of the project showed that the multilingual interviewers experienced high levels of frustration. As Cambodians, they felt deeply for the situations of their people. As socialized Americans, they wanted their people to learn, as they themselves did, the means to self-sufficiency. As human service professionals, they wanted to have access to resources that would enable them to help. In may cases, what they realistically could do to help was limited. There is a city wide shortage of effective programs for Indochinese refugees due to lack of funding, language barriers, the relative newness of the "refugee problem," across-the-board emphasis on African Americans in programs for cultural minorities, and so forth. It is the goal of the Hilltop Council's director to effectively close this gap—thus, the needs assessment project.

In light of these circumstances, a major overhaul in the action plan was necessary. As it turned out, however, the addition of an outreach component actually aligned the project more closely with the objectives of community enablement. To better publicize the existence of the center, we designed a brochure and information packet to send to individual sponsors, refugee families, and other service providers.

Additionally, we developed opportunities and methods for the multilingual interviewers to get out into the community. Strategies included attending adult classes in English as a Second Language (ESL), setting up tables in apartment complexes, and visiting the public schools. The primary objective of these strategies was to enlist the participation and support of the refugee communities in conducting the needs assessment. It was expected that key citizens could be identified and organized to help with this task. They could also assist in motivating social learning. For example, key citizens could help to show friends, relatives, and neighbors that learning the English language would help them *transmit* the values and norms of their cultures, rather than rob them of their heritage and tradition.

Finally, we identified other service providers whose assistance could be secured in providing needed information and training for the multilingual interviewers. We determined they needed information about available housing and housing-related issues, and they needed training in mental health consultation and education. In order for new American communities to become self-sufficient, the interviewers must pass both information and training onto the communities.

We anticipated that these action plans, once implemented, would generate the need for further plans. In fact, we expected much time to pass before community enablement, in its complete sense, would be achieved in this case. Here, time is not perceived as problematic. When changes in everyday community life are perceived by the community as needed and are initiated at the community base, they may be slow in coming, but they stand an increased chance of working.

The Hilltop project has certainly been the most complex and problematic one in which the UCHSD was involved. It was chosen for inclusion here because it illustrates the evolutionary nature of the community enablement process. This particular case study was also chosen because it highlights the need for public education to develop an environment friendly to the social action role. You can erect a building and hope that people will come when you dispense services. You can decide what "the people" need without first contacting them, and then scratch your head in amazement when they do not want what you have to offer. But if you really want your services to be utilized and valued, you could ask the community members you serve what it is they really need, and then teach them how to get it for themselves.

Refugees cease being refugees as soon as they are resettled in this country; appreciating this fact of social life and preparing refugees for the transition to a permanent demographic subpopulation within the United States constitutes the key policy and management issue within refugee resettlement practices. The research we conducted with regard to Indochinese refugee resettlement at the Ohio State University under the auspices of the OSU Department of Communication: Communication and the Public Interest Program identified the following broad issue facing decision makers in the private and public agencies and organizations comprised by the United States Refugee Resettlement Program.

Largely, although not entirely, as the result of the necessary priority given to the task of physically relocating large numbers of refugees, inadequate resources have been applied in areas directly concerned with refugee social integration. As a consequence, the refugee population is, on the whole, ill-prepared in crucial areas of acculturation that are vital for their genuine participation in the American social process. These "new Americans" remain socially isolated and unable to comprehend or to respond proactively to the many complicated demands placed on them for managing the social, generational pessimism that surrounds resettlement.

Enhanced effectiveness and an improved public posture, both with respect to the service population and the American public at large, result from enabling self-confidence and facilitating self-reliance within the refugee population.

Often, funding was made available by the U.S. government for training for persons occupying leadership positions in refugee resettlement agencies and organizations focused on (a) improving the management and the effectiveness of refugee resettlement programming, and (b) promoting the responsiveness and adaptability of existing service structures within a changing refugee resettlement assistance environment. Stated in the most general terms, this proposed research and training design operationalizes these objectives as (a) the production of an information base in a form having practical relevance to key refugee resettlement personnel, and (b) employing a trainer-of-trainers method to address implementing indigenous leadership training and community development techniques.

Research and training should be geared to demonstrating the benefits and incentives for using social enablement strategies from such diverse standpoints as refugee program management efficiency, program monitoring, service delivery, interagency coordination, as well as for improving practical ESL preparation, absorbing the stress created by secondary migration, heightening employability, augmenting community/provider accountability, and improving the public posture for refugee resettlement activities.

NEEDS ASSESSMENT: RESEARCH OBJECTIVES

1. Contact key ethnic refugees and Americans with the experience and the intellectual resources to contribute to the design and establishment of indigenous leadership and community development initiatives.
2. Collect, evaluate, and synthesize information pertaining to:

   - designing, implementing, and sustaining community-based support systems and self-reliance structures
   - introducing leadership enhancement and community development technical assistance into refugee communities
   - effecting coordination and cooperation among social service delivery systems on the basis of community input into these systems
   - employing existing social service, private Voluntary Resettlement Agency (VOLAG) assistance, and Mutual Assistance Associations (MAA) structures to identify and develop existing community leadership resources

- training and obtaining the participation of refugees in the management, monitoring, and needs identification mechanisms of refugee assistance operation—most especially refugees coming from agrarian backgrounds.

Since the passage of the U.S. 1963 Community Mental Health Act, all social planning is supposed to be community based. This means that policy research should be guided by the principle of community sensitivity, and not merely technical or logistical concerns. In this chapter, the general tenets of community-based research are outlined and applied to analyzing the currently controversial issue of what it means for a person or community to be clinically "at risk." Normally, this topic is addressed in a purely technical manner, yet this approach must be altered if need identification is to be consistent with a community's own self-perception, thereby producing valid data.

From 1980 to 1982, a study called The Driving Park Project was conducted at the Ohio State University (OSU). The study can best be described as a community-based needs assessment. This project was somewhat unique in that it was undertaken jointly by OSU faculty members and community representatives. Originally, this research was designed to assess whether the formal legal system was meeting the needs of this particular community because incidences of alleged police brutality seemed to be steadily increasing. As a result of community involvement in this project from its inception, it was soon learned that the traditional objectivistic methodologies were inadequate for assessing a community's needs. Subsequently, the standard sociological theories and methods had to be rethought, so that the data that they generate made sense to the persons who were investigated. Otherwise, information that is objective, yet socially irrelevant, may be all that is produced.

During interviews with mental health planners, they revealed that those methodologies thoroughly distort the social reality as it is perceived by the citizenry. Accordingly, it was learned that the factors which contribute to a person's becoming deviant were not well understood. Thus, these officials were unable to identify who was "at risk" of becoming clinically ill and in need of treatment. Without this type of insight, the delivery of social services is undertaken haphazardly, thereby using resources inefficiently. In order to avoid this, a socially sensitive needs assessment was initiated, one that was not based primarily on the refinement of technique. In fact, the social planners who were interviewed had made this mistake.

According to the Community Mental Health Act of 1963, a new approach to identifying, treating, and studying mental illness was to be initiated. The former state hospital model was to be

abandoned, along with the standard medical protocol for identifying and treating these maladies. Accordingly, a culturally based
understanding of illness was supposed to be adopted. This understanding stresses that the identification and treatment of disease
is a social process. As a result of this change in thinking, disease
can no longer be defined solely in medical terms, but rather all
diagnostic determinations have to recognize the impact of language, cultural traits, and social outlook on specifying the behavior that is considered to be indicative of illness.

This represents a major theoretical reorientation, as the
image of equilibrium that underpins the medical model must be
replaced by a view that is appreciably more dynamic. The medical
model presumed that behavioral norms exist in themselves that
can be applied uniformly, in order to ascertain whether a person's
level of functioning is appropriate. Accordingly, it is thought that
all normal persons strive to achieve or maintain a normative state,
while illness represents a significant departure from this ideal.
Illness, therefore, is considered to be a natural phenomenon that
can be observed readily by any rational person who uses standard-
ized, unbiased diagnostic devices (Ingleby, 1980; Wing, 1979).
Disease is simply assumed to have objective or obtrusively visible
characteristics that can be recorded easily by the trained eye, so
that corrective therapy can be prescribed to restore the equilibrium that has been lost.

This equilibrium model, however, advances assumptions
that are unacceptable to a culturally based rendition of health.
First, a behavioral norm of health is conceived to exist *sui generis.*
Second, behavior is treated as an objective phenomenon which can
therefore be identified properly by merely recording its empirical
traits. And third, it is assumed that illness is a natural occurrence
that is divorced from social and personal considerations. As
should be noted immediately, this model promotes a thoroughly
abstract rendition of health and illness, as it is not sustained by
the judgments of the persons who live in the world but planners
and medical experts. This type of insensitivity, moreover, was supposed to be rejected subsequent to 1963.

Although the passage of the Community Mental Health Act
announced a shift in policy, a clear-cut replacement (theoretical)
paradigm was not available at the time. Currently, however, a variety of alternatives exist. Sometimes this new approach is referred
to as *naturalistic* (Lincoln & Guba, 1985), whereas at other times it
is called *qualitative* (Murphy & Pilotta 1983a) or *community-based*
(Murphy & Pilotta 1983b). Although the terminology is different in
each case, the general aims are identical. That is, they all demand
that behavior norms be recognized as embedded in a social context
that provides them with substance and meaning. Therefore,

behavior cannot be understood by merely outlining its observable features, but, more importantly, has significance only when its social *meaning* is appreciated. This social meaning, furthermore, is determined by the human intentions that serve to specify the dimensions of reality. Thus, values cannot be distilled from research and problem identification, because this type of existential abridgment is impossible. Rather, social phenomena such as health and illness are understandable only within the web of cultural (existential) relations in which they reside. Viewed otherwise, human behavior represents merely an empirical (material) index that lacks depth and significance (Patton, 1980).

Today, public housing, mental health, and resettlement programs suffer from official neglect, chronic underfunding and undermaintenance, and often inefficient and bureaucratic management. It has become an oppressive device for stigmatizing the poor, for maintaining racial and class divisions, and for discrediting the concept of public enterprise in our society. The projects to be covered, regarding the Individual Resettlement, Public Housing, and the Central City Black Community, require a research practice and methodology that generate power and the perceived lack thereof.

This chapter focuses on the functions and manifestations of power in the communication relationships constructed through the research activity. Power, or more precisely, empowerment is conceptualized as a proper communication variable rather than as a poorly disguised analogue of a dimension of physical calculation. This means that we shall not entertain in this discussion the push–pull metaphors so endemic to analyses presupposing the mechanical triad, force–resistance–change. Instead, we shall make some explicit assumptions about organizations and generate a communication evaluation of power.

Following Weick (1979), organization (to substantivise his "organizing") consists of the resolution of "equivocality in an enacted environment by means of interlocked behaviors embedded in conditionally related processes" (p. 91). For our purposes, this working definition of *organization* requires one minor modification, which at any rate probably amounts not so much to a modification as to the selection of a different point of emphasis. We shall apply "interlocking behavior" in the broader sense of the reciprocal obligation of behaviors rather than in terms of Weick's most specific interact–double interact units of analysis that he draws from the relational systems school (Fisher, 1983). What this notion of obligatory reciprocity implies will become evident shortly.

For the present, we need to display definitionally the relationship between our working assumptions about organizations and the communication conceptualization of power. We propose that the interesting dimension of organizations consists not in what they do or the fact that they do anything in particular, but consists rather in their enacting an environment in which and by virtue of which "some thing" inevitably gets done. The condition that something invariably gets done in the environment called *organization* does not depend on either the individual or the collective will of organizational actors. Indeed, things get accomplished often enough despite the volitions of actors. It is this latter phenomenon of doing without willing that contributes to talk about "things" that organizations "do" to people. Organizations are not agents, but they are environments dominated by action, places in which things get done.

Power describes a complicated, multidirectional articulation of relationships, avenues of influence flow, manifesting the communication system of contingent necessitation ("control") embodying concretely and signifying the external and internal contours of the organizational environment for social actors. On these assumptions, power is a property of the organizational phenomenon as such, not a quality of individuals; individuals' power quanta are functions of their respective positions within the network of interlocked behaviors detailing the system's contingent necessity. (The assumptions do not require that such positions are part of formalized intercultural relationships.)

The notion of contingent necessitation follows tautologically from the assumption that organizations are articulated enacted environments of action. It is not at present important how things get done, why they get done, or who does them; instead, all we need to presuppose is that organizations are "doing environments" where tasks (meaningful or not) are accomplished along recognizable (redundant) pathways. We can flesh out the concept of contingent necessitation through indicating its relationship with Weick's "resolving of equivocality." In processing the environment, organizations order informational inputs, much like behavioral inputs are ordered through interlocking, because organization introduces structure (or at least a different order of structure) that establishes for organizational members' restricted (defined) latitudes of discretion with regard to problem solving and decision making. The "doing environment" (enacted domain of activity) generates rules phenomena of all types (social, task, motivational, psychological, etc.) that serve to differentiate organizations from the greater complexity of external environments (Weick, 1979).

We prefer "contingent necessitation" over "rules" because the former is descriptively more precise and conceptually less worrisome. Rules approaches, especially when grounded in sociological conventionalism and unstipulated social contract assumptions, lead analysis into warrantless speculations about deliberation (setting the rules) and knowledge of the rules. We maintain that (a) rules are not formulated but discovered; (b) conscious mastery of the rules constitutes an exceptional situation in an organizational setting, which latter condition itself probably possesses its own characteristic dynamic of contingent necessitation; and (c) rules furnish a necessary precondition of choice, not its proper object.

If one still requires a physical analogy for purposes of visualizing power, one can have recourse to a less anachronistic conception of the physical nature. Just as space expresses the proper geometry of locations in the presence of matter (the "bending" of space), so power expresses a peculiar configuration of behavioral interlocking in an enacted environment. Power articulates a dimension of contingent bonding in human activity much like space articulates the relational motility of "space-occupying" material entities.

In this context, *empowerment* has two communication applications. First, empowerment is coextensive with organizing, inasmuch as an enacted environment predisposes the regularizing interlocking of behaviors effectively regulating the complex mutual necessitation of human interactions. Hence, by definition, to organize is to create power. Second, empowerment occurs in some proportion to the articulation of relationships (interlocking behaviors) with other organizations. According to this assessment, possessing some relationship with another organization means to have at one's disposal some measure of power, however comparatively insignificant, with respect to that organization (to participate at some level in a network of fate/behavior controls).

The sheer amount of prose required here to educe a useful definition of power should not be taken as an indicator of the relative importance of the power variable in this research. To be sure, the "amount" of power actually involved may be so meager that this variable might not in the long run inform the analysis of the project outcomes.

At the same time, it might still be maintained that, even despite its possible insignificance, power is of great importance from the standpoint of at least one component in the research equation, namely, the refugee populations. In turn, one could advance the hypothesis that an organization's own assessment of the importance of its power is inversely proportional to the objective powerfulness of the organization. A weak organization, one capable of only marginally influencing its environment, cannot afford to not be highly "ego involved" in, and so jealously guard, its measure of power. In contrast, a secure and powerful organization can more easily assume an influenceable—even compliant—posture as well as de-emphasize internally the role of power to such a degree that for analytic purposes power relationships have become well concealed. But, at bottom, these surmises are reducible to the proposition that the perceived difference between no power and some power cannot be compared with that between little power and extensive power. Furthermore, it is not clear whether the degree of powerfulness affects theoretically the analysis of power; it may turn out that the increment of power does not meaningfully change the qualitative complexity of the power variable. At any rate, these considerations, although certainly relevant, do not enter directly into subsequent discussion.

EMPOWERMENT

For purposes of exposition as well as for some substantive reasons, the analysis of power requires that the data be subdivided into three units corresponding to the three central and, to be sure, loosely-coupled components in the organizational equation, namely, the target communities, the research, and the project sponsor. In different, but equally important ways, the communication concept of *power* that has previously been sketched can illuminate the relationships taking shape among these components. But for present purposes we shall be assessing only the empowerment of the communities and their local associations. It should be noted that, although it is not attempted here, many of the same phenomena that are associated with empowerment also permit evaluation from a rhetorical perspective concerned with expression, perception, and social perspective as they affect the development of group symbols and interests.

The initial manifestation of community empowerment derives immediately from the communication function of recognition. By mere fact of having been targeted by the city as the first recipient of its jurisprudential largess, the Indochinese community, as opposed, for example, to the Hispanic, Ethiopian, or Korean populations, acquired definition as the principal project focus and the most proximate test of both the city's and the researchers' organizational and interpersonal skills. Because the city envisioned expanding the scope of legal education activities tailored to the needs and interests of resident communities to include additional ethnic populations, the group's initial moment in the spotlight cast a shadow across the entire undertaking in a manner that significantly enhanced their importance both from the city and research viewpoints. In short, the decision to define the task in this fashion constitutes the first stage of a bonding process that promotes by increments obligatory reciprocity—fate/behavior control vis-a-vis both the city and the research interests has been bestowed gratuitously on the refugee communities.

Although the first step in the interlocking of behaviors issues simply from the research directive formulated by the city and the Columbus Area Refugee Task Force, the second step depends on coincidence, identifiability, and limited information. How the communities became defined depended on the representative subgroupings contacted by the researchers. The importance of this factor can be easily demonstrated. As matters evolved, the research component possessed virtually tyrannical control over the equivocality resolving gatekeeping functions with respect to the city. The immediate consequence of the importance of its mediating role left the city with no genuine alternative but to rely on the research component for the information necessary to realize the project objectives. So little knowledge was available, and the opportunities for contact with the target communities so limited, that the research component constituted the vital factor in the project as a whole. Accordingly, owing to the dependence of the research component on subgroups available for interviewing, the communities acquired definition in the eyes of the city on the basis of the viewpoints expressed by these self-selected samples on not only their own communities but on the city and the project as well.

By way of the caricatures emerging through the interview data, the target communities as a whole were drawn into the orbit of the legal system. Community empowerment occurred through subgroup participation in the research component's activity. Even though the degree of empowerment may be relatively minor, still empowerment bears directly on the direction and the implementation of the project and, at the very least, has a potential impact on the communities in ways affecting matters strictly unrelated to the particular objectives of this undertaking.

As far as concerns the project directly, these communities received recognition, inclusion, and therewith consultation privileges immediately influencing the design and execution of an official function; in itself, no small feat. For instance, interview data suggested the value of including crime prevention information and training either as a part or as an offshoot of legal education. The importance of this comparatively minor modification of items germane to the project/research agenda had two interdependent consequences: (a) by promising to respond, the city indicated to the target community that community input serves a role in the formulation of institutional initiatives; and (b) by delivering on the promise, the city provided concrete evidence to the community of the value of participating in the civic process for the sake of satisfying specific community needs. In short, the community gained an awareness that the beneficiary can in part dictate the terms of its benefaction.

But project participation introduces more than just recognition of an institution's influenceability into the target community.

Participation also gives access to and information about mechanisms for exercising legitimate power. From one perspective that is a symbol of city "responsiveness" to community priorities, lending itself to greater sophistication on the part of the community with regard to methods for actively obtaining a response from sources of legitimate power. By displaying its flexibility, especially, as in this case, in a manner that also informs segments of the community about the articulation of the institution in question, institutional authority enables the community to begin to comprehend the means for securing *community-initiated* needs responses from the institution, as well as creating assumptive expectations within the community about the appropriate level of responsiveness of the institution. In other words, expressions of flexibility furnished unilaterally by the institution introduce into the community the presupposition that "responsiveness" constitutes a proper characteristic of institutions as well as suggested ways of going about eliciting responsive behaviors from the institution. The upshot is that the community begins to believe that it possesses at least a *prima facie* credibility that endows it potentially with—and encourages—self-advocacy capability. Taken together, *expectation, institutional insight,* and *presumptive credibility* offer the rudimentary premises for action.

If we look at the community associations themselves, we can see more clearly how the research activity and the project serve to organize and to empower the refugee population. For example, the Vietnamese Association, which existed only for approximately 1 year, had a governing body consisting of an unrepresentative sample of highly educated and largely suburbanized middle-class refugees. The association "represented" a minority of the local Vietnamese population. Project participation held open for this group the promise of legitimation-generating bonds with the city and, if for no other reason, mere attendance at city-sponsored legal information events covered by the local news media contributes to their credentials in the eyes of the greater population of Vietnamese. Almost unavoidably, additional research information resources will be interpreted in light of established bonding implications stemming from the association's research participation. Research participation (research intervention) imparts structure to the community both from the viewpoint of the community as a whole and that of officialdom as the mere function of the necessity for mediating the legal system's outreach activity.

In any event, it serves no one's best interests to underestimate the impact of the project on the target communities. Project participation became a factor in the factious, but most effectively organized, Laotian community, offering a tempting instrument for attempting to manipulate externally the credibility of the competing subgroups within the community.

In this situation, empowerment of the community can proceed only by way of empowering community organizations. Although from the program standpoint, this approach furnishes the most effective, convenient, and durable mechanism for institutionalizing program goals, from the research standpoint this procedure, if not in effect inventing organizational structure out of whole cloth, at least dramatically increases the articulation of the existing organizations. Project participation introduces a clear representative/represented relationship into the community, not simply by reason of providing samples of community needs and priorities, but also politically, owing to their service as mediators diffusing information within the community and as the central providers of project participants. The two primary functions of organization (refugee associations) empowerment that generate representation consequences are patent: (a) the targeting function—organizations form the chief means of gaining access to the community, and (b) the contingency function—research contact mediation produces attendance and participation effects establishing these organizations as the network nodal positions indigenous to the community for purposes, at least, of the project.

But behavioral interlocking extends beyond these minimal conditions. We have already alluded to additional bonding ramifications. Project participation gradually is coming to be identified by the organizations themselves as an entrée mechanism granting community leaders access to institutional power and, as a consequence, solidifying their positions as leaders within their communities by imputing them the necessary credentials to "speak on the communities' behalf" to the research and the project sponsor. Tied into this heightened community–organization articulation is the emergence of a reference group function bestowing organizations with an enhanced capacity for controlling not simply information and aid to community subgroups but also for influencing power relationships within the community. Leadership in the community is diffused through a community subgroup by virtue of having a member participating in the project. The resolution of a rivalry or two will doubtlessly be in part determined on the basis of apparent prominence in research project participation; whoever is relied on by the research and project sponsor components acquires greater influence within the community. Indeed, one might go so far as to say that one of the defining characteristics of the "community" will be the level and quality of project participation.

There has emerged another curious phenomenon directly relevant to the power-generating structural articulation of the community associations. For purposes of this analysis, we shall contrast organizational *task* with organizational *theme*. Organizational task simply names the particular activity or activities undertaken by an organization. In this case, the organizational tasks consist of legal education and related community research. Organizational themes are those symbolic elements establishing the organization as a cohesive entity by supplying the reason for its existence and by registering the significances attached to its diverse endeavors. From the standpoint of the project sponsor and the research components, the tasks at hand unambiguously delimit their measure of interest in uncovering the target communities' organizational thematic compositions. In other words, all these components need is adequate information to make educated judgments about how best to introduce legal education into these communities.

The situation becomes much more complicated when assessed from the standpoint of the community associations. In part, the thematic structure of the organizations themselves was gradually undergoing elaboration and becoming concretely perceived in relation to project participation. We can consider the rhetorical facet of this development on some other occasion; for now we need only suggest its relationship with organizational articulation and empowerment.

The first immediate consequence typically is the reduction of the rationalization utility of the futility prerogative possessed by unenfranchised "interest" groups. New-found access to the legal system institutes, for the associations, the possibility for attracting the attention of the political system, and thereby sets on the associations the burden of "doing something" meaningful to benefit their communities. At this point, success and failure become genuine descriptors from the organizations' points of view. Should the project fail, blame must be assigned; should it succeed, the associations are first in line to claim credit. More than that, success in this instance would reflect upon the viability and competence of the associations both within their respective communities and from the standpoint of legitimate authorities, including more than just the legal system; for instance, social service agencies would have to acknowledge these associations' improved credibility. Finally, organizations representing the interests of other local ethnic communities would be encouraged to take into account a number of additional competitors for the attention of institutional authority and, as a result, open themselves at some level to include the Indochinese as part of their reference group. On the other hand, failure produces a familiar dialectic. The organizations lose their opportunity; this must be rationalized. *Alienation* becomes a meaningful concept at this juncture; so do the associations' ineptitude, researcher incompetence and miscalculation, institutional insensitivity or misunderstanding, and the like. The significant point here is that organizational justification and recrimination reflexive mechanisms have been stimulated within these associations by virtue of their having been targeted, and so structured, by the research and sponsoring agency/components.

The interaction between thematic structure, organizational articulation, and the project task can be viewed in still another connection. The potential for extending their influence within their communities draws the associations toward the city and the project. But the possibility of competition, emanating both from other community subgroups and from other ethnic communities, not to mention the ever-present possibility of project failure, provokes in-group reflection upon organizational themes, if for no other reason than as the means for ascertaining the degree to which it is in the best interest of the associations to commit themselves to the project. Genuine payoffs are at stake for the associations as a whole and for subgroups within the associations.

In the broadest sense, project participation requires reflection on superordinate association goals. For instance, is the main function of the association to promote the preservation of native customs or to advocate the interests, rights, and needs of the immigrant community? Or, should the major concern be the satisfaction of essential survival needs or the social and political articulation of the community? Answers to such questions will influence not only the associations' own self-definitions and thus their internal standards of evaluation, but also help determine which subgroup and which individuals will control the associations and, by extension, "speak for the community." Different emphases require different skills, most especially for immigrant populations, and different criteria of effectiveness. Relationships among association leaders, between the associations and the communities, the associations and the research component, the associations and the city, and, a fortiori, the city and the communities are all affected by the associations' deliberations upon the organizational themes made salient by project participation.

Two additional factors germane to the empowerment of the associations require mention here. We have labeled these factors respectively the *social psychology of the semblance of action* and *the mystique of procedures.*

As we have previously asserted, organizations are more or less articulated "doing" environments. Getting something accomplished creates its own mechanism of rationalization and legitimation. Of course, to be in a state of "not doing," whether as an individual, a subgroup, or an organizational whole, puts into question—primarily by putting out of play—the sensefulness of the organizational enterprise as such. On the other hand, having a task institutes a marvelously effective intersubjective dynamic promoting the formulation of the organization from the standpoint of members and observers alike. For present purposes, it suffices that we acknowledge that the existence of a project in which the associations and the communities are invited to participate in and of itself can be enough to encourage organizational articulation and thereby generate further association empowerment.

Finally, organizational articulation assessed from the standpoint of the incremental interlocking of behaviors can be seen to be embodied perceptually by "procedures." At one level, of course, a task stimulates the formalization of interpersonal relationships through raising to greater explicitness the contingent necessitation underpinning organizational member interaction, both with respect to task proper and to theme and associated symbols. But more interestingly in this case, the associations, while somewhat intimidated, are attracted by the procedural nuances, with respect both to implementation and design revealed to them by the process of constructing the program for legal education. People appear to be attracted to the research component in part because the latter symbolizes a *procedural moment* within the process of generating the requisite materials and plans. In other words, regardless of the problems of relevance and of coordinating the level of difficulty in the materials presented with the linguistic and legal comprehension capacities of the recipients, it is our guess that if the city or the researchers had a ready-made learning package that they sought simply to deliver to the communities, the latter would not display the degree of interest they currently communicate. These people have grown accustomed to assorted "hand-outs" whether on the order of welfare assistance, securing housing and employment, or of various forms of instruction, language and otherwise. But they have always assumed or been forced to assume the role of recipients, pure and simple. Consequently, they have had infrequent exposure to the internal workings of the organizational process. In short, in and of itself, the bureaucratization of decision making smacks to them of legitimacy. Restated somewhat cynically, given this condition, a major ally of the research component in managing this project has been the rather broad latitude available for manipulating without accountability the community associations' perceptions of the bureaucratic complexity involved in accomplishing the project goals.

In summary, we have attempted to suggest some of the complicated interactions occurring among structural articulation, reciprocity, task definition, and selection as they appear to bear upon the roles and manifestations of power surfacing in our project. A synopsis of community-related themes pertinent to the dimensions of power follows.

EMPOWERMENT OF ENTIRE COMMUNITIES

1. Choice of target community and self-perception of status.
2. Project involvement defines community and insinuates the potential for recognition and advocacy.
3. Mere inclusion and avenues of influence deriving from a project underpinned by a research component.
4. Information coupled with access to legitimate power.
5. Reduced utility of the futility prerogative.

EMPOWERMENT OF MEDIATING SUBUNITS (COMMUNITY ASSOCIATIONS)

1. Creation of implicit representation relationships.
2. Targeting function: information and interpersonal (primarily research component) access.
3. Contingency function: attendance and participation (primarily legitimate authority) access.
4. Project definition presupposes community leadership and therewith institutes access to legitimate authority for community leaders.
5. Reference group function: leadership diffused within community on the basis of subgroups, one of whose members participates in the project.
6. Thematic reflection, organizational articulation, and organizational self-interpretation.
7. Semblance of action, organizational articulation, and organizational legitimation.

THREE

Communication as Political: The Covenant Basis of Community Social Action Research

This chapter focuses on the philosophical principles that are either stated explicitly or are assumed tacitly by various political groups and the public norms that such groups promote. The principles that are relevant to political communication in the context of the United States and its form of government are limited to the questions of democracy and the duties of various segments of the public: What are the duties of the citizen with respect to the request for information relevant in making diverse decisions concerning public policy? What are the obligations of the officials, or candidates for office, concerning both the information necessary for public knowledge and the proposed prospective platforms of public policy? What are the obligations of various mass media in providing information regarding official and prospective public policy and issues? Democracy and democratization pose various questions that cannot be addressed without the understanding of the principles on which democracies are based and which imply rights and obligations of diverse social groups. Such groups are engaged necessarily in political communication if they participate in an enlightened and informed democratic way of life.

43

POLITICAL COMMUNITY

Human social relationships are regulated by norms. Some of the norms are conceived to be the results of natural inclinations or even necessities, some are regarded as continuations of moral traditions, still others derive their legitimacy from imageries of superhuman entities, and finally others as impositions by those who are more powerful either by birth or by inheritance of a social position. Various social groups may appeal to one or another type of prejudgment in order to legitimate their unique claims as to the appropriateness of the rules. In some cases, a group may regard its rules to be imperative and even propose that such rules possess a status as the final arbiters among all other social rules, including the legal codes. It is possible, within this context, to argue for ethical adjudication provided that all participants are in agreement on a set of postulated imperatives. Yet, it is the arena of agreement that is usually left out of such ethical debates. If there is a question of agreement or disagreement on rules, even if they may be tainted by one or another type of morality, then there must be a domain in which the members of a society can engage in open contestation and/or consensus. This domain suggests an *ethos* in contrast to moralities. The ethos would provide a framework for consensual practice. Such a framework does not offer ethical rules; rather, it coincides with the basic ways that humans live, if they live democratically. Such an ethos will be related to the task of mass media and its function in a political society that regards itself as democratic. Contemporary debates concerning political rights and duties of citizens, governments, and mass media are in a turmoil because they fail to articulate the base political processes. Despite the contemporary process of democratization, some systems still remain under the guise of being the sole representatives of the real interests of the people.

In the Western tradition, there are posited two fundamental conceptions of the basis for democracy. The first is the classical Greek conception of human equality, based on a shared human nature, and the second rests on the conceptions stemming from various modern views. The latter are subsumed under the title of political enlightenment. Although this title hides a diverse set of conceptions, there are some basic principles that are shared by them all. First, there is a rejection of human nature; second, there is a postulation of a human subject who is fundamentally free both with respect to the natural environment and all social and ethical norms. Because the United States is founded on modern conceptions, this chapter focuses mainly on modern understandings of freedom of autonomy and equality of the citizens of a democratic political community and its ethos. The ethos will imply a primacy of communication over power and domination. In turn, the primacy of communication interconnects the various segments of the public, such as government, the citizens, and the mass media. All three segments are essential for conceiving democracy.

Although socio-historical views might offer analyses of various social, economic, and historical events that "caused" democratic movements, the philosophical task is to explicate the fundamental presuppositions constitutive of democratic political society. It has been well argued that "naturally" and empirically speaking, humans are radically unequal in talents, dispositions, and aims. Such views preclude the derivation of equality. Moreover, such views could easily lead, if not to an aristocracy of the "best," at least to a meritocracy of the most talented to make public policy and decisions for the "good" of the rest of the population.

The principles of democracy, in which free people are the final arbitrator, and free press keeps the public informed, rest on different "conditions." Thus, a question must be raised concerning the difference between relationships that comprise a political community and other types of human relationships. The answer demands a careful scrutiny of the founding of a political community, such that it is the only one entitled to be called democratic. This is to say, only democracies deserve to be called political.

Most types of human relationships rest on numerous common interests. Such interests may become part of a democratic society. Yet there is a difference between such interests and the founding of a democratic community. The founding and the existence of such a community are tied together inextricably. Although there are purposes that may comprise our common aims, the democratic community is its own purpose with an assumed duty by each citizen to maintain it. The reason for human relationships in a democratic community is this very relationship that is identical to its own purpose.

The activity of founding a democratic community, as its own purpose, is not an activity of the past, done once and for all by the founding fathers, but must be constantly maintained by every citizen. We cannot speak of democracy as if it were founded as some "system" perpetuating itself without our participation or merely with periodic participation as "voters." The democratic community is perpetually self-founding and not a structure either imposed on a community or derivable from some other interests. It is a relationship in which the posited equality and autonomy of humans is maintained for its own sake. This means that the very source of humans as equal and autonomous is coextensive with and sustained only in a democratic community. In principle, any other form of community may be based on heterogeneous interests and purposes, resulting in the domination of one social group by another, but such a community would disallow the conceptions of equality and autonomy of every individual. The very notion that humans act socially on the basis of their own interests, leads to the private conception of society wherein either individual or associated group interests are pitted against the interests of others, leading to power and not to free human relationships.

Prior to a fuller understanding of such free relationships, it is necessary to delimit the concepts of autonomy and equality. Critical scholarship shows that the basic principles of modern enlightenment, explicated from Pico through Kant, have rejected the naturalistic and essentialist views of human persons. With this rejection comes a rejection of "causes" in human affairs. But what does this mean with respect to equality and freedom? An understanding of these concepts rests on modern views of a human relationship in the world. Although the modern person is regarded to be rational, modern rationality is defined as instrumental. Thus, the environment must be reduced to material for human purposes. Because the latter are future-oriented, they constitute the human self-conception of what one wants to become. Such a purposive being is free because it does not adhere to the given environment, does not follow the immediacy of internal or external compulsions, powers, and laws, but acts in accordance with its own projected possibilities of a not-yet-existing environment. In this sense, the human emerges as a law giver to the environmental reconstruction. Such "laws" are not derived from the world, and need not have any predecessors or assumptions. They are invented for the sake of reshaping the environment.

This structure allows an intersection of a number of modern political concepts. As already mentioned, the first grants that there is no specific human nature as a source of human equality. Second, equality results from a specific concept of freedom as autonomy. With respect to the latter it means that the laws we posit to shape the environment or to govern our social activities are not discovered but posited. They have no necessary connection to any compelling force. Autonomy must be strictly distinguished from freedom of choice. The choice is seen as a power capable of selecting among options. Yet in the final analysis, the choice is determined by an underlying motive. In this sense, its base is irrational. The freedom of autonomy is analogous to logic wherein the structures are not results of forces, but of rational and free postulations. As already noted, equality of all persons stems from autonomy. If the rules, logics, rational discourses are not derivable from natural states of affairs, there is no criterion by which one could render a decision concerning the superiority or inferiority of one postulate over another. In this sense, they are equal. Autonomous freedom as rational in the above sense results in the equality of persons who are in a position to posit the rules by which they would govern their lives and deal with the environment. Each individual is an equal "law giver" to him or herself and the environment. If there shall be common rules, they will not be discovered but posited and decided on in a public (i.e., political) debate. Third, the modern concept of environment as material, coupled with the view that the human is capable of remaking the environment in accordance with his or her designs, leads to an increasing technologization of the social life and to an all-pervasive technocratization of politics, to political technocracy and bureaucracy.

It is essential for the understanding of the principles of democratic political society and political activities that there can be no other sources of rules apart from those originating with the public covenant. One misunderstanding must be avoided: The autonomy of each individual, as the unconditional source of law, does not imply unrestricted activities. It states that the freely posited rules are not causes that dominate human life but are rationally analyzable systems that can be modified and even rejected. Autonomous freedom means a life under freely posited, debated and rationally achieved rules (Habermas, 1970a). Such an achievement is a matter of mutual public debate and consensus. Indeed, this is the basic sense of the political: a public domain where all members of a community participate in the establishment and maintenance both of this domain and the rules. This is another way of saying that the political is identical with a continuous activity of maintaining, of originating the public domain as its own purpose. This domain is *the most basic political institution* on which all other political institutions—including the establishment of specific constitutions—rest. Without this institution, without each member of society's being able to enter the public domain as an autonomous source of rules, the basic meaning of the political disappears.

No doubt, it could be contended that by living with others, the autonomous individual is limited by the interests of others. Such interests often lead to associations wherein one group's or association's interests and power may dominate others. This is an obvious thesis proposed by both capitalists and socialists. This process may, in fact, lead to a fragmentation of society into classes and their confrontations. In this case, political society vanishes and the public domain is reduced to the dominance of irrational motives and causes. Here the autonomous freedom as a source of public rules also disappears. How is one to avoid this abolition of the political and the public? In face of numerous relationships, the autonomy of every member of the public must be structured by three conditions. First, everyone is an autonomous source of law; second, all laws are proposed and discussed by the members of the public in order to reach a reasonable consensus; third, all laws must be applied equally to everyone (i.e., they must be designated as universal). These conditions constitute the rights of every member of the public, and the rights are secured by mutually obtained laws. The latter regulate the freedom of everyone with respect to all others.

One of the more important assertions is the universality of law. The universality is a guarantee of rationality or the absence of contradictions in a given law. This is, every proposed and approved law must be accepted by all, including the one who proposed it. If one proposes a law against stealing, then he or she too must freely subject him or herself to the law. If a person decides to make an exception to him or herself, then he or she contradicts him or herself because in this case the law ceases to be universal. Any public claim to the universality of a law must exclude such contradictions. But in this sense, there is assumed freedom and equality of persons as the ground of law. The universality of posited laws implies a more basic principle: If one proclaims that he or she has the autonomy to be the source of laws, then he or she must universalize this claim to include all members of a political community—all are equal sources of law. Without this procedure, one would face a reverse contradiction: No one is the source of laws, but I am the source of such laws.

It must be understood that such a ground has very little in common with any kind of naturalistic ontology or metaphysical and moral explanations of human political community. As already noted, it is obvious that naturalistically and even morally, there are great varieties of individuals. Persons differ with respect to interests, abilities, and aims, and left to function in such a context, society would be a sum of confrontations and antagonisms among interests, leading to inequalities. Given such a context, laws would depend on the powers of interest groups. In this sense, not all societies are political, despite the numerous writings about the political actions of personages such as Hitler or Stalin, Reagan or Mao Tse Tung. If such persons were engaged in the support, protection, or enhancement of specific interests, or if they abolished the public domain and public participation in the rational debate concerning the laws, then one could speak of power confrontations but not of politics. Strictly speaking, politics has one major task: an open domain in which every member of the community participates in deciding public questions. Of course, such a position also implies that all community members are equally duty-bound to participate in all public affairs. The term *duty* should not be read morally. The concern is with an ethos, a way of being political and of constantly keeping the public arena open for public participation. It is known that the Athenians of ancient Greece regarded those who failed to participate in the public affairs not as "nonpolitical" but as "incapable of being." Therein lies the goal of community social action research. As we conceive it, communication is politics.

The net result of the distinction between the political and the social–private is the conception that human autonomy requires political community where the individual's freedom is guaranteed by a free establishment of laws and a free acceptance of such laws. Public and free establishment of laws is, simultaneously, an establishment of a political community as its own purpose (i.e., the presence of the freedom of each individual to participate in the establishment of laws and the maintenance of the right of any individual to be an autonomous source of laws). This framework allows the discussion of all other purposes. One may establish other institutions, such as legislative, administrative, and judicial, yet they too have the task of guaranteeing that in the final analysis the autonomous being remains the final arbiter or all public rules. There is a hidden condition of this guarantee: In the public arena, all social and economic differences become disregarded and everyone enters the public domain as an equal.

In a political community, a person acts from respect for the law. What is the composition of such a respect? First, it means that a person respects freedom and is not subject to causes and impulses; second, respect for law draws its nourishment from the requirement to maintain the autonomy of everyone and thus to maintain the public arena. In this arena, laws are not given as if they were natural necessities, but depend on public participation in their continuous preservation. Third, their continuity means that freedom is not merely one of the social factors, but a condition that is equally established and maintained actively. Fourth, the maintenance of political freedom and the public sphere, requires legitimate force capable of preserving the public arena against private interests and individuals who reject the freely obtained laws. Such persons have rejected their own autonomy and become subject to impulses and causes, to irrational forces. This should not be taken as if it were a moral question; rather, it reveals the ground of what is a political community and the necessity of its preservation if the human is to remain autonomous. Moralizing edicts depend on private threats and fears, punishments and rewards, in brief on singular interests, but freely established laws are everyone's affair. Those who are appointed to maintain the public domain cannot be the keepers and imposers of their own morality. Given numerous moralizers, the public officials would be at a loss concerning the proper morality in a given case. Rather, political community has its own ethos with respect to rights and duties in the public domain. The ethos requires a free, rational public debate and agreement on laws, issuing from mutually autonomous persons and their understanding of the necessity of maintaining the rights of all. This ethos allows for tolerance and the view that laws are not eternal. On public agreement, they can be altered or rejected. Because the posited laws are practical, they must meet the previously mentioned conditions of public approval and universality.

Although these considerations may imply that humans are social beings, it is quite clear that the latter can only function at the level of individual and group aims and interests, and is not yet coextensive with the concepts of autonomy and equality as fundamental conditions of the public domain. The political is established in society as the basis of social freedom and as an appearance of human autonomy and free associations. In brief, the political is an essential expression of a creation of society as political and free, and not as a sum of motivated interests and aims. In the social–private domain, one may follow various moralities, whereas in political society one is bound to the political ethos. Although what has been said may sound somewhat different from the usual conceptions of the political, it is, nonetheless, the most basic political institution and the condition of any democratic revolution and constitution. Without this condition, one could not grasp the current frustrations, cynicisms, and so on, about politics.

POLITICAL COMMUNICATION

In principle, the institution of representative government is not democratic unless certain conditions are met. First, any person appointed by the public is bound legally to accomplish what the public requests. All other activities claiming to be for the sake of the public are illegal. This stems from the conceptions that the sole source of legality is the public and the decisions to which it binds its own members and the public officials. The public official is not to "lead" but to serve. Second, election is a dialogical process. Persons running for public office offer their proposals on public questions; such proposals become a covenant in case the official becomes appointed. That is, because the public agreed with the proposals and thus appointed a candidate to a public office, the public official is duty-bound by that very covenant to carry out the proposals. Any failure to do so is equivalent to the breaking of a binding and communicated agreement. Such officials must be dismissed from the office immediately, and perhaps should be prosecuted for criminal activities. Third, a candidate for office should not only offer his or her proposals, but due to public discussions, should modify his or her proposals based on public input. Ideological dogmas comprise one person's proposals, and should reflect possible modifications once they are exposed to public discussion. In a political society, the duty of the candidate is not to expound on "future hope" and "grand visions," or even "my dream of better life," but in the first instance to communicate his or her public concerns and the concerns of his or her constituency and to offer either practical or legal solutions to such concerns. This means that political communication, if it follows the structure of autonomous public and its free domain, is responsible for the statements made. Yet in this sense, private interests, motivated by causes and irrational drives, hide, if not abolish rational, logical and free discussion of public issues. Such a discussion need not be simplistic or without controversies. Yet one principle is important: Political communication consists of a triadic structure. There is the subject matter of concern that is addressed by a speaker and the public or an opponent of the speaker. What is to be avoided is the surface view, often paraded as "objective": It is assumed that if two opposing opinions are presented, then the public has an understanding of an "issue." Yet a serious dialogue requires a thorough exposition of the subject matter of the arguments prior to its obfuscation by the so-called "different viewpoints." A simple exposition of viewpoints does not constitute information; the subject matter of the viewpoints is fundamental. In turn, the public participation in the public arena requires that it too should be cognizant of the subject matter of discussion and not be a simple sum of yet "other views" to be taken into account. Full rationality requires no less. It would be nonsensical to debate public policy on nuclear energy without first explaining what such energy is, what it does, what are its effects, and how it functions. It could be argued persuasively that the duty of the public, and above all a candidate for office who claims to possess an ability to serve the public, not only is to be well-versed in the subject matters that are of concern to the public, but also to be able to present the subject matter to the public.

It must be understood that "political communication" is not about "politics." The political is the public domain of autonomous and equal persons. Given this base, political communication is about the subject matters that are of importance to or relevant to the public. Such an understanding would exclude all informal arguments and all efforts at psychologization of the issues. The term *psychologization* covers emotional coloration, theatrical rhetorical exhortations, such as rituals, images for impact, and slogans. Instead of revealing, they obfuscate public issues; they assume that the members of the public are not rational and autonomous, but react to causes. Soliciting such reactions is one mode of modern, but not classical, rhetoric. In the former, a detached reasonableness and the political process vanish. In this context, one could claim that if the publicly appointed figures, or figures running for public office, engage in this level of rhetorical obfuscations, creations of imagery, and sloganeering, they disqualify themselves from public office. This claim carries not moralistic undertones; it simply follows from the principle of the political as essentially public, concerned with proposals for public discussions of public matters as their sole task. No such justification as state secrets, known only to the leaders and prohibited to the public, can be claimed to either prevent public debate or to avoid the facing of important public concerns. Such practices presume that only the officials are in a position of deciding what is of public interest. This is paternalism and is modeled on the mistaken view of the political state as a family. Indeed, there are temptations not to mix in politics and to leave such matters to the officials. In this case, the citizen has duties, but ceases to have rights. This tendency may appear even in a representative democracy if the representatives begin to assume that all public affairs can be managed by the wisdom—and in most cases an ideology—of the leaders. This is obvious in cases of a popular representative's appeal to the public. Such an appeal allows the official to pursue undebated his or her ideological dogma, leading to disastrous results.

POLITICAL TECHNOLOGY

In political society, the public has the right and the duty to know. Given the emergence of technological concepts in the domains of production, research, efficiency, control, and their complex interrelationships and power, there emerges a need in the public domain for persons capable of managing such complex relationships. Such concepts and relationships are premised on material, psychological, economic, and power interests. In brief, the question of autonomous public decision begins to be changed into interest-laden obfuscations and an interest-laden concept of knowledge, resulting in a legitimation crisis. In order to grasp these concepts, it is necessary to delimit an underlying structure of technocracy that has become a dominant theme both of the critical as well as the general systems schools, specifically in relationship to democratic institutions and communication.

What is known as modernity, inclusive of the political as well as the scientific enlightenments, is premised on the concept of human ability to reshape the environment to suit human needs and designs. The reshaping requires the exclusion of the experienced world in favor of quantitatively constructed models imposed on a purely homogeneous quantity of "matter." Such an imposition does not occur on the basis of mere mathematical thinking; it requires human physical and practical intervention as means, as labor power capable of shaping the "raw materials" into desired results and products. Extensive scholarship has traced and explicated this complex "desire" in epistemological and metaphysical-scientific thought of modernity. The entire struggle of the critical school, the seemingly irresolvable issues in Habermasian thought between instrumentality and ideality, are composed on the ground of this trend. The latter not only leads to the mechanical conception of the world, but also to a constant incrementation of power "over" the environment and a continuous division of human functions toward most diverse disciplines and technical expertise. Thus, a view emerges and takes root that only experts can manage the specific domains, ranging from changes in production, agriculture, biology, chemistry, psychology, social affairs, economy, physics, mathematics, linguistics, propaganda, and even communication. Such experts must, of necessity, assume not only a technical model of the world, but also the ability and power to change the material processes (including humans) in the domains of their expertise in accordance with causal principles. Setting up of conditions in order to obtain the projected result comprises a mode of understanding that is basically instrumental. Thus the very principle of operation in all areas is control, manipulation, and power. All events can be used for the setting up of conditions to obtain any desired result to the extent that the conditions are controlled by experts in specific domains. One should be careful to note that the experts are not interested in what is the case, but in how to fashion the case for obtaining the desired results.

The technological presumption extends equally into various public domains, leading not only to a requirement for experts in the management of public affairs, but also to the public demands of the appointed officials to be in a position to offer solutions and fulfillment of private wants. No doubt, "private" wants are a part of social life, yet once such wants are introduced into the public arena, they become a matter for public adjudication and not one group's social power to prevail in imposing its interest on the public. In principle, the introduction into public arena of an interest is coextensive with submission to public decision. This very temptation to introduce one's private interests into the public domain tends not only to split the public domain into private spheres of influence, but also to reduce the function of public officials to adjudication of diverse, and at times opposing, interests of the populace. In addition, such a reduction includes a temptation among the holders and prospective holders of public offices, to engage in non-public commitment (i.e., promises of private well-being to diverse and contradictory interests). These promises have an appearance of sincerity, because the officials make a claim to technical expertise in managing such interests. However, the public domain is being reduced to the domain of private interests and thus to the abolition of the public domain as a place of exercising autonomous freedom. This constitutes the legitimation crisis.

The latter comprises a complex, although interconnected set of issues. First, the presumption that the experts (*qua technical*) are in a position to solve the material issues leads the publicly appointed officials into a temptation to offer solutions to the individual-private, or group–corporate questions. In this sense, there appears a contingent of "experts" or basically technocrats to manage the private affairs of the public. Second, the public's demands are equally reduced to the level of material well-being. The perceptual structure of the public is composed of interests that are basically private–social, but not public–political. Thus, the public demands that the appointed officials also manage the affairs of the public at the level of numerous interests—not at the level of the management of the institutions that guarantee human autonomy—with a full participation of all in the affairs of the public, and as public. Third, because interests are different and are backed by differences in social power, then the socially and privately more powerful interests dominate the public arena and the writing of laws. The result is not only the emergence of winning interests, but also the division of the public into classes and pressure groups. Such a division results in public apathy and cynicism. Fourth, these factors imply that the only legitimate government is one that manages private needs; if the elected officials fail to keep their promises in such various areas as economy, jobs, medicine, and so forth, then such government is deemed illegitimate. It is irrelevant whether one is in a so-called capitalist or socialist society; one tends to think of the appointed public officials as being in charge and as having expertise and a right ideology that can guarantee material and even psychological well-being. The obvious result is a political technocracy without the political ethos. It views itself capable of adjudicating public affairs on the basis of material interests and technical expertise. Obviously, this form of management of the public is regarded as "factual" and thus ethically "neutral." The presumed neutrality opens the door to various moralizings of the practices of the technocratic establishment and the debasing of the public domain to private moralities and various mythologies. The public officials equally fail in this respect, and attempt to use their myths in order to shape public policy. Together such practices abolish the public arena as a domain of free and equal participation.

The technocratic attitude extends toward the management and promotion of the images, rhetorics, and designs for effect during political campaigns and enhancements of office holders. There is an accepted assumption that the political figure, whether in office or campaigning for one, will surround itself with numerous media experts capable of designing appropriate rhetorics, poses and positions, objects of attack and images of placation, indeed an entire gamut of statements, expressions, and gestures, cultic enunciations and moralizing pronouncements, to suit the given occasion. At this level, the experts are not interested in doing research to discover truths, but in producing rhetorical images or constructs for specific audiences and specific effect. Such a production could be subsumed under the general term *political theater*, capable of solving, as if by the wave of a magic wand, all the ills afflicting such an audience.

The technocratic operations in this setting follow from the more general set of modern assumptions that the material world can be reshaped by technical experts to produce desired results, whether they are commodities for daily consumption and enjoyment or guarantees of well-being and health. In this sense, the factual truths are producible in accordance with human wants. Truth, then, is a result of technical, economic, and political power. Such a production can range from desired crop yields, new technologies through genetically planned "new humanity," to images and incantations that would comprise the conditions of production of the desired effects, resulting in positive public reaction. Indeed, one produces even public opinion including accusations that mass media also engage in ideological rhetoric to "shape" public attitudes and behavior.

The complexity, variety, and conflicting claims of abilities to produce different results by political figures, the numerous instrumental rationalities, defy the ability of ordinary language to offer an encompassing mode of public autonomous reason, and lead the citizen to his or her enclave of specific material wants and their fulfillment. Such an enclosure leads to the treatment of the public domain as an arena of power confrontations, interest laden demands, and calls for leaders who can fulfill such demands. The leaders, in turn, will have expertly designed images and rhetorics that make them into figures capable of producing all the desired results demanded by the public. This is the collapse of, and the fragmentation of, the public domain and the democratic ethos into private moralities, ideologies, myths, and interests. Given this context of political technocrats and theatrics, what is the role of mass media?

JOURNALISM

In a political society, the role of mass media is not merely "free," with rights to print or show anything at will, but above all it is *public*. It speaks to the public and presumes to report states of affairs as they occur. No doubt, there are numerous epistemological arguments concerning the possibility of reporting the "given" without interpretive mediation, and no doubt these arguments should make the public take notice and remain critical. Yet the principle remains, specifically in the domain of public affairs: In order to participate in the public domain, the public should know the states of affairs that are of concern to all. Mass media, as transmitters of such knowledge, are among the most fundamental public "institutions" of democracy. Indeed, one could plausibly contend that they are coextensive with the continuous origination and maintenance of the autonomous source of all laws and legitimation. The uninformed citizen is hardly in a position to grasp public issues and to form a rational judgment. Moreover, the very information is a condition for public dialogue, debate, and adjudication. Democracy, as an incessant self-maintenance, includes in its core the necessity for open information, present and available to everyone, not simply for the sake of extraneous purposes, but for its own sake as part of the ethos of democratic activity. This may be a difficult point to convey in an age that assumes interest-laden, technical and purposive rationality; yet to speak in terms of mass media, it could be argued that irrespective of the type of information, the latter is offered for its own sake as an exercise of public freedom to bring into the public domain a voice or voices that comprise the continuous origination of the free public domain.

The activity of journalism, in this sense, is coextensive with political ethos. If journalists assume the freedom to report and to inform, then they also assume the obligation and duty of maintaining the public arena wherein open and uncompelled debates are carried out in public. They are part of the public and also a facilitation of the public's participation in all political affairs through the very media and information they provide. To speak in terms of the democratic principles explicated so far, mass media and journalism are political communication to the extent that they are geared toward information and thus the public. In this sense, there is no such thing as apolitical reporting. This is to say, in political society journalism is principally political communication—prior to questions of ideology or other agenda.

While being a major avenue of political communication, apart from public gatherings, journalism is not restricted to reports of what the public gatherings are doing or what the appointed office holders are saying. In terms of the understanding of the public domain, it is obvious that any activity or proposal that enters the public domain, even if such activities or proposals are of "private" interest, of necessity becomes a public issue to be adjudicated publicly. In this sense, even private enterprise is an aspect of political agreement to delimit what areas shall be private and what will be seen as public—and thus what is private is equally a public decision. Thus, the common wisdom—claiming that free enterprise might lead to freedom—must be subverted; the very notion of private is a political understanding. This means that in democracy no one should claim the sanctity of private economy. Such a claim would require that a particular enterprise does not demand anything from the public, such as an access to public roads, and so forth. If such an access is sought, the enterprise enters the public domain and its interests become the purview of the public. In this sense, once the private interests enter the public domain, they become of public concern and thus journalistic concern. The public must be informed and the ethos of journalism in democracy requires the reporting of all such entrances in order to activate the participation of the public in public issues. Crucial to the concept of coextension between democracy as its own purpose and journalistic mass media is the principle that whenever journalists appeal to a right of free access to, and a publication of information, they are in a process of origination and maintenance of the autonomous public domain. Such a demand is not natural or social but political. This is to say, taking into account natural wants and social interests, it would be more convenient to subject oneself to the requests of the officials to serve their own or the interests of their friends for rewards, pleasures, or position. Yet, precisely such a subjection becomes instrumental, purposive, and interest laden, and thus social and not political. Journalists subject to these conditions are no longer a part of the political domain but are marketers of specific commodities that are adorned with the signs of the interests of the seller. They are in an advertisement business and sell "designer news," or more bluntly speaking, they sell technical training for other than political reasons.

No doubt, one must report the "given," but in the contemporary sway of political technocracy and candidates by design, one must go beyond the so-called reporting of the given (e.g., statements or pronouncements by public figures, their posturings, performed rituals, and at base, rhetorical theater). In democracy, political journalism is, above all, duty bound to inform the public about such obfuscating theatrics, and what ignorances, indecisions, equivocations, they are hiding. In turn, journalistic political communication, within the ethos of democracy, must articulate and expose what is or is not relevant for the public, what is private and particular, of no public concern, and what is essential in the proposals of current or prospective public figures. If such a public figure offers a technical solution to some public concern, the task of journalistic communication is not merely to repeat what such a figure stated, but to raise questions whether the statement is an accurate and adequate comprehension of a given subject matter relevant to public concerns. Indeed, the task is to inform the public that a given public officer has no comprehension and is merely using generalities to obfuscate his or her ignorance. To say the least, this is a heavy burden on political journalism, yet given the temptation of public figures to offer theatrical rhetorical "solutions" to public issues, it becomes the task of political journalism to maintain the public domain clear of obfuscations and theatrics for democratic, rational decisions. Such journalistic practice not only provides information, but also guarantees that any public figure is called on to account for his or her rhetorical theatrics, introduction of myths, moralities, and even ideologies into the public arena.

The importance of the function of journalistic communication for political society cannot be sufficiently emphasized. Despite the constitutional forms, governmental functions and divisions it may take, free press, in the delimited activity just discussed, is *the* sole and unavoidable institution in all political societies. It is, to say most emphatically, coextensive with the ethos of democracy and the very public domain wherein autonomous individuals make informed decisions. Perhaps this emphasis is more required today than at previous historical junctures—in light of the attacks by public figures on the press. In order to deflect such attacks and to insure the trust of the public in political journalism, members of the press must be equally up to the task of their own calling. That is to say, they must know what they are talking about in order to tear the veil of rhetorical theater from the postures of public figures. Those who accept the burdens of this task must also be cognizant of the ethos of political society, of democracy.

POSTSCRIPT

Political communication is strictly distinguished from social and individual activities that are interest-laden and thus lack the autonomy to be political. The latter belongs solely to political societies that are democratic. Indeed, there must be a strict restriction of the use of "political" to a public domain in which every member of society participates in public debates and decisions. This participation is the continuous origination and maintenance of the political domain as a guarantee of human autonomy and equality. This equally suggests that the publicly appointed officials are bound by the democratic ethos to maintain such a public domain and thus are called on to communicate the public issues; any communication that is designed for effect, for rhetorical obfuscation, is interest-laden and hence designed to advance the motives of an individual or a group and not the concerns of the public. In various ways, such a communication, and those who in their expertise help in its design, adds to the legitimation crisis that leads finally to public cynicism. Political journalism, as part and parcel of the originating and maintaining of the political society, is designed to serve the public by providing information that is of public concern. This is not to say that gossip columns of social interest are to be excluded from mass media. Rather, the primary task is information—despite the tendency of the public officials and their experts to obfuscate and mislead. One could, in fact, argue that political journalism and communication is, by now, the primary instrument of continuing the origination and maintenance of political (i.e., democratic) society.

FOUR

Dialogical Structure of Social Relevance: Establishing Social Validity

One of the more troublesome issues confronting social scientists who share a broadly phenomenological outlook on social science concerns the nature of the relationship between social scientific knowledge and social scientific research. Stated in the broadest terms, the issue forms part of the larger paradox constituted, employing Apel's (1980) analysis, by the "disjunction between the value-free objectivity of the sciences and subjective private morality" (p. 253) within the modern liberal consciousness. We propose to limit the question to that of the dual role of the social scientific researcher who is the creator and possessor of social knowledge as well as a social being who unavoidably participates in the social process of democratic politics and power relations. Although this question about the relationship between social knowledge and social being can be, and has been, posed for the social scientific community, as a whole, we shall further restrict the scope of this question by considering only how it can be addressed within the context of phenomenological social science.

PHENOMENOLOGICAL REFLECTIONS AND THE THESIS OF THE LIFE-WORLD

When it embraced Husserl's concept of the life-world, phenomenological social science relinquished the various epistemological and methodological privileges associated with the disembodied, historyless *ego cogito* underpinning the scientific consciousness. In its place, it accepted the principle of life-world situatedness and, thereby, became formally obligated to seek out criteria for meaningfulness and validation that are clearly related in the social process out of which social scientific reflection has emerged. From the standpoint of conducting social scientific research, the life-world thesis has at least the following general implications:

> Phenomenological understanding means that there is no pure social science or scientific theory which is not influenced by the socio-historical tradition from which it emerged. The social researcher, using theories and techniques for investigating social phenomena and the meaning of social relativity, is a part of the phenomena and activity and hence is influenced by them. The social researcher cannot claim immunity from social norms and influence, and hence his or her theories and methods are equally influenced by the socio-historically acquired norms and linguistic prejudices. After all, it is the social researcher who formulated the theories and methods out of the socio-historically acquired fund of understanding within which he or she lives. Both the social researcher and his or her theories are second level constructions which are understandable only in terms of the socio-historically acquired understanding from which they were originated. (Mickunas, 1983, p. 18)

Rephrased in the shorthand jargon of phenomenology, the conduct of social scientific research cannot be separated from the ongoing social process by which such activity is permanently and necessarily substructed and informed, and only by virtue of which the research activity obtains *prima facia* legitimacy as a possible mode of activity permissible within a given social organization of life.

The formal methodological question that usually arises at this point concerns the cognitive problems of scientific presuppositionlessness and the complications associated with the modes of "giveness" peculiar to social scientific data. But the problem does not end here. That is to say, given the life-world premise, phenomenological social scientific inquiry must not only *speak from* the social process as the condition of conducted experientially grounded inquiry, it must also return to that very social process as the only available resource for establishing its authentically intersubjective veridicality or, if you will, its claim to social truth. Phenomenological social scientific inquiry must also *speak to* the life-world community composed of social actions as the conditions for its gauging both the cognitive adequacy of its determinations and the social validity of its conclusions. Only in this way, by both speaking from and speaking to the life-world, does phenomenological social scientific inquiry do justice to its acknowledged situatedness within the sociohistorical process of a living human community.

Phenomenological social scientific inquiry constitutes a mode of *praxis* given within the social process whose completion presupposes its interpretation within that social process. The circle of understanding (from and to the social process) described by the life-world situated accountability of phenomenological social scientific reflection sets a distinguishing mark of lived concreteness on phenomenological social science (and prevents it from lapsing into bourgeois social science and into positivized Platonism).

The primary orientation of phenomenological social science must be the domain of actual social practice, because for actual phenomenological social science, at any rate, this life-world domain bounded by lived social practice constitutes the methodological basis for its essential insight, and distinguishes it from "worldless" scientific rationalisms.

The methodological initiatives established for the research projects in which we are engaged have been framed in terms of the set of concerns just described about establishing social validity within the context of phenomenological social scientific research practice. The remainder of this chapter briefly summarizes the broader methodological structure of this research. The organization of the following discussion proceeds from the general to the specific. It begins by differentiating in broad strokes the phenomenological research perspective from alternative research and analytic viewpoints, then outlines some key methodological principles underpinning the research, and finally suggests some important applications of these discursive moments within the project design and research practice.

SOCIAL SCIENTIFIC OBJECTIVES AND SOCIAL SCIENTIFIC OBJECTIVITY

This discussion reviews two of three alternative methodological viewpoints from the standpoint of their adequacy to the constitution of the life-world and, in that light, assesses them with respect to research practice. Although the authors regard communicative accountability or community social action research (see subse-

quent section) as the preferred methodological standpoint for both
phenomenological and practical reasons, it should be noted that
we do not think that these viewpoints are altogether incompatible
(alternatives in the strict sense), nor are we asserting that the two
methodological viewpoints discussed in this section are irrelevant
or wrong, but merely that they are inadequate from the standpoint
of phenomenological social science.

Methodological standpoints constitute formalizable discursive strategies exhibiting the social scientist's process itself. The
nature of this challenge is aptly portrayed by O'Neill (1975):

> Science always obliges us to forget what we know. In this way we may
> learn much though we may still lack wisdom. In the case of the nat-
> ural world, our power over things is compensation enough for the
> separations of knowledge. But in the social world we cannot start
> with any certain distance between what we know ordinarily and the
> reports of sociology. For the social order does not wait upon the con-
> structions of scientific reason. It makes sense from the first day until
> the last in the all-day and everyday surroundings of others whose life
> we share. Nothing lies outside of this circumstance, neither its igno-
> rance nor its fears, neither its joys nor its injuries. The mystery of
> this circumstance measures the poverty of sociology. (p. 39)

The social scientist encounters a world that is not only made
ready-to-hand in Heidegger's sense but which also has always
made sense of itself completely, and the sedimented sensefulness
of which will continue to thrive regardless of the presence of a
social scientist within it. The scientific consciousness reconstitutes
the social world through an original act of objectification that sets
the world at a mute distance in hopes of recouping the lived world
in the form of a known world by populating the resulting inter-
stices between things with the discursive productions of the scientific intellect.

Among the various pathways of intellectual indirection, the
social scientist may take the cognitive reacquisition of the lived
social process; the most frequently traveled one has been staked out
by objectivist social science. Objectivist social science has created a
kind of semiotic of social objects, complete with an explanatory and
predictive semantic, a highly mathematized syntactic, and a social
survey and quasi-experimental pragmatics. The chief advantages of
methodological objectivism are its methodical clarity and analytical
tidiness, which issue from its carefully crafted *a priori* determinations for defining, measuring, and evaluating social facts.

The litany of objectivist social science's faults, both cardi-
nal and venial, has been regularly rehearsed in the literature, and
so need not detain us here. For present purposes, it is only important to recognize that methodical scientific detachment does not

guarantee epistemic objectivity as much as it ensures existential disengagement from the social process. The methodological stance of objectivist social science has the advantage of being teachable. Unfortunately, the language game of cognitive domination is virtually inaccessible to all but the initiated (Widman, 1982). For these reasons, although undeniably professional, its data and its conclusions are incomprehensible from the social situation of human beings and consequently generate minimal social self-understanding for them. Because its significance is almost entirely exhausted toward the discursive assumptions of hypothetico-deductive predictiveness and methodological rationality, social scientific objectivism tends to *speak for* and *about* human social existence rather than *from* it or *to* it.

In contrast, the methodological outlook that we are labeling *social scientific objectivity* emphasizes descriptive accuracy and narrative-like detail in the study of the social process. Despite producing data possessing a high degree of verisimilitude and richness, in many ways methodological objectivity has substituted a reiterative and empirical, in the narrow sense, orientation toward the social subject for the detached cognitive manipulation of social objects characteristic of social scientific objectivism. The preoccupation of social science objectivity with qualitative fidelity in the scientific representations of its chosen objects can make it exceedingly difficult to detect a theoretical interest within the research.

This phenomenographic, as distinguished from phenomenological, preference for exacting description of the meaning structures revealed within the life-world can be found in phenomenological social scientific as well as *Verstehen*-oriented literature The phenomenological disclosure of the life-world—one might also say its legitimation as a object for social scientific inquiry—as a region of phenomena which had hitherto remained "anonymous" lent the mute social objects of objectivist social science a voice that occasionally approaches cacophonous proportions.

In light of the new-found importance of the social subject, an apparent reversal of the researcher/researched tends to take place, sometimes framed in the vocabulary of partnership, which masks the true nature of the social scientist's continued aloofness from the social situation. In brief, the phenomenographic orientation tends to reify the social present that it so skillfully describes by reducing it to the totality of events and meanings circumscribing the situation *qua* situation. (Pilotta, 1982). Research populations learn soon enough, whether we are talking about a minority group, wage laborers, corporate America, or even a comparatively naive refugee population, that highly descriptive qualitative research often exhibits—much like a novel by Robbes Grillet—quite a bit of scenery but not much of a plot. The notion of part-

nership implies mutual advantage. Quickly enough, research populations begin to ask, quite legitimately, about what is in it for
them. In the absence of a meaningful response from the
researcher, the population will endeavor to avoid or to manipulate
the research condition.

Illumination of a social situation does not inform that situation unless it modalizes the situation by opening up genuine possibilities within it and recovering the original selectivity undergirding
it. This modalization introduces socio-historical reflectivity, which
recasts the present condition as the future of some past and the past
of some possible future (Mickunas, 1977). The fundamental temporal
dimension and its correlate of critical selectivity go untapped in these
largely retrospective analyses. The social researcher typically exits
the research situation; the researched seldom has that prerogative.
Information is power even and perhaps most especially when it
derives from interpersonal or dialogical exchanges: Social knowledge
is readily translatable into social control.

Social scientific objectivity overlooks important elements of
the social process in a different, although related, sense. The
return to the subject from whom information has been garnered
for the purpose of confirming its accuracy and validity constitutes,
depending on whether one adopts a Kantian, a Husserlian, or a
Sartrean perspective, either infinite regress or a futility. At the
same time, it is not enough to say that every understanding is "different," or similarly that "realities" and "perspectives" abound
(Apel, 1980). The inner unity of the social situation must be drawn
forth from within it by means of an ideational moment, whether in
the fashion of Husserlian "essential insight" or Schutzian "ideal-
typical" construction (Schutz, 1967). Otherwise, the unity of the
research object constitutes merely an artifact of its textual compilation. "We must keep in mind that the self-interpretation of the
human event is not identical with the behavior of a specific human
being" (Pilotta, 1982, p. 51). The individual human being can only
be grasped within a mutable horizon of temporal mediation whose
modal contours can be apprehended against the fixed background
constituted in self-critical reflective thematization—in short,
through a theoretic interest having temporal significance from the
standpoint of the researched.

COMMUNICATIVE ACCOUNTABILITY/COMMUNITY SOCIAL ACTION RESEARCH

Speaking generally, communicative accountability designates a
research strategy that endeavors to mediate the distance between

the predominately objective (*objectivism*) and the predominately subjective (*objectivity*) methodological standpoints, and by doing such, to actualize a social scientific complementarity of researcher/researched in a manner consistent with the fundamental unity of social knower and social being manifested in the discursive polarity of speaking from and speaking to the concrete meaningful situatedness of life-world experience.

In this section, we shall discuss the main principles underlying methodological communicative accountability and address some of their implications for conducting phenomenological social scientific research. In the interests of brevity and of maintaining the primary methodological focus of this chapter, we shall refrain from extensive illustration drawn from current research activity.

A research procedure premised on communicative accountability attempts to illuminate equally from the empirical and the discursive points of view the chief state and dynamic properties of the social situation and to engage the research population in an open-ended dialogue about the accuracy, appropriateness, and value of the research process. These two tasks are not separated operationally, rather they are mutually reinforcing simultaneous agenda whose objectives are tapping into the social reflectivity present within the modal qualities of the social situation. This procedure makes three assumptions: (a) it is necessary that social research data and its outcomes establish social knowledge that generally reflects community interest, (b) social research needs to involve technical assistance or policy features and must be responsive to perceived needs and concerns of the research population, and (c) social research must not obstruct or attenuate but hopefully promote community self-determination. In summary, the social researcher acknowledges his or her participation within the significative configuration of a social life-world and actively engages this experiential *a priori* as a constitutive criterion for the social scientific validity of his or her research pursuits.

An immediate consequence of this viewpoint is the elevation of social historicity and a temporal orientation toward action to a prominent design and assessment function both from the standpoint of the research activity itself and from that of the community. This discursive methodological premise of actual or potential action-centered engagement, as distinguished from an adventitious or psycho–personal action orientation, becomes thematic and operational on the basis of the concept of enablement.

It is against the background of enablement that the social being emerges as a limited (and intelligible) possibility within a temporally pre-constituted social world where, as a kind of "oriented possibility," social existence "emerges as a product-producer, the locus where necessity can turn into concrete liberty (Merleau-

Ponty, 1968, p. 104). This concrete temporalization of the research process generates a historically/ethically obligating partnership of research/researched, a cooperative working-out of some future. In the words of Husserl, "The future is for the I of its possibilities and the I of the present which opens itself toward the future is the I can: its original corporeal practicality" (Piana, 1972, p. 114).

The world is never given as a totality but always contains a "more" that is enacted before it can be represented by thought.[1] The social structural liaison of researcher/researched is founded on a pre-reflective inter-corporeity that sets taken-for-granted meanings into relief against a background constituted by a shared practical interest. From the standpoint of securing useful social scientific data, the accessibility and the reliability of the information increases proportionately with the mutual investment of each party in the other. In the conduct of our research, valuable, accurate, and—as we have determined—unique information has been shared with us because we are doing something and therefore need to learn how things really work. In a similar fashion, needing-to-know, willing-to-listen, and in-order-to-do modes soon become experientially correlated. Enablement is constructed on a basic corporeal motility that already inhabits the world and that has already responded to the call of things long before thought reaches forth to grasp them. The openness of space and the pliability of time are extensions of an essential corporeal motility (Merleau-Ponty, 1974).

A second important consequence of communicative accountability is an effort to employ "relevance" as a standard guiding the selection of strategies for eliciting information and for creating favorable implementation conditions (Schutz, 1964). At the same time, these strategies must contain the potential for stimulating critical self-comprehension. Accomplishing this requires the researcher's being leery about overindulgence in well-rehearsed and highly convenient modes of self-articulation—of a reiterative stance that would absolutize the merely present. Uncritical empathy can secure the staging ground for domination. As Lingis (1982) observed:

> If it is only our needs and wants that get articulated in signs, in herd signals, that is not only because it is the only common form of our impulses that can be understood by others, but because the others want to hear only our needs and lacks. For our needs and lacks are apprehended by others as appeals to themselves, expressions of dependence upon them, declarations of subservience, invitations to subjugation. It is through our needs and lacks that we appeal to the will in the others—the will to power in the others, the will to dominate. (p. 168)

---

[1]See Schutz (1967), the "because motive" and the "in order to motive."

The Nietzschean moment within client-servicing social and administrative institutions is only too well-known to the social scientist. But the central difficulty to be gotten around here is that empathic understanding, however well intentioned, can lead to the disengagement of the social scientist's legitimate claim to truth. Moreover, in dealing with individual needs and social situational lacks, it is presupposed that the corrective is not to be found with the existing conditions because it is precisely these positive conditions that are deemed inadequate by the social agents. Such a judgment asserting the inadequacy of the present is grounded on a not-yet-realized, and so modal, possibility. In this circumstance, not simply an interpretive effort, but a response verbal or otherwise, is incumbent on the researcher. Functional standards for ascertaining relevance that promote recipient autonomization provide an avenue transmuted into interpersonal domination.

The method by which the researcher goes about accomplishing these ends can be adapted from the phenomenological concept of the dialogical. As operationalized within the research process, communicative accountability, in contrast with social scientific objectivism and social science objectivity, invokes a concept of communicatively constituted interobjectivity. It is not the persons' meanings, or the intentions of the communicators, nor is it the objective social circumstance of the communication. Instead, it is the articulation and critical analysis of shared social objects, in the form of the premises and the referents of possible social action, as they are addressed to and thought through with the researchers that furnishes phenomenological social scientific research with an intersubjective focus and with interpersonal accountability.

At this level, the research proceeds through the identification and elaboration of key, situationally relevant themes. In our community action research, for example, letting the community speak has emerged as an important theme. But it is not merely the opportunity to speak as such, but rather the invitation to speak about something in particular and for some end that has generated a kind of meaning-core around which various concerns come to be articulated and analyzed.

Themes are resident in overlapping topics, in the recurrence of metaphors or adjective groups, and also in what is consistently *not* spoken. Some thematics are most or first visible in a certain incongruence between what is spoken and what is done. It is the emergence of themes that guides for the researcher the development of research questions, and shapes the project's progress in a way that will help ensure the vaildity of the research conclusions in terms of the subjective understanding of the social actors. This is because the identification of themes involves a dialogue of sorts between the field researcher and his or her interlocutors; for as the researcher works by sorting through notes, speculating, and discussing ideas with colleagues to extract potential themes, he or she must test out these suggested themes, refine their potentialities by tossing them out directly or indirectly into the very environment from which they have emerged. Interpretive methodologies are not interpretive in the sense that they balance solely on the idiosyncratic interpretation of the researcher, but rather they are interpretive in their insistence on the acknowledgment of the actor-subjective meanings, and their utilization of that knowledge to inform the actual research and research products.

Thematics point to a different, unarticulated, and frequently imperfectly understood or acknowledged level of social reality. They are signs and so part of a communication code—a pattern of signification. They have primary meaning while concurrently carrying out additional embedded cultural, social, and historical meaning. Thus, thematics hint at the forest beyond the daily lived reality of the individual trees of life, or, in this case, of the organization. The forest is paradoxical in nature; genuine understanding of it requires both the lived experience among these metaphorical trees as well as a hawk's view of the collectivity.

The thematic meaning-core secures a generalizable motivational basis allowing for personal, organizational, and institutional autonomy, and so the pursuit of private interests, within the framework of a collaborative, symbolically mediated orientation.[2] This generalizable thematic core is not synonymous operationally with a superordinate goal, precisely because the meaning of the thematic core can vary widely among the different participants. The intentions of the researchers, for example, and what they see in the research process is significantly, if not altogether, different from the intentions and understandings current among the many individuals, communities, and institutions involved with the research project.

If we liken the thematic core to an overdetermined symbol suffusing a field of action, then the symbolically generalized action system is permeated by multiple meaning potential, inscribing a system of possible orientations that allow the various social agents to particularize their experience and acts. As the consequence, the field of action subtends a horizon of possible meanings that surpasses its specifications by virtue of ordering thematically the various meanings and acts but yet does not exist apart from its multiple particularizations. The symbolically suffused action system can be centered from any point within the system and then spread (interpreted) from that point in any interpersonal, temporal, and practical orientation. Individuals and groups actualize (enact) available meaning contin-

---

[2]This principle is drawn from Niklas Luhmann (1975, 1982).

gencies, and thereby idiosyncratically reproduce communicatively generalized social processes; the many realities represented by individual perceptual systems periodically undergo the push and pull of reconciliation and resignification. In this manner, the *many* and the *one* of sociality collaborate and understand one another while pursuing their distinctive orientations.

The community action social scientist begins from the premise of the incontestability of life-world experience. But, at the same time, the critical distance to that pre-scientific world of sedimented intentionalities can disclose—amidst the everydayness of taken-for-granted meaning structures—the possibility of its transformation as well as the fundamental temporal accomplishments that sustain it. In the movement from the life-world to reflection, the social scientist recovers acts of social expressions underlying human social arrangements. In the movement back from reflection toward the life-world, phenomenological social science brings clarity and essential insight, but highlights most of all the need of the researcher to confirm his or her theoretic predisposition through concrete engagement in the social organization of action.

RELEVANCE AND NEED

Every cultural being lives within a scheme of interpretation and orientation incorporated into a system of relevance. Every consequential decision that people encounter brings them face to face with what is relevant to them. The questions of whether and how a technology is to be introduced into one's own culture as well as the questions of whether and by what methods one should introduce a technology into another culture require reflection informed by knowledge about relevant variables of social communication and of cultural value selection.

The concept of *relevance* designates the composite of values, their interconnectedness and the functional unity they express within a society. Relevance is what matters to a specific sociocultural group and forms part of a network of "all that matters" to it, including the history of the group's past commitments. A system of relevance exists at every historical moment and is part of a people's social heritage, transmitted through their specific educational process to all its members (Natanson, 1970). Relevance functions: (a) to determine what facts, events or problems are to be treated with equal or unequal value; and (b) as both a scheme of interpretation and as a scheme of orientation for each member of a group, constituting patterns of meaningful conduct and discourse (Schutz, 1964).

We can be responsive and responsible to another culture or community only if we come to understand our own system of relevances as they have been identified and articulated by the human and social sciences and only if we understand how, in turn, the human and social sciences influence the system of relevances. Moreover, we can only communicate competently with another culture or community if we understand how the relevance embodied in social technology and theories about development and assistance is meaningful in another culture that is the intended recipient of the intervention. The possibility for successful and social–cultural communication rests on establishing the congruence of pertinent relevances. This means that a common scheme of interpretation and orientation must be found, one shared by the deliverer of a social–technology and by its receiver. In order to communicate competently with the recipient culture or community, genuine relevance is a necessary condition for successful communication. Finally, cultural relevance as a criterion of inquiry and of communication can enhance the viability of policy intervention in the community.

One important implication of this redefinition of the communication relationship between the donor and the recipient involves the re-evaluation of the role that *needs* play in assistance projects. Typically, needs are taken to represent objectively occurring insufficiencies that can be identified empirically on the basis of culturally neutral socio-economic frameworks. In fact, needs assessment technologies are imported into minority communities and developing nations and employed on the basis of pre-established, principally Western, liberal contract theory assumptions about social and cultural well-being. In contrast, from the standpoint of the phenomenology of social relevance, needs constitute culturally specific organizing functions that select historical aspirations of social actors by establishing a temporal structure that is composed of expectations differentially attuned to the range of available social features, thereby managing the complexity of the present in relation to the past.

For this reason, need offers a functionally interpretable interface between two cultures that structures the exchange of values taking place between them. In this case, recipient self-determination and self-selection must be encouraged for the sake of identifying interculturally reliable needs and discriminating among various possible solutions on the basis of a dialogically constituted horizon of expectations.

Mattelart (1983) framed such an approach as a "demand"-side policy:

> In terms of policy on experimentation in communication technology, a problem of the new technologies and their diffusion (videotext, electronic directory, optical fibers) has been approached from the "supply" side, analyzing the economic stakes, and the means of ensuring the social penetration of the techniques of communication. In this light, when the social aspect is only seen as an after-effect, experimental research has been conceived of as mere product testing. "Demand" which, on the contrary, starts from the analysis of individual needs and questions the ability of new technologies to respond to them, is only now beginning to be explored. (p. 4)

Given the requirements of dialogical expectations, the recipient community must particularize its needs, making possible the refraction of cultural assumptions and the reflective determination of the original selections implicit within them. In light of an interculturally established criterion of need, it becomes possible to respond cognitively to the available technological and scientific options. It is, however, not inevitable that modifications of response patterns to technology take place. But it is crucial that indeterminacy be introduced in order that a stimulation of existing social mechanisms of reflection occur.

Needs do not exist in a socio-cultural vacuum; they embody relevance structures rooted in social processes that link the future with the past. As part of a dialogue, needs can be employed by functions enabling the recipient culture to particularize the range of possible social and technical futures in a relevant way. Given cultural diversity, there is no *a priori* reason for supposing that "needs" identified by the donor and the "needs" of the recipient are compatible. In short, need must be negotiated and communicatively constructed rather than assumed to be factual and empirical. Moreover, because the social technology methods of research policies themselves are laden with temporal selections— they are *pasts* selecting expected *futures* from among available *presents*—temporal articulations cannot be assumed to be compatible cross-culturally.

Assessing need makes salient boundary-maintenance performances that must be fulfilled on the basis of the reflective mechanisms serving various subsystems of organized activity within a given society (e.g., political institutions, family arrangements, and social topographics). For this reason, need offers a functionally interpretable interface between two communities that structure the exchange of values taking place between them. In this case, recipient self-determination and self-selection must be encouraged for the sake of identifying interculturally reliable needs and discriminating among various possible solutions on the basis of a dialogically constituted horizon of expectations.

HOW IS RELEVANCE ESTABLISHED IN THE INTERVIEW?

Relevance is determined along the lines of an individual's presuppositions and anticipations. The interviewer establishes and reveals his or her relevancies on the basis of what matters. What matters is relevant as part of a context of all that matters socially. In the case of the interviewer, what matters is a part of the context within which he or she works. For example, organizational utility is an aspect of what matters. Relevance also has a biographical dimension that connects the evaluator's present and past commitments. The interviewer may take X as personally relevant. This relevancy becomes part of the interpretive context and is a part of the interviewer's perception of the respondent's situation. What is seen as important is therefore imputed to the subject in terms of the observer's (interviewer's) reality. She or he *thinks* that is the case, but it might not be the case. Something is truly relevant when the respondent takes as relevant that which coincides with that which the interviewer views to be relevant. This is an interpretative agreement. The agreement is interpreted to be the reality of a mutually defined understanding of what is going on. Objective knowledge then is established in the interview. The danger is that the interviewer from his of her point of view may impose his or her criteria of relevance on the respondent, by simply assuming that those criteria hold good for many individuals of a certain type. This is an example of defining a situation and attributing to it a general meaning in terms of a particular system of relevance. Cicourel (1964) develops this point:

> . . . both interviewers and respondents can be viewed as [generally] social types and that [sic] they treat each other as such. Thus, though certain subjects and some observers can control the imputations attached to others, they cannot always control their actions or suspend the relevance of the imputations for the purpose of the brief encounter. We find that continuous situational imputations, strategies, and the like occur which influence how actors treat each other and manage their presence before each other. Now, these are precisely the conditions found in everyday life. (p. 27)

When two individuals communicate, they interpret each other's views and experiences, which results in the development of a basis for a communication to other individuals. Therefore, in the interviewing process, theories cannot be seen as merely conceptual and useful for analyzing the situation indifferently. In the interview situation, the evaluator's social definitions assume the form of a theory that influences the subject, who in turn influences the theory. Under the scientific code of conduct, however, theory is at best a labeling or ordering tool, which is generally constructed and subsequently thought to be valid for assessing all data.

Since theoretical statements such as "deviant," "addict," "indigent," "criminal," "good guy," and so on, are not necessarily connected to a particular corresponding reality, and these labels can serve to describe various kinds of people, then the connection between the labeling process and the particular reality must have someone to connect the two. The evaluator becomes the connector, and the connection is based on someone's interest or presuppositions about the nature of social reality. If the connection of social labeling is based on a connector's interests, then the evaluator is engaged in a selection process. This selection process assumes that characteristics are chosen as relevant or irrelevant, based on what matters or what is perceived to be socially relevant. The selection process makes evaluators become aware that they do not deal with purely objective data. The evaluator is social and therefore must already understand the individuals he or she is about to question. To already have understood is to presuppose that linguistic categories do indeed remain indigenous to the interview situation and therefore cannot be thought of as inherently abstract or objective. Therefore, interview situations assume a mutual interaction situation comprised of the evaluator and his or her source of data (the client), which is substantiated on a common understanding of that situation.

The interviewing process demands that there is a cooperation or co-orientation based on a selecting process. Speaking and listening, speaking and answering, is one event with various phases. Questions and answers are unified in a reciprocal movement. Questions initiated by the questioner reach their aim in the countermovement of an answer by a respondent who fulfills the intent of the original question. When an evaluator addresses the respondent about something, the evaluator assumes an active initiation on the part of the respondent. When he or she asks a question, there is already an expectation of an answer that fulfills the question and that contains the various possibilities of accepting, rejecting, or correcting the answer or rephrasing the question. The response is contained in the interviewing process from its inception. This is directly counter to what Patton (1980) presumes to be the case in his view of the phenomenological approach to interviewing. Rather, a phenomenological view of interviewing assumes this mutual shaping of question and answer. Evaluator and respondent are interrelated. Every initiation of a question is a simultaneous expectation of a response. The interviewer gives the correspondent something to understand, and this allows the respondent to listen and to become immersed in the question in his or her own way. Listening is itself an invitation. When the interview opens, the subject is already participating, and the subject's inability to accept a question can indeed hinder the interview. In the reception of a question, the subject is already propelled toward an expected answer, which is a response toward certain events, or toward certain future possibilities where the answer is accepted, rejected, understood, or questioned. While listening, and at the same time formulating an answer, the listener interweaves this passive and active listening in order to formulate a response. This intermixing constitutes a single process which involves the evaluator, the respondent, and the topic of concern.

The act of verbal communication is based on a reciprocally endorsed contract between the evaluator and the respondent. It must now be assumed that the linguistic exchange between the evaluator and the client is continuously listener-oriented and monitored in accordance with assumptions pertaining to the development of a common social world and convergent modes of categorization.

The structure of taken-for-granted anticipation and expectation which assumes the interrelatedness in the form of a common social understanding between the evaluator and the respondent is related to a crucial interviewing problem that was identified by Hyman (1954, p. 30):

> While the role is prescribed by the agency and usually maintained by various enforcement measures or by the interviewer's sheer acceptance of it on the basis of knowledge of the agency's demands, there may well be conflict with other definitions of the role proceeding from a variety of sources. For example, the interviewer may have views as to what other interviewers or his immediate field supervisor or particular respondents regard as proper interviewing behavior. While we have no evidence as to such direct social influences on the definition of the role, we do have considerable evidence that the definition may often proceed from certain beliefs the interviewer has as to the nature of attitudes, the nature of respondent behavior, or the quality of the survey procedures, although there is the possibility that they may also provide gratification for the various needs. (p. 30)

Hyman notes how various sources of data alteration can be induced by an agency's structural or managerial constraints, formal theories, and undocumented presuppositions, and the everyday social world *while* they are collected.

INTERVIEWING CONSTRAINTS

The constraints of the social organization can aid in the organization and classification of individuals who enter the agency. Social organizations as a rule label or generalize in terms of typically acceptable statements concerning the nature of social life. A generalization is presumed to operate effectively to maintain the social order of the organization. Clients are admitted, classified, and organized properly into some type of order. Yet, social individuals do not necessarily organize their lives around the ordering process of an organization relative to the way they define their social worlds.

Presuppositions made on the part of individuals in an organization are motivated by the belief that their organization is an evolutionary or organic system that develops naturally; then, the classificatory categories or labeling processes are presumed to be the natural logic of the organizations. When this is a major organizational presupposition, the classificatory ordering process influences how individuals are defined, as well as constructing typical questions that are thought to be of relevance for any individual who enters that organization. The "natural logic" of the organization can therefore influence and shape the cognitive expectations of the evaluator's very questions, and in turn shape the client in terms of typical responses.

Zimmerman (1969), in his research on the intake procedure at a California welfare agency, shows that the type of administrative knowledge required to run this particular welfare agency was not believed to be naturally valid by its front-line employees. These front-line employees (case workers), moreover, were "socialized" or forced to use an administrative frame of reference when interviewing prospective clients. The process of socialization or learning how to keep records was used to secure an accurate knowledge base used for the proper selection of clients who were in need of welfare. To be socialized into knowing the process of securing a knowledge base meant, in this case, learning a methodology used for documenting client information imposed by the administration of the agency. In order to assure that accurate information could be obtained, the logic of the methodology was followed by the interviewers at the intake office under closely monitored conditions to ensure the procedural rigor of data collection. This is a forced method of standardization that contains its own logic; yet this procedural logic may not conform to the logic of the situation as viewed by the client. Yet, as "standard procedure" it was viewed as "official." This study points out that a methodology can go unquestioned if all interviewing procedures are viewed to be in a one-to-one correlation to the organizational presuppositions pertaining to the inherent, natural, evolutionary development of an agency. When this is the case, the "standard" practices are thought to be natural and hence command obedience in the form of official practices. The interview procedure may reflect the agency's need for organizational maintenance, and therefore may not provide knowledge relevant to the client's situation in the agency.

Based on this model of interviewing, expectations are a part of the interaction process present in everyday life, in which observation, questions and answers, and biographical and institutional arrangements interact in the process of selecting data in terms of their relevance. In the interview, the presuppositions of formal or informal theories function as prejudgments or prejudices that in turn guide definitions of adequate and inadequate information. To be governed by prejudgments is not to be viewed as necessarily negative, but as an affirmation of the need to develop a common understanding that binds an evaluator to a particular framework of cognitive expectations and orientations that may or may not be foreign to the agency of which the interviewer is a member.

For example, the intake interview in a mental health center may be used to ascertain the need for counseling. If the function of determining appropriate counseling is governed by the motto "know thyself," the intake interview would necessarily be oriented to the client's own enlightened self-understanding. Yet, if the intake is already presupposed to be a medical or therapeutic interview, then the implied attitude pertaining to changing the client's situation presupposes the kinds of questions that will be asked. In this case, the client's self-understanding is necessary only to evaluate a psychological situation, in order to achieve "good health" by adjusting to the situation. Yet, adjustment to a situation may not be viewed by the client to be in his or her best interest. If information is collected by the evaluator in the interest of social adjustment, then a set of prescriptions are already established that outline how a client's or subject's responses should be evaluated. These prescriptions inadvertently detail what responses are considered to be indicative of good health or proper adjustment. Yet, another theory of psychological health may result in an identical behavior being viewed as entirely different in terms of its acceptability. The point here is that an interviewer may define a client's behavior without really understanding how the client views his or her own behavior.

The following interview strategy is based on "communicative competence," for it is designed to allow the interviewee's expressions to be understood on their terms. It is based on a natural communication model, which allows for mutual clarification among the parties. Immediate intersubjective or interlayer reliability is possible, thus ensuring that a mutual understanding of possibly competing validity claims is secured, in order to increase the worth of all information collected. The following outlines both the rationale for this interview process and the logistics of its implementation. For the interview sessions conducted, we developed an interview technique. This strategy is called the *multiple interviewer verification strategy*. Each interview session employs two interviewers for the following reasons: single interviewer sessions are quite clumsy when attempting to coordinate questioning and writing; single interviewers cannot pay adequate attention to the conversation in which they are engaged, thus creating a highly contrived situation; and single interviewer sessions offer minimal opportunities for the clarification of information. The general thrust of the multiple interviewer verification strategy is to create a comfortable situation that allows information to be exchanged and documented without jeopardizing the continuity of the interview, while also allowing for information clarification.

It is the information clarification facet of this interview technique that ensures the operationalization of "communicative competence" in each interview session. In any communicative exchange, two individuals might register a piece of information, yet with each party, meaning might be totally obscured. Many theorists argue this occurrence can be avoided by having a person interviewed by different persons at different times. The purpose of this protracted type of interview is to allow the subtleties of any communication to be teased out and elaborated, in order to increase interpersonal understanding. Yet, as more than adequately illustrated by the work of Garfinkle, when one party in an exchange continually questions the other to secure further clarification, the relationship eventually becomes adversial and communication terminates. However, Simmel (1964) has shown that when three persons are present, the situation is suddenly conceived to be more public, and requests for clarification are perceived as more acceptable. In addition, requests can be alternated between interviewers, thus creating a situation more consistent with natural communication in a public place.

During each interview session, a type of "public" testimony is required, allowing all information to be understood in the terms of the intention of speaker. When one speaker in the interview session is addressed by another, a second-level discussion about that original communication can be initiated by a third party, thus allowing for the intricacies of the initial exchange to dilate in a nonchallenging or nonthreatening manner. Simply, "talk about talk" can be generated unobstrusively, without the interviewee feeling his or her statements are continually under scrutiny by an adversary. Through this type of public or open talk, communicative competence is operationalized, in that the inner or intended meaning of a communication can be apprehended. As in the course of any natural, public communication, more indepth insight can be obtained without truncating the communicative process.

This interview strategy incorporates a process of reflection that allows each member in a discussion to recognize that the assumptions he or she is making about communication may not be shared by everyone. When this awareness is engendered, real or sensitive communication can begin, for each person feels the need to explicate assumptions that are not universally adopted at the outset of an investigation. A legitimate need for additional clarification is present, illustrating that requests for such clarification are not merely indicative of academic curiosity. Instead, as in any non-contrived communicative situation, the need for clarification is recognized and the additional information required is provided. This multiple interviewer verification strategy is designed to address this need for discussion about the assumptions of communication, so that intensive dialogue can be initiated among communicating parties. Dialogue and intersubjectivity are fundamental axioms of communicative competence.

The research projects presented in the following chapters utilized this process of interviewing. The "clarification" interview is particularly important, for it not only produces socially valid and reliable information, but it increases the public character of the action research for the interviewee and "other" members of the community of concern. At a very basic level, it shows a true commitment, an investment in the community, as well as providing a measurable "success" for the community members by establishing that they have something *significant* to say.

FIVE

Case Studies

The following case studies are presented in the form of the actual reports that were submitted to the communities of relevance: the citizens of concern, agency officials, politicians, legal authorities, media personnel, and so on, as well as the academic administration. The actual documents are presented here (with modification of tenses) in order to demonstrate that the "report" has a public character and is the mechanism for creating not only rhetorical differences, but motives for action and countervailing action. The writing of the report has been crafted to manage all the competing interests involved if significant action is to result beneficially to the community of concern. All reports will immediately be cast into a political action framework with analysis and competing strategies created. All documents of action need to be crafted to meet the context of all other documents related to the community. The documents will be viewed not only as documents for the marketing of power but will be perceived by the media as documents of power, framed as such to "mobilize the media" as accomplices to the demands of the documents and to which the media will gladly comply. Lessons to be learned on community-based marketing and how the media can participate appear in the last chapter.

DRIVING PARK PROJECT

Background

In August 1981, the project "Assessing Nonintegrative Law in the Black Community" was initiated in the Driving Park area of Columbus, Ohio. The estimated population of this area is 13,000 (descriptive comparative statistics for Driving Park can be found in Appendix A). Driving Park is a city-chartered commission that is chaired by Khari Enaharo.

The Driving Park Commission and the project director, Joseph J. Pilotta, collaborated in developing a unique community-based research project in accordance with Ohio State University's premise that university research expertise can be useful to the community at large in developing a research/service project that genuinely reflects the community's interests. The information that was gathered for the Driving Park project can be utilized to establish open channels of communication with human delivery systems that have been designed to tend to their specific needs.

Residents of Driving Park view the area itself as having made progress in recent years. However, in the 6 years prior to the project's inception, there had been a rapid increase in crime (see Appendix B) which alarmed the citizens and created an atmosphere of powerlessness in terms of developing concrete social action to reduce crime, which is necessary for maintaining community development.

A Black male was shot by the police during a robbery in Driving Park. The shooting generated tensions regarding the issue of police using "deadly force." In response to this event, the commission set up a community–police relations board to mediate and eradicate potential conflict between the police and the predominantly Black Driving Park community. Because of the establishment of a community-police relations board, there was a genuine receptivity for a community-based project that could yield information in an effort to reduce crime and, in turn, that could facilitate systems which were responsive to their situation.

The title "Assessing Non-Integrative Law in the Black Community" indicates that the legal system is a human delivery system consisting of all social communication that is formulated in reference to the law, including daily life in which citizens raise legal questions or register or repudiate legal claims. Therefore, the validity of police practices, the negative orientation of those seeking to violate community norms, the problem of curtailing crime, and so on, are within the legal system to the extent that it is communicated about or there is anticipation of communicating about it. To the degree that the legal system and its auxiliary, the mental health system, does not foster social cohesion or is not responsive to it, can be termed *non-integrative*.

It was the attitude of the Driving Park Commission that law is a power that can create community development (social cohesion) as well as produce tension and fragmentation when it does not meet citizens' needs. Therefore, information obtained from an evaluation, such as this, could furnish a basis for the Driving Park project and the legal system to engage in mutual recognition practices.

Purpose and Aim of the Project

It was the commission's intent to evaluate the perceived source of social stress in the Driving Park community. The stress was attributed to the legal system. Subsequently we wanted to develop a working model aimed at enhancing communication between the citizens and the representatives of the legal system. In this way, we believed we would assist in the facilitation of community self-determination.

Rationale

The purpose of law is to be integrative, which means to create social cohesion and trust. The legal system speaks to a community in various ways: through statutes created by legislators, judicial decisions, police behavior, and so forth. If the legal system is viewed as being neither responsive nor relevant to the community's needs, sentiments, and sense of justice, then social stress develops within the community.

In these circumstances, *social stress* is defined as the discrepancy between the way the legal system addresses the community and the way the citizens think the system should communicate itself to the people in order for it to be trustworthy.

Database and Data Analysis

Information was obtained through "key citizen" in-depth, open-ended interviews, and observations at community forums, and block-watch training sessions in the Driving Park area. The staff interviewed 41 key citizens from the area and 23 mental health and social service personnel.

Interviews were open-ended, allowing as much information as possible to be obtained. The questions asked were not preformed but were developed and refined in the preliminary stages of the project in order to capture the concerns of the citizens in the community and also to ascertain the most fruitful way of phrasing the questions. This ensured that the questions asked were *relevant* and *comprehensible* to the citizens. Questions were not developed to capture attitudinal information but rather to assess the extent to which people believed in the legitimacy of the legal system and whether these perceptions of the system may increase social stress. Each interviewee was paid an honorarium for his or her time.

All interviews were conducted by using a "cross-referencing" team approach. (Pilotta, Murphy, Jones, & Wilson, 1981). Two interviewers from the project were present at every interview, with one person conducting the interview and the other serving as a sounding board for clarification. During the interview, the person functioning as the sounding board raised points and issues in a typical conversational manner by using a public verification procedure that ensured that the interviewee's response could be rendered understandable. Following the initial interview, each respondent was contacted again for another interview but with one member of the interview team changed. Changing one member allowed the already collected information to be clarified in terms of a different frame of reference. Due to this strategy, the data obtained can be considered valid and reliable.

One of the major criticisms of the key citizen method is that key citizens may not be representative of a community at large. In order to avoid this criticism, a form of network analysis was employed. Each citizen interviewed was asked to refer us to one or two persons who would be knowledgeable about specific community issues. Each citizen needed to be identified as knowledgeable about the issues by other citizens as well. This procedure was used also to identify mental health and social service personnel.

All community forums and block-watch training sessions in Driving Park were monitored by teams, thus using a cross-checking approach to validate the collected observations and information.

In addition to our own data collection, other data sources were consulted that could have implications for the Driving Park project. Sources consulted were *Ebony Family Expressions*, *The State of Black Columbus*, and *The Client Profile 1980*, which were all produced by the Columbus Urban League. Also, the *Columbus Area Social Profile* (CASP) and the *Community-Originated Studies* (COS) 023 were utilized. (COS 023 was directly related to the Driving Park community; see Appendix C.)

Data was analyzed through triangulation (Patton, 1980) for the purpose of establishing "meaning" in its appropriate context. The criterion of analysis was to understand how the Driving Park community understands itself in terms of the legal system as well as how the legal system understands itself in terms of the Driving Park community. This allowed us to understand the forms of communicative action (Habermas, 1970) each social group takes in relationship to the other and the possibilities for altering these social relationships.

Format

The following sections are based on the relevant concerns of the Driving Park community. The recommendations offered are based on citizens' and agencies' perceptions of practical possibilities for social action in Driving Park.

PERCEIVED FUNCTIONS OF SOCIAL SERVICE AGENCIES

The Community's Perception of Social Service Agencies

The concerns the Driving Park constituency expressed regarding the community mental health system serving it can be separated into two interrelated categories: access to services and community input into the overall planning of these programs. Typically, the citizens of the Driving Park area felt they had little or no influence on the planning of mental health services in their neighborhood, and, subsequently, they were equally uninformed about the services available to them. As a result, most Driving Park citizens overwhelmingly summarized their view of the mental health system as not meeting the needs of the Black community.

This allegation should not be seen as trivial, for a deep-seated feeling exists on the part of this community's members that they have been overlooked by the mental health system. Considering the fact that since 1963, mental health services were supposed to have been community-based, this is a serious deficiency. This mandate has been in effect for almost four decades. The fact that the residents of the Driving Park area believed they had been excluded from the mental health system can be seen as an indication that social and community planners have not paid attention to the issues of importance to this community.

Community members contended that Blacks are "isolated" from social service programs. Therefore, these individuals saw planning activities as being extremely haphazard, resulting in services being provided that were unknown or considered inadequate when they are known. The argument is that planning groups have not taken the time necessary to accurately assess the needs of the Black citizenry. Black community leaders interviewed said they most often learn about proposed plans through newspaper articles and are always surprised by what they read. At best, Black community leaders had been consulted only subsequent to the formulation of any plans and were then merely asked to endorse programs that are already scheduled to be implemented. Plans and proposals were never submitted to them on a regular basis for their approval before such pursuits were undertaken. When Black leaders were invited to participate in "high-level" planning sessions, they felt they were not given adequate time nor the information necessary to make a meaningful contribution. In short, these Black community members viewed the social planning process to be extremely "paternalistic" and therefore unacceptable.

Black community members also felt the methods used to assess its needs were too abstract, and therefore tended to ignore the "context" of all plans. Others simply said planning was too "generalized" and not "localized" enough. The result of this was that planning was not "comprehensive," and, therefore, citizens felt the federal funds that were received were not used appropriately. Some community members believed planners were making their decisions on the basis of "erroneous information." The general sentiment of the community members contacted was that planning was too "technological" and, accordingly, did not tap the elements in the Black community that could provide planners with the required information to properly understand its needs.

When citizens were asked if they knew the location of the social service programs that are designed to serve them, none could say with any certainty where they could be found. Sometimes these persons did, however, make an attempt to identify services, and when they did, they said they were located at their neighborhood commission or library. Upon making inquiries at those locations to determine whether services were available, it was discovered that the persons in charge of these institutions had no knowledge of providing such services. Additionally, when community members did attempt to identify the actual services they might need, they could only guess what they thought should be available. None of the citizens contacted could provide the actual name of any of the social service agencies serving their neighborhood.

These citizens were also asked whether they had ever been directly contacted by a service provider in their vicinity. No one reported ever receiving such a contact. At community forums conducted in the Driving Park area, citizens in attendance were never asked to serve on the board of directors of any of the neighborhood agencies. Some citizens said they could vaguely remember some notices in the newspapers about these agencies holding meetings, but they considered this type of notification to be insufficient for two reasons. First, they failed to provide adequate information in that citizens could not recall *exactly* what they pertained to; and, second, they were not sufficiently visible to attract a significant amount of community attention. While attending Driving Park Commission meetings, it was determined that none of its members had ever been asked to participate in planning the service delivery system for their neighborhood or had been personally contacted to attend any of the meetings those agencies might have convened.

The citizens interviewed felt they should be contacted before planning activities were undertaken. In general, they wanted service providers to communicate with them on a more regular basis. At minimum, citizens maintained that planners and policymakers should consult their neighborhood commission before initiating any program. Driving Park citizens said they could make a greater contribution to their community and feel more "worthwhile" as citizens if they were contacted more regularly by social service agencies in an effort to solicit citizen opinions about the social services needed in their neighborhood. It was also believed that community residents would participate in such planning activities if given the opportunity. Because they had not been offered the chance to voice the needs of their community, they felt helpless or "handcuffed" relative to solving the problems they were facing. Moreover, the citizens interviewed believed they were supposed to have this type of "input" into the planning of social services, and they felt they were being cheated because their opinions were not actively sought.

Most importantly, Driving Park citizens did not know where to go when they did have a problem. Community members often reported to their neighborhood commission with lists of problems that were well within the purview of the local service agencies, yet the procedure for voicing their concerns to these organizations had not been made clear. As a result, unnecessary barriers were erected, prohibiting citizens from finding solutions to their problems. In raising this concern, these persons did not believe they were making an unreasonable or unusual request by asking their local service provider to take some interest in their needs. This community believed some type of "substation" placed in the heart of the Driving Park area could enable its members to have closer contact with their social service agencies. In one citizen's words, some "nice walk-in centers would be nice."

During the meetings that were conducted in the Driving Park area, the following unmet needs continually surfaced:

1. Drug and alcohol services should be more visible.
2. More social services for the elderly should be provided.
3. More joint parent–child activities should be planned.
4. Counseling should be provided for persons who are suspended or who drop out of high school. (Many believe desegregation activities have resulted in increased problems of this nature.)
5. Vocational counseling is needed for the neighborhood's youth.
6. Localized employment assistance should be provided.

Additionally, many citizens have ideas where local walk-in centers could be established making the aforementioned services available on a regular basis.

In summary, all the citizens contacted said social services were going to be needed in Driving Park more than ever as a result of the budget cuts initiated by the Reagan administration. Accordingly, they hoped social service providers would get involved in the community in order to minimize the possible deleterious effects of that economic trend. However, the citizens of the Driving Park area maintained their needs were not taken seriously by social service providers who were supposed to service their neighborhood.

The Social Service Agency's Perception of Social Planning

It is important to note that the social service programs that were contacted were also hurt by the same budget cuts affecting the Driving Park area. Program directors had to trim their staff; therefore, many services were curtailed. As is traditionally the case, those activities that are considered direct service were maintained, whereas support programs were eliminated. When a program is supposed to be community-based, however, such cuts also prove to be problematic. Those areas hardest hit by budget retrenchment were consultation and education, outreach, and staff development programs. This approach to budget cutting results in agencies losing the services that keep them in touch with their communities and also affects the number of in-house workshops offered to staff, which would better prepare them to handle their clients' problems (i.e., cultural sensitivity training).

Most of the staff persons interviewed expressed the belief that Reagan's economic policy pushed their program to the point of crisis, demanding that the overworked staff meet increasing community demands with reduced resources. Nevertheless, it was discovered that many additional problems existed with the strategies used by the agencies in the Driving Park area in planning services for that community. There is no doubt that some of these problems were the result of the budget cuts. Yet, even if this were the case, they must be remedied if real community-based planning is to ever be realized in Driving Park.

To use one staff person's words, "we [the mental health system] haven't been discriminatory, but we haven't been affirmative either" when dealing with minorities. This type of sentiment adequately characterizes the style of social planning undertaken by the social service programs that were contacted. What this means can be stated as follows: Planning activities have been conducted to meet the letter of the law, but certainly could not be considered community-based in nature. Community-based planning requires that "community sensitivity" serve as the standard to guide all planning activities. This has not been found in the programs that were contacted.

For example, overwhelmingly the type of needs assessments conducted by local agencies used "computer models" or "mathematical models" to make projections about the treatment needs of the Driving Park area. Considering this approach to planning, it is understandable why community members viewed this process as being extremely abstract. When this type of methodology is used to predict a community's needs, assumptions are advanced about social behavior that may or may not be corroborated. These models in and of themselves, therefore, cannot be considered community-based unless supplemented by more direct contact with a community's members. Most staff persons believed planning to be based on old data or on information that had not been collected first hand by local agencies. New "surveys" were believed to be sorely needed. Specifically, it was agreed by mental health staff that there was too much reliance on data produced and disseminated by the Franklin County "648 Board" (Community Mental Health and Retardation Board) for planning.

Staff persons immediately recognized the need to conduct studies designed to assess the problems of the Black community so the proper treatment services might be provided. Nevertheless, it was immediately stated that money did not exist for this research to be undertaken. Even though this type of planning was urgently needed, it was also argued that such activities were not the "in thing" or "where the money is" and accordingly would probably be ignored. Other staff members said administrators of the mental health system were "afraid" to address the issue that the needs of minorities are not currently met. To use the words of another respondent, the leaders of the Columbus area mental health system seemed to be "petrified" of the Black community.

Most staff persons understood that their agency's board of directors could supply an avenue for securing contact with the community that their organization was supposed to serve. Nevertheless, the individuals interviewed did not believe the board members of these programs actually represented the community. It was maintained that board members were "self-selected" in that they tended to be drawn from an "old boy network." The attitude that was manifested also confirmed the opinion that just because a person is Black does not automatically guarantee membership in the Black community. It was believed that Blacks chosen for these positions were picked by persons inside the mental health system and, therefore, did not represent the Black community. These boards, accordingly, were not viewed as offering the type of linkage they were originally established to provide.

This type of under-representation of citizens from the Black community in key planning positions is not limited to membership on boards of various agencies. Additionally, it was discovered that the staff composition of most agencies did not reflect the populations in the areas they serviced. It was mentioned by staff that this problem had continually been brought to the attention of agency administrators but that the issue was avoided by their continually shifting the point of reference used to make all comparisons. For example, if a program's staff did not reflect the demographic composition of its catchment area, the populations cited for comparisons may have been the "Columbus area" or "Franklin County." Also, it was reported that most staff persons did not reside in the catchment area serviced "and consequently have little contact with or insight into the problems in those areas." Some agencies, however, did have, on paper, mechanisms that allowed citizens to convey their ideas and concerns directly to an agency's administrators. When staff were asked about the logistics of these procedures, they were described as highly complex, requiring numerous steps to be taken and contacts made with an agency before an item could even be placed on the agenda of an agency's board meeting. It was stated that such an approach to securing direct community input does not encourage citizens to voice their problems.

From the staff members interviewed, it was determined that programmatically few opportunities were provided to familiarize them with the needs of the Black community. As mentioned earlier, it must be recognized, however, that the budgets of most consultation and education and in-service training programs were sharply cut. Nevertheless, little cultural sensitivity training was available to counselors in order to help them interact most effectively with minority clients. In point of fact, staff repeatedly commented that administrators of programs continually attempted to "play down" cultural differences as a method of avoiding all racial issues. The result of this is that the possibly unique concerns of the Black community were systematically overlooked or misrepresented.

In short, these findings indicated that the community mental health system and the Driving Park area were not well integrated. In order to remedy this situation, the following recommendations were advanced.

1. In order to become familiar with this community's needs, a series of community forums should be conducted.
2. Members of the community mental health system should attend meetings of the active neighborhood commission that exists in this area.
3. These neighborhood commissions are very active throughout Columbus and should be used as a viable source of community-based board members for social service agencies.
4. A variety of community-sensitive needs assessments should be conducted, using theories and methodologies that allow for all data to reflect the voices of a community. Only this type of information is worthwhile when attempting to directly assess the needs of citizens. Abstract mathematical models are cheaper in the short run, but over the long term the insensitive knowledge they produce proves costly if involvement services are to be developed.
5. Community mental health centers should streamline the procedures they have for allowing citizens to directly address their administrators and boards.
6. Planning proposals should be more widely circulated among the leaders of the Black community so its members can be more intimately involved in the formulation of plans of action.

COMMUNITY PERCEPTION OF CRIME

The basic sentiment of the community toward crime was a general attitude of powerlessness in the face of it. Crime was viewed as something that could not be stopped, and citizens were skeptical as to whether it could be reduced. The expression of such doubt does not mean that Driving Park citizens were unwilling to "fight crime," but rather points to the ambiguity regarding how it can and should be handled. Such ambiguity stemmed from a public affairs announcement and the crime prevention units' directive that the police cannot stop crime, only the community can. Clearly, budgetary problems were a primary reason for the police department's reliance on the community, but shifting responsibility to the com-

munity, specifically the Driving Park area, raised the question that
then faced the citizens: "How can this be achieved?" The citizens
interviewed in Driving Park accepted the responsibility of performing
the task. Specifically, the citizens saw the Driving Park Commission
as having primary responsibility for providing direction.

Crime had been a concern for the Driving Park citizens for
a number of years. When citizens were interviewed regarding how
they determined what counts as crime, they responded by describing how they felt crime was produced in the area. They believed
crime was produced where sewage and litter in the environment
were not cleaned up; where loitering of youth and adults was
prevalent, particularly outside of grocery stores; and where motor-
cycle gangs raced their cycles up and down the street "causing
noise," which meant "they must be up to no good." Citizens viewed
these as signs of disorganization in the neighborhood. From the
community's standpoint, these undesirable features of the neighborhood were fear-producing. The signs of community "disorganization" were viewed as a part of the Driving Park area (DPA) definition of community crime that, in turn, meant that citizens expanded their definition of crime prevention. Driving Park residents saw
physical, social, and city disservices in their community as part of
the crime-producing problem.

Such activities as city traffic passing through areas of the
neighborhood contributed to an atmosphere conducive to crime,
according to some citizens. Heavily trafficked streets could be
viewed as belonging to outsiders rather than residents, thus creating an environment for offenders. Physical and social signs of deterioration or disorganization generally created a fear of crime that
kept people off the streets, reducing informal surveillance of the
community and weakening social contact with neighbors. It must
be remembered that as signs of disorganization or deterioration
increase, citizens may become less committed to their neighborhood. This means that concern about crime must be considered in
relation to signs of crime that produce fear in citizens. From citizens' points of view, crime and how it is produced were linked to
signs of deterioration.

According to Driving Park area members, it was also generally believed that crime was generated by those who lived north of
Livingston Avenue. It was perceived that north of Livingston is a
"pocket" area of crime. This designation is interesting inasmuch as
citizens generally felt crime was committed by those who lived outside the community, yet they designated north of Livingston
(which is part of the Driving Park area) as the source of crime. This
led us to believe that Driving Park area citizens viewed the community as being divided by the main traffic route of Livingston
Avenue.

Specifically, designated areas that citizens believed needed to be cleaned up were the area of Fairwood to Whittier avenues, Kelton Street to the freeway, and Fairwood and Seymour streets. The area of Fairwood to Whittier to the Freeway was considered a general trouble spot; Kelton was targeted as an area for prostitution; and Fairwood and Seymour streets were labeled by youth, who were interviewed, as "streets for drinking and drugs." It was overwhelmingly expressed by the adults in the Driving Park area that most crime is drug related, and that youth are responsible for crime in the area. The citizens within the Driving Park area felt that crime came from outside the community, and youth and drug-related crime was generally seen as "out of control."

The youth in the Driving Park area had a much more acute perception of the crime problem and its reasons. Their focus on crime was not property-related but a concern for personal safety. They reported numerous incidents of being "shot at" walking to and from the recreation center in the evening. They claimed that these activities had been reported to the police, but the police "don't show up" and shootings continued intermittently throughout the evening.

The selling of "hot goods" and drugs was common, and "drug selling" was rapidly increasing in the area. It was reported that one could get anything one wanted on the streets and even in the schools. According to those interviewed, a few of the teachers in the schools were selling drugs to their students and "smoking" with their students in school. It was also reported that a local ice cream truck vendor sold marijuana from the truck to the kids in the area. The children did not report these activities because they feared that if they told anyone they would be "beat-up or worse." For them, drugs, their sale and use, were part of their life, as was fear for their personal safety.

The children were very concerned with the number of women fighting in the community—especially when "they fight with razor blades." The youth believed women fought as a result of "drugs and alcohol" and "adults don't care, no future here."

The adults in the area viewed vandalism as a sign of disorganization in the neighborhood; the children viewed vandalism as the top crime problem in the area, and the reason for vandalism was "revenge and boredom." As a part of the overall context, revenge and boredom point to an interpretation of crime and violence in the Driving Park area, which is the lack of a future. From the youths' point of view "nothing can reduce crime," for crime occurs because there is no future for those involved in the crime.

Recommendations

1. Community crime prevention is viewed by the community in broader terms than merely reporting suspicious activity; community clean-up programs and maintenance can be viewed as crime-prevention activity.
2. City services must be aware that picking up trash and sewage is part of the community crime-prevention program and a poor response will be in violation of the Driving Park program.
3. Merchants should be enlisted in maintaining the "environment" as a part of the overall crime-prevention definition of Driving Park citizens.
4. The children believe that more lighting should be placed around the recreation center and on he streets that are most traveled by youngsters to and from the recreation center.
5. The fear the children have for their personal safety must be dealt with. Youth should have regular input in a youth board that can identify persons who harass them in the streets. A youth mediation board could be set up to deal with disputes between youth and parents without fear of recrimination.
6. A youth employment service for babysitting, house sitting, vacation sitting, and so forth, could be set up to encourage an economic future.

COMMUNITY-POLICE RELATIONSHIPS

The general sentiments that capture the history of the Driving Park population as well as their ambivalent attitude toward the police is the following statement, "Citizens want someone [police] who respects them and protects them, not someone that suspects them." Generally, the citizens felt that the relationship with the police department had improved. The improvement was a result of the establishment of the community–police relations board, and more recently the block-watch program developed good feelings toward the police. In talking with the citizens of the Driving Park area, they continued to see police brutality toward Blacks as a constant issue. One citizen expressed the reason for trying to establish good police relations as well as the Black community's reticence: "Blacks in particular in most communities do not trust the police and never have. But if you don't trust them, nothing will get done."

Police Perceptions

When we interviewed police officers who were connected with the area, their perceptions were

1. There are fewer juvenile problems or youth problems in the area.
2. Police see that people in the "Driving Park area are lax about giving information unless it relates to them." This view was justified by a White male citizen of Driving Park. "Blacks won't give information to police—because of their long history of being downtrodden."
3. Police perceive there is "not a lot of domestic violence" in the area.
4. Police believe that the drug problem is "no more a problem than [in] any other area." The police generally tend to construe problems in the area as "just like any other place in an urban area."
5. Police have noted an attitude change on the part of Driving Park citizens: "People don't care about race. It used to be that a Black wouldn't turn in another Black, but now they seem to be willing to turn in any criminal regardless of race." The police cite this as evidence that relationships of cooperation have been enhanced.
6. Police see Driving Park's biggest problem as being *fear.* Police have not specified the fear but seem to assess the individual citizen as being fearful, rather than the social environment *creating* fear.

Citizens saw their relationship with the police department as having directly improved due to crime seminars, meetings with the safety director, and meetings with the chief of police. In other words, interpersonal contact and increased knowledge of the system have helped create a climate more conducive to *trust.* The citizens of the area realized their own attitude change toward the police. As one commission member suggested, "before—police presence was viewed as something must have happened in the area," but now, "they [the citizens] expect the police to be there."

Police Perception of Community and Citizens' Views on Specific Issues: Differences

1. Police perceive few juvenile (youth) problems in the Driving Park area. This is contrary to the citizens view of who is responsible for crime, and it is directly at odds

with the way youth understand the crime problem and
the reasons for crime in the Driving Park area as discussed in the section on citizens' perception of crime.
2. Police do not consider domestic violence in the Driving
Park area to be a priority issue. This conclusion does not
concur with the way youth in the area view family life
and violence.
3. Police feel that drugs are not a big problem in the area.
The citizens and youth of the area believe the situation is
worse and selling and using cocaine is escalating. (The
youth population of the area is the most emphatic about
this issue.)

Agreements

Police and citizens agreed there was a change of attitude resulting
in better police relations with the community. However, this view
was not held by the youth interviewed in the Driving Park area.

Citizens' Suggestions for Community–Police Relationship Improvement

These suggestions included more visibility in the community, the
ability of police to handle domestic squabbles better, and an
increase in police sensitivity to the role violence and drugs play in
Black youth culture.

        These suggestions are not law enforcement directives on
the part of the citizens. Rather, these directives point to the fact
that the citizens of Driving Park saw the police as necessarily having a social service function in the community. In other words,
they believed the police should have this function. This meant that
more cultural sensitivity training and better mediation skills were
vital if the police were to continue to improve their effectiveness in
the community. In addition, the suggestion that police should be
more visible in the community indicates that citizens saw police in
the role of policing a neighborhood rather than merely acting as
law enforcers. Policing the neighborhood, for instance, can include
such activities as moving along the people who loiter in front of
grocery stores. This would, in turn, generate an atmosphere of
public safety for residents, especially senior citizens.

Interagency Relations

Interagency relationships and their view of each other have impact
on the services delivered to a community. In most cases, mental

health employees voiced strong opinions about the police department and parts of the legal system. Our questions did not necessarily direct these employees to comment on their perception of the police. But, the topic of the legal system's impact upon the Black community created a context which brought police–Black relations to mind. A credible source in the mental health system said that "because mental health and police have financial contract relations, training police to be sensitive to racial barriers is rejected because the police perceive that it is not a problem, and we don't want to lose our contract." Persons associated with the mental health system believe that police refer more people to mental health as "tensions" grow. Mental health sees this as an "easy out" for the police in determining how to deal with people as they come into the criminal justice system.

Those who are both members of the mental health profession and who have been part of the legal system have concluded that minorities fall through the cracks in both systems, and the inability to access either system means that minorities generally feel "they don't want to deal with the system, they just want to get it over with." According to agency persons, the cultural background and educational training of minorities make it difficult for such personnel to work with the system, and the opportunity to deal with the system is not available.

Police in the Driving Park area said they had no contact with social service or mental health agencies and thus had not established any forms of cooperative relationships with them, even in the case of domestic violence or youth problems. A major mechanism that had been instituted to keep minorities and the poor from falling through the cracks of the system was the night prosecutor's office. When we asked the citizens of Driving Park if they had heard of the office or if they knew where it was, the overwhelming response was no. Those who had heard of it neither knew where it was located nor its specific functions. (Generally speaking, there were no formal communication channels between the major delivery systems for the Driving Park area and the night prosecutor's office.) The previous discussion points out that delivery systems were inaccessible due to the lack of communication between those systems and the citizens of Driving Park. Additionally, there seems to be little formal communication or cooperation between delivery systems. The agencies entrusted to serve the community have made little or no attempt to develop an intimate knowledge of the Driving Park community.

Recommendations

1. Police should be trained in *community* relations and not in public relations.
2. Police–community relations should be developed along a model of communicative competence, which is based on understanding what is socially and culturally relevant to a community and how the community understands itself (e.g., its aims and interests).
3. Police training should emphasize the function of social service in addition to law enforcement.
4. Police should become *more* community based in terms of organizational planning by listening to and incorporating the citizens' suggestions regarding the ways in which the police can best serve the community.
5. Police must become more aware of how community members view police visibility and how *policing* reduces fear within the community.
6. A linkage and outreach program should be instituted between the Driving Park commission and the night prosecutor's office.
7. A linkage between the police and Driving Park, as well as its commission, should be established to aid interagency communication, specifically focusing on youth problems.

THE BLOCK-WATCH PROGRAM

The community or neighborhood "block-watch" is one particular type of community response to crime that has gained popularity. The information that follows was generated by evaluating the January 1982 implementation of the block-watch program in the Driving Park area.

Information was obtained from citizens in the Driving Park area who did and did not participate in the block-watch program. Crime-prevention officers were interviewed regarding their perceptions of the program. The research staff also observed numerous block-watch training sessions in the area.

During the initial stages of implementation, the general attitude of the population toward the program was that it was "very good" and that the relationship between the police and the community had been enhanced. After the training sessions had been completed, however, citizens expressed dissatisfaction with the program and felt confused because they lacked direction from the police. For example, they had been promised, but did not receive, designator numbers for reporting crimes. This was further complicated by the fact that many citizens did not know the identity of their block captains. The citizens wanted procedures to recruit new members and a concrete measure of success. As one citizen said, "if this [block-watch] fails, the police won't take the blame, they'll blame us."

On the basis of citizen evaluations of the block-watch program and the research staff's interviewing of the Detroit Crime Prevention Unit, we present a brief description of the program, and we offer recommendations for its improvement.

Description

In response to the Driving Park request, the police, via the crime-prevention unit, initiated a block-watch program in the community. The program was an adaptation of the one instituted in Detroit. The police considered this to be a pilot project and hoped that it would eventually be established citywide. For this reason, the block-watch program became the main priority of the crime-prevention unit, and staff was relieved from other assignments in order to perform various functions in relation to the new program. Through this project, the crime-prevention unit was hoping to illustrate the importance of its work and to "build a case for the addition of more personnel to its department."

Observations of citizen training sessions by crime-prevention officers were conducted by six researchers who attended meetings in groups of two or three. In this way, the reliability of data gathered was enhanced by cross-checking notes. Each research team was assigned to a particular training group and then followed that group through the training program.

The crime-prevention unit divided the community into three areas called zones, with each zone being headed by a coordinator. Within each zone block, captains were to be elected by the citizenry. They were to be assisted by monitors. The way in which the coordinators and monitors were to be selected was never discussed in meetings or in the material describing the program.

Instead of organizing the residents' meeting on a block basis as was done in Detroit, the crime-prevention unit decided to work on a larger scale and included the residents of two or three streets within one group that would undergo training together. Each Monday, crime-prevention officers canvassed the area assigned for that Thursday's meeting and invited all residents to attend the first meeting. In other words, the officers went door to door in order to contact as many people as possible. Because this was done during normal working hours, flyers were left for those who were not home. Neither local figures nor residents of the area accompanied the officers on their rounds. Although the Detroit program stipulated that 50% participation was necessary for any block-watch program to be effective, the crime-prevention unit had set a goal of 75% citizen involvement. Turn out at the initial meetings was far less than 50% of the population in the targeted areas. By the conclusion of the training sessions, attendance had dropped rapidly (e.g., from 35 people present at the first meeting to 23 at the second and to 16 at the final meeting). When the officers were asked if they could explain this poor response, they said people were "fearful of leaving their homes" and "the cold weather" stopped them from coming. Although these answers have some merit, they do not fully explain the reason for the decrease in citizen participation and the overall low level of involvement in the program. An answer may be found by looking at the structure and content of the program itself. It is our contention that the police's conception of *community* was not founded on a real understanding of the term and that the effectiveness of this program was severely limited by virtue of this fact.

The block-watch program was based on a territorial (geographic) concept of community. The police envisioned an area lying within certain arbitrary boundary lines as a "community." In other words, because those who lived within these designated boundaries were all nominally residents of the same community (e.g., Hillcrest, Glenview, or Sunnyside), the police assumed that those residing within this spatial domain comprised a community.

The belief that a "community" existed simply because the area was geographically designated as one was reflected in both the planning and implementation of the block-watch program. No measures were taken to generate solidarity among the residents, and thus, a sense of community never emerged.

This fact became apparent during the block-watch meetings. A crime-prevention officer presided over each meeting, and the program followed a lecture format. At the initial meeting, each person introduced him or herself to the audience. One person commented, "Even though I've lived on my street for 11 years, there are people here who live on my street that I've never seen before." Others made similar comments in response to this remark. Yet, meetings did not present the opportunity for the attendees to mix with one another. This could have been achieved simply by serving refreshments. In the earlier meetings, residents attempted to add to a statement made by officers by recounting personal experiences that illustrated the point. Such contributions were discouraged by the officers through nonverbal behavior and such comments as, "Well, we'd better move on because I have a lot

of material to cover, and I don't want to hold you too long tonight."
Thus, the sessions did not allow citizens an opportunity to share
their problems and achieve a feeling of commonality among them
based on similar experiences. Due to this factor, citizens did not
view their personal "troubles" as part of larger public "issues." This
thwarted the development of any "community" response to crime
because such an action must be founded on a common orientation
to the problem.

As part of the program's structure, each street was to elect
a block captain who would act as liaison between the police and
the residents in his or her area. Block captains were elected during
the first session. In one instance, a participant questioned this
procedure by asking how a captain could be selected when not
everyone was familiar with other members. The officer attempted
to ignore this remark. On each occasion, no names were offered in
nomination for the positions. After a few minutes, someone would
volunteer to fill the position, to which there were no objections.
Thus, these people were not necessarily "leaders" within their particular area but rather were individuals willing to assume this
responsibility because they were retired or had more time and
thus were in a position to handle this task.

Even though the neighborhood block-watch was conceived
as a community program, no provisions were made for any community input and feedback. The residents were not included in the
planning process. In other words, no crime-prevention committee
was formed so that police and citizens could work together in the
development of a program specific to this community. With the
possible exception of speaking to the commissioners (members of
the neighborhood association's board), there was no avenue
through which residents could voice their concerns and interests
as to what the block-watch program should focus on and eventually accomplish. Consequently, residents had little, if any, opportunity to participate in the formulation of the objectives and goals of
the program. Police personnel determined the priorities for this
block-watch program. Evaluation of this program's success was
based entirely on the crime statistics in the area, which were monitored by the police.

In like manner, the police did not involve the citizens in the
implementation of the project. Crime-prevention officers conducted
all meetings and citizen training. Residents were not phased into
training roles so that they could instruct others in crime-prevention measures. In addition, residents were not drawn into becoming a part of the program by serving on subcommittees that, for
example, would help the elderly install locks or take care of
refreshments at the meetings. This type of involvement would have
led to interaction among the residents and would have spawned an

identity with the program and community. However, the police did not utilize these types of interactive mechanisms.

Because the police had a territorial concept of community, they perceived it in terms of a "thing"—an entity. To them, it was a place that one could specifically point to on a map, not a network of relationships based on commonalties that stemmed from shared needs and concerns. Due to this fact, they overlooked the importance of utilizing the existing channels of communication within the neighborhood to publicize their program. Communication about the program was not fed through the community's networks.

The training films also revealed the fact that the police did not perceive this community in terms of the people who comprised it. The films dealt with middle-class White America and were produced by such organizations as a lock company and the National Rifle Association. In none of the films were the central characters Black, although in one instance the perpetrator was Black. In all of these films, the focus was on the individual as a victim of crime. Consequently, these movies portrayed a personal, not a group, response to crime.

Although the theme of this block-watch program was "you are your brother's keeper," the police made no effort to cultivate any sense of responsibility for others within the community. Instruction was conducted on a personal level (i.e., in terms of home security and self-protection), and group approaches to community crime prevention never emerged. In summary, the police attitude was one of "take care of yourself and the 'community' will be taken care of." The fact that the police viewed the community as an abstraction, "a thing" rather than a network of relationships, is evident in this program and can be cited as a primary cause for the lack of support and frustration on the part of Driving Park citizens.

Recommendations

1. The block-watch program summoned varying types of commitment from citizens because the crime prevention unit merely posed that the community has a common problem: crime. Yet, what makes crime their common problem was never seriously discussed. It was assumed that the area residents viewed crime as a problem merely because it was affecting the specific locale. Subsequently, the block-watch program was organized around the crime issue, but not on a sense of community responsibility that might specify why this particular problem should be viewed as one that is held "in common."

The issue of crime does not necessarily solidify a community if a sense of community does not already exist. Therefore, the block-watch program might have been better from the citizens' point of view if it had been organized around already existing institutions in the area that had engendered a sense of interpersonal commitment on the part of their members (e.g., social clubs, church organizations, school clubs, etc.). In this way, the project would have established a strong base of commonality, which would have allowed a problem to be viewed as one that is common to all. By failing to foster this sense of community solidarity, the block-watch program may serve as a temporary deterrent to crime but not succeed as a preventive strategy for confronting crime. From the citizen's perspective, crime prevention refers to a collective or social action that allows each individual to lead an unencumbered life (not barricaded in his or her home) while simultaneously reducing the neighborhood's vulnerability to crime.

2. Block-watch leaders must emerge from a community's "domain of commitment" if they are to be effective. Because the block-watch program was constructed *ad hoc*, block-watch leaders who were elected did not really represent the community. For the most part, the leaders were those who were the most vocal at a particular meeting or who volunteered for service (because no one else did). If block captains are selected in this way, it does not automatically mean the eventual demise of the project, but it does indicate that additional time and effort must be spent enhancing the solidarity of this *ad hoc* group.

This can be accomplished in various ways. The block captains can allow the group to "come out." Coming out is accomplished when persons who do not really know each other are permitted to talk to each other about the crime problem in terms of their personal experiences and possible remedies. Through this endeavor, individuals gain an affinity for other persons in the group. Allowing individuals to come out transforms what citizens initially believe to be private "troubles" into public "problems" that warrant a collective response. Accordingly, the private and public regions merge into an interpersonal "domain of commitment" based on the ability of each individual to be attuned to the plight of others.

All who attend the block-watch sessions should be allowed to fully participate in all planning activities. This activity will elicit a "buy-in" response from each participant because all group members need to feel responsible for the development of the block-watch program and its eventual success or failure. In order to encourage involvement, block captains, once chosen, should initiate all plans, disseminate information, and be at the center of all communication.

Cell groups within a community can increase their solidarity by instituting a mild form of competition between themselves. This competition, however, must be supplemented by erecting a superordinate goal binding all groups together if this "in-group" solidarity is to be maintained over a prolonged period of time. Citizen solidarity can be promoted on two fronts, by (a) establishing common goals, and (b) promoting mild competition between individuals (or "cell" groups) to achieve those goals.

The key, however, is that these goals cannot remain nebulous (such as reducing crime), but must be formulated in terms of clearly defined aims whose achievement can be readily measured. Because the block-watch goals were not clearly specified at every step of the planning process, the Driving Park project began to flounder and antagonism toward the police department increased. The goals should be the community's own and must be articulated in the language of the community if the goals are to have meaning. These goals should have been clarified at the outset of the block-watch organizational activities in order to set the community's aims clearly in sight.

3. The community should not be divided in terms of police precinct maps, structural boundaries, or highways. These "networks" are certainly official and easily established, but they may not actually reflect the communication channels that are already in place.

Community members were told that they must monitor their community, but the observational strategies were not well conceived. Citizens should be assigned "sentry" schedules to watch over particular individuals to whom they are committed, thereby drawing on the already existing domain of commitment in the community. Eventually, these highly specialized networks can be expanded in order to include a broader range of persons. Driving Park citizens perceived that they should "survey the community at large," which caused confusion.

Although it is true that interpersonal networks in the community might have to be created or fostered anew (they may have deteriorated long ago), this task should not be ignored.

Communication channels should be direct, not hierarchical. Within police departments, hierarchical communication is most effective; on the community level, it is quite unnatural. Neighborhood communication is conducted between persons who share a self-identity. Therefore, the most effective style of communication is that which proceeds through a network that "represents" the boundaries of these identities. Communication channels should assume two forms: (a) within neighborhood "cells," these communicative avenues should follow the flow of interpersonal commitment of the "in group," whereas (b) the "out groups" should be connected in terms of those citizens who have commitments to other groups. These cross-group commitments provide a natural method of uniting "cell" groups yet overlapping domains of commitment. For example, there should always be persons who are part of more than one group in the community who act as communication liaisons between them. Hierarchical or bureaucratic channels severely limit the effectiveness of informal channels. Yet, it is precisely the "informal" channels that provide the community with its structure and ensure its unity. This type of communication is a "linkage" format that allows direct communication between community members.

4. When Driving Park residents began to mobilize for the block-watch project, training was needed for success. The police supplied this training. Given the approach taken, the police trainers and community residents should be aware of the following issues.

It should not have been presumed that the police knew the community, even though it might be argued that they did. As Bent (1974) maintained, public relations for the police is "a prepared, one-way channel of communication designed to influence community opinion favorably on behalf of a police department" (p. 41). As part of their overall approach to police–community relations, the police crime-prevention unit developed an idealized stereotypical view of the community on which they based their knowledge and actions (Lundmann, 1980).

The material presented and instruction offered should be relevant to the social context of the community. Citizens who were interviewed after the completion of the three training sessions remembered little about the specifics of crime-prevention practices portrayed in the films or the information presented in the oral presentations. Visual aids were not employed in the crime-prevention instruction. These would have enhanced understanding, set a pace for instruction, and allowed opportunity for questioning. Therefore, before any police training is initiated, the police must be tuned in to the community's customs and standards so that rational contact can be maintained between the two groups. If this type of awareness is not generated between the community and police, sensible communication may never take place. Repeatedly, the chairperson of the Driving Park Commission admonished the police, "you cannot treat the community in a bureaucratic manner. Remember you [the police] are addressing a Black community." This is especially important in communities, such as this one, which have a collective historical memory that has ambivalent and hostile sentiments pertaining to prior police actions in the community.

As part of the training package, citizens felt training should concentrate on reducing the barriers that separate the community and police so that each might gain an accurate perception of the other. The training package did not contain this element but merely attempted to physically unite the police and community members in hopes that some type of support would automatically develop.

5. When block captains emerge, they should be trained so that they can begin to direct all training activities. (This was recommended to the police department; see Appendix D.) This type of strategy accomplishes a variety of important aims: (a) community residents will feel more committed to a project that it establishes; (b) community members can be required to meet with each other on a regular basis, thus generating community solidarity; (c) community members will begin to develop confidence in their ability to organize themselves to achieve their own goals; and (d) as a result of such direct participation in its training, community members will gain the expertise necessary to operationalize their own training, so that they do not have to rely on "experts" in the future. In this manner, the community will gain a sense of solidarity that will extend beyond the crime-prevention program, which, in turn, will facilitate the implementation of any future projects.

6. All community training should, consequently, proceed in accordance with the community's needs and at a pace acceptable to its members. The block-watch program was initiated as a "quick sell" approach that only momentarily drew community interest. All ideas pertaining to the development of the block-watch program should have been tested out on the citizens, and if evaluated as acceptable, should have been built from the "ground up," and not from the "top down." Police should not treat the program as merely an administrative task but instead must demonstrate that they are willing to rearrange their administrative priorities to meet a specific community's needs. For example, the Driving Park community indicated at block-watch meetings that police patrols should be changed or manpower shifted for visibility. Police trainers did not seem willing to seriously entertain this suggestion. This lack of police receptivity can lead community members to feel that the program is only another bureaucratic trap created by and for the benefit of the police.

7. Most importantly, the community needed to have all the information necessary for its members to make cogent suggestions about the direction the block-watch program should take. This can only happen if a project is erected on a community base (neighborhood commissions) beginning in the initial planning stages—a top-down sell job will produce only momentary success and will eventually alienate a community.

For example, all training materials should be community based and should reflect the community's standards of behavior. "Official" police training films should not employ actors not representative of a specific community, thus, avoiding situations that are irrelevant or entirely contrived. If a community cannot make its own film due to prohibitive costs, then maybe a few inexpensive slides could be made that actually depict the community in question. The point is that the circumstances presented in the training materials and the solutions to a community's problems that are advanced should reflect the concerns of the citizens. If this does not occur, then the training materials that are used will have little or no impact.

Moreover, any training that is employed should stress the idea that crime is a social and not a personal problem. If this understanding is not promoted, then once training is concluded, community members will again resort to merely personal solutions (like bolting doors or

buying firearms) to remedy what is actually a social problem. All training materials should stress ways in which a
group can mobilize itself to undertake projects that will
lessen its vulnerability to crime. This notion of collective
action must be stressed, or any training materials that
are used will contradict the purpose of a community
block-watch program.

8. Finally, every training program and organizational tactic
should be constantly evaluated from its inception.
Optimally, this type of evaluation should be formative in
nature so that a community can be aware of its successes
and errors while a project is in operation, thus allowing
correction to be immediately applied as it is needed. This
type of continuous evaluation permits a community to
monitor itself so that it has some indication if it is achieving its stated goals. Feedback of this kind helps to maintain citizen motivation, in addition to making information
available that may be useful for planning future projects.

Summary

A block-watch program will only work if community solidarity is
generated. Communities must replace feelings of powerlessness
and isolation with a sense of control. If a block-watch program is
to work, a sense of "community responsibility" must be engendered that reflects a "collective identity." This type of identity can
be promoted through plans of action that require that a community utilize its own resources (manpower, ideas, initiative) in a communal effort to solve its problems.

The Meanings of Crime Prevention and Communicative Incompetence

It is not surprising that crime has become a major issue within the
Driving Park community. Yet, integrating this concern regarding
crime into a form of action that could curb criminal activities was
perceived by the residents as being a cumbersome and almost
insurmountable task. From their point of view, those agencies and
organizations that could aid in such efforts often impeded the
achievement of such goals. This is not to say that the public service sector was intentionally uncooperative. However, the attitude
expressed by the citizenry was indicative of the type of community–institutional relationship that develops when services are
divorced from the sociocultural context of the community.

Within the community, the meaning assigned to a service, then, may be related to issues other than those envisioned by the providers (i.e., it may pertain to a domain of relevance which has heretofore remained unknown to providers). The community may ascribe roles and functions to such services that fall outside the purview of the provider's awareness. When these different interpretations are not mediated through communication (i.e., dialogue), the community and service sector may not act on the same set of assumptions and expectations. For this reason, they may interpret the same phenomenon differently. In particular, the significance attributed to the absence, delay, or negligence in the delivery of such services may be related to other issues within the domains of relevances in that community. Thus, this dissatisfaction that citizens may feel about one service may color their attitude toward others. However, the reason for this sentiment is not recognized by those providers associated with these other services simply because they stand outside the community context and therefore fail to identify the domains of relevances prevalent within it.

This becomes more evident when residents' complaints about city services are examined. In a meeting with the neighborhood commission, a city-chartered association, citizens voiced great dissatisfaction with the maintenance and upkeep activities performed by the city. Attendees recounted such incidents as the city taking 2 years to tear down a dilapidated building, having to call the trash department 4 to 5 times to get garbage picked up, and the failure of the housing authority to mow grass in front of vacant homes or on vacant lots.

On the surface, such problems may seem to typify those that any community combats and on this basis may be quickly dismissed. Such a conclusion, however, minimizes the impact that these conditions have on the lives of these residents, as revealed by respondents' answers to a question regarding the factors conducive to crime. Overwhelmingly, interviewees cited the presence of litter, run-down buildings, abandoned cars, and poorly kept homes as being indicative of a potential crime area. In the minds of these residents, then, there is a correlation between crime and the environment. Therefore, crime prevention is, in part, dependent on city services.

This finding concurs with the results obtained by the Center for Urban Affairs at Northwestern University in a 5-year study of citizens' fear of crime. Through interviews with residents in 10 neighborhoods located in Chicago, San Francisco, and Philadelphia, it was discovered that citizens felt that the physical condition of the community itself played an important role in crime prevention. "Local residents see physical, social, and service improvements in their neighborhoods as effective crime prevention mechanisms" (Lewis & Salem 1981, p. 414).

The inability or failure of city services to respond to requests is cause for greater anxiety and anger than providers might anticipate. Citizens feel they are more susceptible to crime because they seem to be incapable of correcting those elements within their environment that increase the potential for crime: "Fear is induced not only by crime, but also by many other signs of social disorganization that indicate to residents that their community is changing in threatening ways" (Lewis & Salem, 1981, p. 418). The sense of urgency and frustration that residents express over the inadequate delivery of such services is not simply the sound of a disgruntled, overdemanding public, but rather reflects fear for one's continued well-being, a fact not readily understood outside the community context.

Yet, it is in terms of this context that these services are evaluated. When residents related their stories regarding inadequate service delivery to the commissioners, others responded that this absence of action was "typical." Remarks like these indicate that such experiences are considered as more instances in which city service providers have fallen short of their responsibility. These stories are assimilated into a typification of city services as being unresponsive to residents' efforts to keep up their community in an attempt to protect its vulnerability to criminal activity. This negative assessment of city services, then, is incorporated into expectations regarding future encounters with this group, as well as any other area of the public sector which is involved in crime prevention, that is, which pertains to the same domain of relevance.

From the community's perspective, there are a number of public sector organizations that perform an important function in preventing crime. In addition to city services, the justice system and mental health agencies were most frequently mentioned. Taken together, these services form a constellation of meaning regarding crime-prevention activities, making one integrally related to the others.

In order to understand the meaning assigned to crime prevention within this community, then, each organization must be appraised not only on the basis of its own work but also with respect to those other agencies whose activities are directed toward reducing crime. In other words, the part can only be understood in terms of the whole.

The public sector, however, seems to be unaware of the community's definition of crime prevention. There seems to be a lack of awareness on the part of many that the service offered by a particular office is related to other concerns beyond the realm of the task at hand. Consequently, the significance that residents attribute to inadequate service may be underestimated or simply go unnoted.

Institutionalized Inequality

To the extent that these services fail to deliver the assistance requested, access to crime-preventative measures is barred. This inability to gain entry to the system is not only due to the failure of services' to respond to citizen requests in a reasonable amount of time but is also the result of other factors.

Among these factors is the physical separation of such services from the community itself. Poor people and senior citizens often do not have the transportation available to get to such offices. Women who are single heads of households may also confront child-care problems if they attempt to go downtown to lodge a complaint. Just getting to the appropriate office becomes a major undertaking.

Yet, even discovering where to go can be difficult. When services are physically isolated from the community, people frequently do not have any information about them because they are not part of their frame of reference. Respondents reported that residents knew where they could get food stamps and welfare but generally had no idea what to do if they were having problems with their landlord, spousal abuse, and the like. When respondents were asked if they knew the location or name of the social service agency in their area, only one interviewee was able to answer the question. Similarly, only two residents had heard of the city prosecutor's night program, which was originally instituted for the purpose of offering citizens an opportunity to settle disputes outside the courtroom. In fact, interviewees were even unaware of CALL, an organization that assists people in tracking down appropriate services.

When asked whom they would contact if they had a problem they did not know how to solve, respondents cited their minister as the only resource who could possibly help. For those who are not associated with a religious group, then, sources of information appear quite limited. These two factors—the lack of knowledge regarding available services and the problem of physically getting to them—create a climate of individual helplessness in the face of difficulties.

This sense of individual powerlessness was thematic throughout the interviews conducted among area residents. When subjects were asked if they thought they could have any input into the police department or social service agencies, the negative response was unanimous. No one thought that any individual's views or concerns would affect the activities of these organizations and many cited personal experiences that substantiated their perceptions.

Feelings of individual impotence undermine one's self-esteem. When one's self-worth is threatened, defensive behavior often follows, which moves communication away from a dialogic mode and to an adversarial form. Community residents see themselves fighting for their rights in a battle with the service sector fighting for their rights. One respondent made this very point when he said action was only taken in this city when 10 to 15 people called about a problem at the same time or if complaints were taken to the media. From their perspective, then, these citizens were being ignored by a system that was unresponsive to their needs. This led to outrage over the seeming injustice under which they were suffering or resulted in attitudes of resignation that may culminate in withdrawal from the system. In any case, a sentiment of disenfranchisement prevailed.

Such a situation becomes more critical when service providers are alienated from the community due to a physical and psychological isolation from the taken-for-granted world of their clients. Although this distance can be lessened through educational workshops, no sensitivity training has been offered to personnel working within the public sector of this city. This includes mental health professionals, police, and mediators employed by the prosecutor's night program. Because individuals are not required to reside within the area in which they work, the only opportunity to acquire such knowledge is on the job itself, through the personal encounter. Because such contact is generally made at a time when the citizen is dealing with a problem of some consequence, this hit-or-miss method can have serious ramifications.

This point was made by an interviewee who was associated with the mental health system for a number of years. She noted that minority access to social services is blocked when providers do not adapt to the cultural differences among their clientele. Among the examples she cited to substantiate her claim was an instance in which a woman brought her teenage niece to the center for counseling. After meeting with the case worker, the woman was informed that center personnel would only provide services to the teenager if the parents would meet with the counselor. Despite the fact that the parents lived in another city and the woman was responsible for the welfare of this child, no exception was made in view of these circumstances, even though the woman continued to request services. From the respondent's perspective, "The therapist did not understand this person was not just an aunt but *the* aunt. Service was not given to a person who needed it simply because the therapist didn't understand the family structure of the minority culture."

Incidents such as the one just described occur when providers assume that each client operates within the same realm of typifications and relevances as they do. This oversight has the effect of denying the existence of the other because the self has been removed from the culture in which his or her identity is defined. When the individual is addressed not in terms of the self he or she knows but on the basis of other schemata of meaning, other systems of typifications and relevances, the legitimacy of the self is questioned. The client perceives that his or her valuation of personal integrity is being undermined. If an individual

> is compelled to identify himself as a whole with that particular trait or characteristic which places him in terms of the imposed system of heterogeneous relevances into a social category he had never included as a a relevant one in the definition of his private situation, then he feels that he is no longer treated as a human being in his own right and freedom, but is degraded to an interchangeable specimen of the typified class. He is alienated from himself, a mere representative of the typified traits and characteristics. (Schutz, 1964, p. 257)

> Peoples everywhere have developed symbolic structures in terms of which persons are perceived not baldly as such, as mere unadorned members of the human race, but as representatives of certain distinct categories of persons, specific sorts of individuals. (p. 303)

In this way, one is "cast out" by a system that was originally instituted to serve his or her interests.

By relying on standard operating procedures, rules and regulations, it is presumed that each person is treated equally. Equal treatment is interpreted as meaning the same treatment. This approach seems to characterize the public service sector. Across the board, the professionals interviewed stated that cultural differences are played down within the system in order not to exacerbate racial issues. More specifically, they spoke of institutional fear over the possibility of "stirring up" the Black community. It appears, then, that efforts to homogenize cultural differences are considered to be the best tactic for protecting institutional vulnerability. By treating each client the same, allegations regarding discriminatory practices can be countered: Equality is insured because each person is treated the same.

In point of fact, this solution contradicts the fundamental meaning of equality. By expecting each person to act in accordance with a particular set of typifications and relevances, service providers are assuming that each client operates on the basis of the same socio-cultural context. "Typification consists in disregarding those individual features in the typified objects, facts, or events which are irrelevant to the actual problem at hand" (Schutz, 1964, p. 239). This indicates that the socio-culturally constituted reality of an individual is not considered to be a key feature that distinguishes different types of clients and is therefore viewed as irrelevant.

However, as the previous discussion pointed out, meaning is assigned in relation to a socio-cultural context, one that includes its own structure of typifications and relevances. The effect that this may have on service delivery becomes evident when a more specific situation is examined, for example, the therapeutic one.

If therapy is to assist the client, it must be relevant to the individual's life-world. When the social worker ignores or unconsciously overlooks the client's socio-cultural environment, the therapy given is only helpful to the extent that the client can relate the counseling he or she has received to his or her personal situation. This therapy, then, is not adapted to the individual's needs and circumstances. Rather, the client must synthesize the counseling he or she is given into the realities he or she knows. When therapy is not sensitive to the client's socio-cultural world, those people whose reality differs most dramatically from the one acted on by the therapist have the greatest burden placed on them. In these instances, the client's inability to integrate the counseling he or she is given into his or her own life does, indeed, block his/her access to the services (i.e., the help he or she needs). When this occurs, communication is not meaningful because the message is not relevant to the client.

For this reason, the client is not receiving counseling that is equal to the assistance given to one who shares the therapist's socio-cultural world. This is due to the fact that delivery of the service, in this instance counseling, has been typified because it is presumed that each client is the same. Such an assumption is erroneous as the story of the aunt illustrates; the typical therapeutic approach does not always pertain to the same domain of relevances for each person. Therefore, counseling that is administered in the typical manner may actually violate the concept of equality.

Schutz points out that equality can only be applied to homogeneous elements that fall within the same typifications. This condition has not been met in the situation just discussed because the clients are not homogeneous under that method of typing. If a person is to receive equal treatment, he or she must be addressed in terms of his or her socio-cultural understanding. Although this solution to the problem of equality requires that other typifications be constructed, it enables each person to be recognized on the basis of the same criterion and thus establishes homogeneity that precedes any assessment of equality.

Community-Relevant Programming

In this section, it is pertinent to repeat some of the suggestions cited in the report in an effort to remind the reader that the recommendations are critical.

Community programs have been undertaken on the basis of similar assumptions. Although community grows out of shared experience—a commitment to common goals—planners and policy makers have not been sensitive to this fact. Community has not been defined in terms of a network of relationships, mutual objectives or aspirations, a shared constellation of meaning based on a common historical experience, and so on. Thus, community was not interpreted in light of a specific context but rather took on an abstract character. Such vague notions of community limit the extent to which communication is possible and, thereby, pose an obstacle to the delivery of relevant programming. This not only significantly affects community–institutional relationships, but also strips the community of its power to exercise control over its environment.

The police's attempt to institutionalize a block-watch program within the community studied is a case in point. The block-watch program was initiated at the request of the neighborhood commission in the hope that it would aid in the reduction of crime. Although the police had been working on such a program, this was their first opportunity to implement it. This was, then, a pilot project that they believed might serve as a "model" to be used city-wide. Given this goal, it is not surprising that the program was designed as a "package" that could be delivered to any community, thus involving little, if any, adaptation to the particular needs and concerns of a specific neighborhood. One community was basically interchangeable with another.

From their point of view, the "community" was a place that one could identify on a map, not a network of relationships based on commonalties stemming from common interests and a mutually experienced past. In other words, the police typified the "community" as being an area lying within certain arbitrary boundary lines.

This territorial (geographic) conception of community may explain why the police did not take advantage of the channels of communication existing within the neighborhood in order to publicize their program. Information about the program was not fed through the community's organizations, such as churches, schools, senior citizens' groups, and so on, nor was the support of these groups solicited in order to enhance the legitimacy of their program. By involving local organizations in the block-watch program, its visibility would have been enhanced, making it more accessible to the public. This would have also provided a base on which the police could have built the solidarity needed for their program to be a success.

Yet, rather than take this tack, it was presumed that social solidarity is a natural consequence of territorial proximity. Given that those individuals who lived within these designated boundaries were all nominally residents of the same community, the police concluded that those living within this spatial domain did, indeed, comprise a community. This belief shaped the way in which residents were addressed, which, in turn, elicited certain responses from the citizenry. This became evident when observing police behavior at the block-watch meetings. The crime-prevention officer from the police department presided over each session using a lecture format, indicating that, from the police's perspective, this program was to be "presented" to the public, meaning that they envisioned their role to be one of information dissemination—not information exchange.

In this way, the meetings did not offer the residents the chance to share their problems and achieve a feeling of commonality among them based on similar experiences. Consequently, citizens did not have the opportunity to discover that their personal problems were part of a larger "public" issue. This seriously impeded the development of a "community" response to crime.

Despite the fact that the precautions that were suggested are important, this strategy emphasized the individual's vulnerability to crime and did not foster the development of a plan of action by which the community could gain control over crime. Thus, the individual was depicted as being pitted against an awesome adversary—crime—that he or she might confront anywhere at any time. As such, one's helplessness in the face of this pervasive threat was thematized.

Such feelings were intensified when the solutions presented to citizens as protection against crime were not viable alternatives. Several individuals, many of whom were single heads of households and/or elderly, stated that they could not afford to spend $30 for a lock for each door. Others added that they were unable to follow the recommendations made due to physical impairment, lack of know-how, or inadequate tools for doing such work. Yet, no assistance was offered, nor were other options presented to these individuals. Thus, this information heightened these people's awareness of the severity of their plight for it emphasized their inability to combat crime.

This situation illustrates another important point—a program must be relevant to the community in order for it to succeed. By neglecting to draw on the insights and suggestions of local residents, factors of major concern to participants were overlooked. Due to financial limitations and a lack of technical know-how, a number of the recommendations offered did not lie within the spectrum of possible action for many of these people. As such, these crime-prevention activities remained inaccessible to them.

Although the block-watch meetings continued for several weeks, the level of commitment to the program began to diminish.

One of the reasons accounting for this decline in participation stemmed from the fact that residents felt they had been placed in a precarious position. As one person stated, "The police are taking a lot of credit for the success of the program. If it fails, however, the area will be blamed. It is very unfair. It will hurt the community and its relationship with the police." From the residents' perspective, the absence of input into program development and assessment deprived them from receiving recognition for their contributions to its success. This program was not theirs; they were simply the recipients of it. Even so, the program's failure was perceived as being the community's fault, despite the fact that some of the measures proposed were not feasible tasks to be undertaken by many. Thus, many people felt they were caught in a double-bind.

Fear grows out of an awareness of vulnerability, which is the inability to exercise control over a situation. Although the police seemed to be cognizant of this fact when informing individuals of how they might "protect" themselves against crime, this point was not taken into consideration when attempting to establish this program within the community. Even though the neighborhood block-watch was supposed to be a community program, no provisions were made for community input and feedback. Residents were not afforded an opportunity to participate in program planning, implementation, and evaluation. For example, no crime-prevention committee was formed so that the police and citizens could work together in the development of a program specific to this community. With the possible exception of speaking to the commissioners, members of the neighborhood association's board, there was no avenue through which residents could voice their concerns and interests regarding what the block-watch should focus on and eventually accomplish. Consequently, the people had little, if any, opportunity to participate in the formulation of program objectives.

By being excluded from this process, community members were barred from a role that would allow them to respond to those threatening factors that were disrupting the quality of their lives. When community members are not able to exert any influence on those forces that are impinging on their welfare, the situation seems out of control. The community is powerless, thus making it vulnerable. This, in turn, raises the level of fear within the community, a conclusion also reached by Lewis and Salem (1981): "Fear increased as a function of the perception of change in the area when local residents had little opportunity to control that change" (p. 415).

Differing Domains of Relevance

One explanation for why community input has been neglected in the planning and implementation of such programs can be found in an examination of the domains of relevances under which these institutions are operating. Every program is created with the intent of fulfilling some purpose that is expressed through both its form and function. This purpose is but a part of a larger context in that it is constituted on the basis of certain domains of relevances. These domains of relevances reflect particular interests (Schutz, 1964). In light of this fact, some factors are deemed as being important to the maintenance and advancement of these interests, whereas others are not and are simply disregarded. According to Schutz:

> Since the system of problem-relevances depends, in turn, upon the interests originating in a particular situation, it follows that the same object or event may turn out as relevant or irrelevant, typified or untypified, and even typical and atypical, in relation both to different problems to be solved and different situations within which the object or event emerges, that is, in relation to different interests. (p. 236)

In many instances, community participation in program development, institution, and assessment is not considered to be crucial to the success of such projects because citizen involvement is not related to ensuring or furthering these interests. The city prosecutor's evening program clearly illustrates this point.

This program was initiated through the actions of the city prosecutor in response to "the justice system's difficulties in handling minor civil and criminal disputes" (McGillis, 1986, p. 64). Cases have since been limited to those involving criminal disputes, but the purpose underlying the program has remained the same: offering some relief to the courts that are presently taxed beyond their capabilities. This is not a community program, then, despite the fact that this project is viewed as being part of the neighborhood justice movement.

Although the philosophy underlying the community justice concept is one that advocates greater citizen control over those forces affecting these individuals' lives, this point of view has not been adopted in the Driving Park situation. Community input is not solicited but is, on the contrary, somewhat discouraged. Although this organization had a community board at one time, the head of the program stated that it was disbanded because too many views were expressed, thus making it ineffective. Many citizen proposals conflicted with the rules and regulations set forth in the state's revised code and thus could not be acted on. This appraisal of citizen recommendations suggests that the program director considered these ideas to be "unknowledgeable" and therefore irrelevant.

With the exception of offering complainants the option of meeting in the evening, the city prosecutor's program did not attempt to provide citizens greater access to the legal system, a goal of neighborhood justice centers. Referrals were primarily made by the police or the city attorney's office. In other words, citizens did not seek this service and enter the program voluntarily; rather, they were sent to the center. This lack of interest in improving citizen access to the justice system is also indicated by the low priority given to follow-up. For this reason, little, if any, follow-up was undertaken in order to assess the degree of citizen satisfaction with the process. The emphasis, rather, was placed on handling cases as expeditiously and efficiently as possible, for it was in terms of number of cases resolved that this center justified its existence. In addition, the majority of cases mediated were not selected on the basis of their relevance to the community but, instead, were ones that would alleviate the workload of the courts. As such, a predominant number of cases dealt with bad checks. McGillis and Mullen (1977) note that this center handled more than 10,000 such cases in 1977 alone.

The absence of a community orientation was also reflected in the hiring of mediators. These individuals were not chosen in accordance with a criterion that insures community representation but were selected in terms of their education. The center's director pointed out that the mediators had 6 to 7 years of education beyond the high school diploma and that a substantial number had studied law.

By examining the various aspects of this program, then, it can be seen that this project had been constituted in relation to a particular domain of relevances: to reduce the overburdened courts. Given this intent, community input into the process was not a necessary element in the achievement of its goal. As such, community input was disregarded, a fact that was clearly revealed in all facets of the program.

The problem this presents, however, is that all groups do not organize reality on the basis of the same domains of relevances. From the community's perspective, it was important that residents gain some control over those events affecting their lives. Programs like that of the city night prosecutor precluded this possibility and thus alienated the community from the legal process.

Conclusion

Social scientists and practitioners are needed to engage in community translation. Schutz (1964) noted that

> the outsider measures the standard prevalence in a group under consideration in accordance with the system of relevances prevailing

within the natural aspect the world has for his home-group. As long
as a formula of transformation cannot be found which permits the
translation of the system of relevances and typifications prevailing in
the group under consideration into that of the home-group, the ways
of the former remain un-understandable. (p. 246)

This discussion focused on the "translation" that occurs when one
is addressed by the other in terms of a different system of typifications and relevances. In the instances explored, the message was
interpreted in accordance with domains of relevances that differed
significantly from the service deliverer's. Consequently, the meaning assigned by one did not concur with the meaning that the
other believed was assigned. For this reason, there was no mutual
understanding. Thus, communication was incompetent.

The desired "formula of transformation" can be discovered
through dialogue that is conducted in the spirit of the ideal speech
situation described by Habermas (1970b). Such communication is
competent for it is contextually specific and is, therefore, sensitive
to those domains of relevances that structure the other's perception of reality. This, in turn, allows one to respond to the other in
terms that are appropriate, in ways that are relevant to the other.
Such is the purpose of responsive law. Nonet and Selznick (1978)
point out that this law embodies civil politics, which is

politics that affirms the central value of citizenship—the principle that
no member of a genuine polity may remain unprotected. Its special concern is the maintenance of a moral community . . . in a political context
where individuality, diversity, and hence conflict are presumed and
accepted. There is a commitment to widen the sense of belonging and to
avoid postures that read people out of the community. (p. 90)

This section has attempted to point out the ways in which communicative incompetence undermines these goals. As such, attention
has been given to those factors that alienate the community from
the legal system.

The key themes that emerged from the Driving Park project
are as follows:

1. The legal system and its auxiliary support systems were
   divorced from the Driving Park community. Through
   their communication practices and forms of needs
   assessment, the delivery systems revealed a distorted
   perception of the community and addressed the community in a manner that created mistrust and inhibited possibilities for creating social options that would enhance
   the quality of life for area residents.

2. The citizens of Driving Park did view the delivery systems as potential mechanisms for increasing social commitment in their neighborhood and reducing crime. For instance, citizens expressed the views that mental health has the *potential* to *prevent* crime; also, in *principle*, the block-watch program was highly desirable because it could increase citizen involvement in social issues beyond crime.

3. Concern for the future of the youth population was high. The youth, too, were concerned about themselves and how they could have a future at all.

Our research findings in Driving Park are generalizable. They are consistent with the findings of the federally funded Reaction to Crime project (1975–1980) which was conducted by the Center for Urban Affairs at Northwestern University. This study indicates that "when a community cannot assert its values, its residents become "fearful" (Lewis & Salem, 1981, p. 418). The increase in fear results in a self-fulfilling prophecy, whereby withdrawing from active participation in a community is promoted, thus facilitating increased community disorganization and opportunities for crime. The vicious cycle between citizen involvement, fear of crime, and the production of crime has direct bearing on the issues of the responsibility and responsiveness of the legal and mental health delivery systems. Again our findings are confirmed by the Reaction to Crime Project:

> Our examination of fear of crime in ten neighborhoods in Chicago, San Francisco, and Philadelphia revealed a broad range of concerns that included but were not limited to the crimes considered by those working within the victimization perspective. Respondents questioned about crime problems described a range of what we have labeled "incivilities" as undesirable features of their communities—abandoned buildings, teenagers hanging around, illegal drug use, and vandalism. In most instances, these other problems appeared to generate at least as much concern as did the crimes customarily considered by scholars examining fear of crime. And the concerns appeared to be equally potent in generating fear of crime. Therefore, local residents see physical, social and service improvements as effective crime prevention mechanisms. When delivery systems do not competently address and fulfill the relevant needs of the community, they must share in the responsibility for producing fear and crime in a community which, in turn, contributes to social disorganization. (Lewis & Salem, 1981, p. 414)

Implication for Action

The Driving Park Commission was willing to assert itself, and it began to seriously rethink many facets of the quality of life in this area. The commissioners' questions and responses directed them to re-evaluate and reformulate the meaning of the role of community organization in relationship to social planning in Columbus. Their motivation was reconfiguring public institutions to be responsive to the delivery of legal and social justice that is community relevant This was a call for responsive law on the part of the Driving Park community.

Throughout the country, the idea of responsive law has gained popularity and has been operationalized in the form of community justice centers (McGillis & Mullin, 1977). The philosophy underpinning responsive law states that law must be *relevant* and must *produce social solidarity*. This can be accomplished if law is based on the exigencies or pressing needs of community life. Law will only be supported when it reflects a community's standards of morality and sense of justice. Therefore, the legal system's practice must be viewed as a part of the community's organization. Only when the law embodies the collective experience and history of the way a community views itself will it be respected. If it does not, law is a disruptive element, negatively affecting the community's social cohesion. Responsive law advances a new vehicle for dispensing justice. This vehicle is the community justice center, which is located within the community and operated by residents of that area. Community justice is a forum consistent with the ideals of responsive law; that is, of having both knowledge and skills readily available to the community so that the use of the legal system can be optimally facilitated.

From the information that we have gathered, it appears that a *responsive* conception of law that is representative of community justice would *greatly* reduce the social stress situation that has existed in the Driving Park area. A community justice model that is truly community-based would allow for increased community input into the operation of the legal system, while simultaneously diverting many individuals, especially the youth population, from the criminal justice system (see Appendix E). Also, this model would serve as a communication vehicle between the community and the police department and promote the transmission of the community's standards of morality and justice to the police "on the street." This would aid in more effective and efficient law enforcement and policing that would affect community and police morale. We believe that the creation of a community justice model would benefit both the community and the legal system which would be cost efficient (see Appendix F). What must be recognized, however, is that this "responsive" type of legal system operates in accordance with the principle of social cohesion and community relevance that is different from that which underpins the traditional standard of law and justice. The community justice model can be referred to as *participatory democracy.*

The idea of participatory democracy is not entirely new, yet its implementation requires long-term planning and sound principles of operations. (Ironically enough, the operation of community mental health centers is based on this principle.) For instance, our research has pointed out, Driving Park cannot be understood in geographic terms but rather must be seen in the ways in which the community comprehends itself on the basis of its needs and interests. Responsive law requires emphasis on participation and is guided by "communicative competence," which means that effective interaction can only take place when the socio-cultural backgrounds of all parties are recognized in the dialogue between the legal system's representatives and the community. Accordingly, this conception demands that community organizational efforts must be viewed differently. Organizational appeals initiated by the police, the community, and mental health agencies cannot be made by merely invoking a rhetoric of "common" issues that are supposed to be important to everyone. Instead, it must now be realized that organizational efforts succeed only when they pertain to the real needs of a community, not general conditions.

Finally, social institutions cannot be conceived in a bureaucratic manner, for if this is the case, "participation" is impossible and community justice cannot be properly employed. When institutions such as community organizations, police, and mental health agencies are "linked" by interaction, the participants in these organizations are trained in different ways to cope with social stress, conflict, miscommunication, and crime. This type of training provides the greatest opportunity for resolving existent problems. Consequently, the successful implementation of responsive law through citizen participation is a fundamental principle for community self-determination and modern urban development.

APPENDIX A: COMPARATIVE DESCRIPTIVE STATISTICS
FOR THE DRIVING PARK AREA—1970

- Eighty percent of the population was non-White.
- Only 15% of the geographic areas of Columbus had a lower median income.
- Eighty-five percent of the families in this area were classified as living below the poverty level.
- Only 8% of the areas in Columbus had a higher rate of single-parent families than this area (indicative of high neighborhood instability).
- Only 20% of the areas of Columbus had a higher adult–child ratio (which is indicative of high family instability).
- Only 8% of the areas in Columbus had more unemployment (which signals a high unemployment area).
- Only 20% of the areas in Columbus had more underemployment (a very high underemployment figure).
- Only 28% of the Columbus area had fewer years of completed education (which indicates a low level of education).

APPENDIX B: SOCIAL STATISTICS FOR DRIVING PARK
AREA—1975

This summary was requested by Ann Luther of the Hope Lutheran Church and was prepared by Steve Ballard of the BENCHMARK staff. The study looked at selected questions on housing, child care, social services, crime and justice, physical health, and the community for residents of the Driving Park area (census tracts 55, 56.10, 56.20, 5900, and 87.20). Responses of residents of this area were then compared to the responses of residents from the remaining parts of the metropolitan community. This study was released to the user on March 21, 1975, in the form of a computer printout.

In general, this information shows that residents of the Driving Park area reported behaviors, practices, and attitudes that are fairly similar to those reported by residents of the remaining metropolitan area. With respect to overall satisfaction with housing, child care, social services, personal safety, and health, about the same percentages of residents of Driving Park reported dissatisfaction as did residents of other areas.

Of the residents of the Driving Park area, 35% indicated a need for child care for children 3 to 5 years old, in contrast to 25% from remaining areas reporting this need.

Residents of the Driving Park area generally reported slightly more concern with crime and personal safety than did residents of other areas. For example, 41% of those from Driving Park said their neighborhood was less safe than it was 1 year earlier, compared to 27% from remaining areas who felt less safe. Although 65% of the residents of Driving Park had taken precautions to protect their family from crime, only 49% from remaining areas had taken similar precautions. Residents of the Driving Park area had very positive images of the police (e.g., with respect to being well-trained, fair, courteous, honest, strong, gentle, quick to respond, and calm), and these images are slightly more positive than those found among residents of remaining areas.

APPENDIX C: REPORT ON MEETING BETWEEN DRIVING PARK COMMISSIONERS AND COLUMBUS POLICE CRIME PREVENTION UNIT

EARL BURDEN, CHIEF OF POLICE   May 20, 1982

Captain Robert L. Smith #2015, Community Relations Bureau

Meeting with Driving Park Commissioners on Block-Watch Program

Sir:

On Monday, May 17, 1982, a meeting was conducted to discuss ways to maintain the momentum of the block-watch program in Driving Park. Persons attending the meeting were:

Khari Enaharo—chairman, Driving Park Commission
Dr. Joseph J. Pilotta, PhD.—Department of
Communication, O.S.U.
Earl Burden, Chief of Police
Sergeant Norman D. Haggy #2207, Crime Prevention Unit
Howard Wilson, Crime Prevention Unit

AREAS OF CONCERN

A.   Should the juvenile bureau become involved in the block-watch program since young people in the Driving Park community have shown an interest in wanting to take part in the program?

Recommendation: At the present time, Driving Park does not have a controlling structure to organize, supervise, and direct the activity of its youth. However, there are plans for youth-structured programs in the near future. Therefore, it is recommended that the juvenile bureau provide an officer to attend the monthly block captains' meetings for the purpose of exchanging information as it pertains to juvenile activities.

B.   Block captains need additional training in their duties and responsibilities in order to maintain interest in the block-watch program.
       Action to be taken: Develop and publish a block-watch captains' guide, target date for completion: May 31, 1982.

       Set up meetings with block captains to conduct training—during the first week in June 1982.

       Schedule monthly block captains' meetings with the following persons in attendance:
       a.   Block-watch captains
       b.   District crime prevention officer
       c.   District officer from patrol bureau
       d.   Crime prevention and patrol sergeants (when appropriate)
       e.   Officer from juvenile bureau as needed

C.   Could the mayor's volunteer program be used in the neighborhood block-watch program to provide a qualified person to train block captains, when a block captain is replaced and/or when the crime prevention unit has moved to another community to start another block-watch program?
       Action taken: Mrs. Poling, coordinator for Mayor Moody's volunteer program stated that this is the type of long-range pilot program in which they would like to be involved. A meeting is planned to brief the board on the block-watch program and how the volunteer trainer can fit into the block captains' training program.

D.   Should or can transportation be provided to senior citizens to daytime block-watch training?
       Recommendation: Recommend that existing transportation be utilized (i.e., American Red Cross provides free transportation to people, age 60 and over, who live off of bus routes and within the I-270 outer belt, and C.O.T.A. for those living on bus routes). Detailed instructions for obtaining transportation will be included in the block captains' guide.

E.   Can or should double cylinder deadbolt locks be obtained at a discount price or free for families that cannot afford to purchase them?
       Action taken: CHORE program under the Department of Community Development will provide free of charge and

install deadbolt locks for senior citizens, 60 years of age or older.

Individuals other than senior citizens can purchase double cylinder deadbolt locks at a discount. The crime prevention unit is in contact with dealers who will sell the locks at a discount. It is suggested that Driving Park Commission canvass businessmen in their community for possible financial aid to families that cannot afford to purchase locks. Mr. Angel, Department of Development CHORE program has agreed to provide someone to train our Explorers to install the locks and/or provide tradesmen from the retired seniors volunteer program to install the locks.

F. Personal surveys conducted by Dr. Pilotta indicate that the use of cocaine has increased among teenagers in Driving Park both on the street and in the schools.

Action taken: narcotics bureau confirms that cocaine is available in the Driving Park area, but believed the cost of cocaine prohibits a significant increase in usage among teenagers. They felt that marijuana and prescription drugs are still the largest abused substances.

Methagualone (commonly known as sopors) is also available in the Driving Park area both in the liquid and powder forms. The powder form can easily be mistaken for cocaine. Principals and school nurses at South High School, Barrett Middle School, and Kent Elementary stated that "pot" and pills are still the leading substances being abused in that community.

Because drug abuse is a concern of the Driving Park residents, it should be a topic for a block captains' meeting within the immediate future.

Finally, I would recommend that a division directive be published outlining procedures, duties, and responsibilities for all bureaus for the neighborhood block-watch program.

Respectfully submitted,

CAPTAIN ROBERT L. SMITH #2015
Community Relations Bureau

RLS/HLM/mkr

cc: Khari Enaharo, Chairman, Driving Park Commission
Dr. Joseph J. Pilotta, PhD, Dept. of Communication, OSU

APPENDIX D: COURT WATCHING STUDIES REVIEW

The Citizens' Study of the Franklin County Municipal Court (1975) was a court-watching study conducted in 1975. The purpose of this study was to gather information through courtroom observations on such things as courtroom conditions, procedures, the behavior of defendants, the behavior of court personnel, and the disposition of cases in order to measure the quality of justice in Criminal Arraignment Court.

A follow-up study of the juvenile, municipal, and common pleas courts was conducted in 1979 ("Court Watching Project," 1981). Again, data was obtained through systematic observation of courtroom activities and conditions.

The nature of these studies and their conclusions provide useful information in assessing the impact of the court system on the citizens of this area. The information examined, as well as the conclusions of these studies, are summarized in the following table. A critique of each study is included.

The result of these studies suggest that the court systems may be producing some stress among the minority populations. In this event, the reported information has direct consequence for the study "Assessing Nonintegrative Law in the Black Community" (see Table 5.1).

APPENDIX E: ADVANTAGES TO THE MENTAL HEALTH COMMUNITY

1. Responding to the perceived needs of their community.
2. The immediate possibility of abating civil strife and violence.
3. Expanding and actualizing the 1963 Mental Health Act.
4. A visible image of a place in community responsibility.
5. Needs and priorities can be acted on with some immediacy, at least on the individual level.
6. Responding to the State of Black Columbus Report that parallels the National Black America Study. Therefore, a possible national impact.
7. The first study ascertaining the mechanisms and effects of law as a stress producer.
8. Development of training packages for the mental health center and community groups in order to help them become more self-sufficient.
9. An avenue to clarify repressed needs of a community that can be useful in individual counseling.
10. Immediate access to the effects of government cutbacks in social services in terms of the community's needs, thereby indicating alternative program development areas.

Table 5.1. Assessing Nonintegrative Law in the Black Community.

1975	1979
Data:	Data:
This study examined 1,395 criminal nontraffic cases in Criminal Arraignment Court between January and July 1975.	From January to June 1979: 612 preliminary hearings, 293 trials, and 363 disposition hearings in Juvenile Court 917 felony cases for bond in Municipal Court observed 852 felony case dispositions in Municipal and Common Pleas Court.
Conclusions:	Conclusions:
1. The majority of defendants were young, poor, White, and male.	1. Juvenile Court: The seriousness of the charge, the sex, and the age of defendants were the critical factors in case decisions.
2. The defendant's <u>race</u> and <u>class</u> were prominent factors in determining preferential treatment. In felony cases, Blacks were treated much more severely than Whites. In the case of bond, Blacks ($4,104) had to pay almost <u>twice</u> as much as Whites ($2,150) to be released. "Blacks received sentences <u>more than twice as severe</u> as Whites for similar charges" (see Figure 5.1). Furthurmore, Blacks with no criminal record received sentences more than twice as severe as Whites with no prior record (see Figure 5.2). The data also indicate a trend for lower-class defendants to be treated more harshly than middle- or upper-class defendants (see Figure 5.3). Lower-class defendants had their charges dismissed less often, were found guilty more often, and were given harsher sentences and fines than were middle- or upper-class defendants.	2. Municipal Court: The seriousness of the charge, the judge presiding, and the presence (or absence) of an attorney significantly affected decisions in these cases.

Table 5.1. Assessing Nonintegrative Law in the Black Community (cont'd).

3. Most defendants were uninformed of court procedures and therefore intimidated by courtroom activity.

3. Felony cases in Municipal and Common Pleas Court: The seriousness of the charge, the judge presiding, and the presence (or absence) of an attorney also affected the outcomes of these cases.

4. The court provided little or no information about procedures or appropriate behavior to the defendants.

Criticisms:
The major limitation of this study was that the statistics do not reveal the number of defendants who might have been discriminated against for more than one reason, for example, being poor and Black.

Criticisms:
The study did not indicate the number of Blacks versus Whites, males versus females, or lower- versus upper-class defendants. It seems that important areas were glossed over.

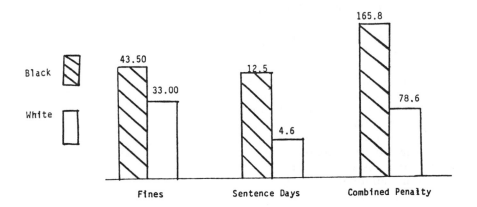

Figure 5.1. Variation in penalty by race.

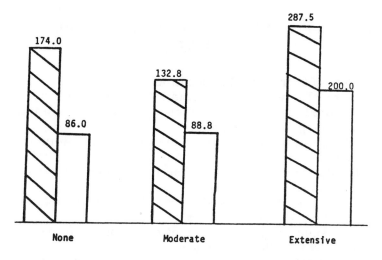

Figure 5.2. Variation in penalty by race according to prior record.

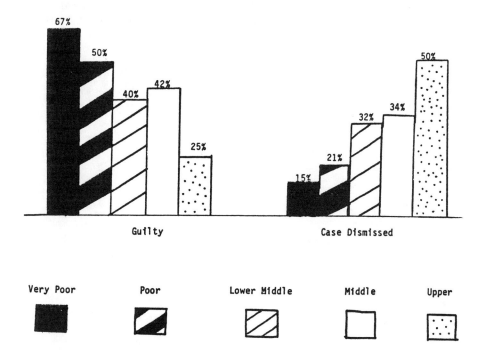

Figure 5.3. Variation in disposition by class.

APPENDIX F: ADVANTAGES TO THE CRIMINAL JUSTICE SYSTEM

1. More efficient use of police time.
2. More effective police contacts with the community.
3. Ensure better human relations between the community and the police department.
4. Police can be better trained to meet the community's needs.
5. Docket backlogs can be reduced, thus ensuring more efficient processing of clients.
6. The criminal justice system can devote more of its time to dealing with serious crimes.
7. The community can be organized to combat crime and to support the efforts of police.
8. Communication channels can be opened between the police to ensure effective community planning and utilization of available resources.
9. Close formal collaboration between the police and the community can assist in securing money for further projects.
10. A mechanism will be in place for the reduction of social stress by facilitating a community-responsive criminal justice system.

SIX

Legal Education Through Cultural Dialogue

The immigration of thousands of Indochinese refugees into this country presented various branches of the social service delivery system with an enormous and cumbersome task, in addition to that system's daily struggle to provide services while juggling ever-changing resources. Issues of shelter, food, clothing, and medical services loomed large and eclipsed other issues not directly related to survival (Office of Refugee Resettlement, 1982, 1983).

And yet, in accepting refugees of any nationality, the U.S. government, and hence its people, make an implicit commitment that exceeds that of physical relocation; that commitment is to the effective assimilation of those refugees into American culture. It is obvious that "cultural assimilation" is intangible, and as such is a great deal more difficult to deliver than tangible support services (i.e., food, medical attention) by which the social service delivery system is known. In this chapter, we argue that the close relationship between self-sufficiency and cultural assimilation has not been appreciated by refugee service delivery systems.

It is because the U.S. social system can be characterized to a large degree by a certain "legalistic mentality" that our research experience with the Indochinese refugee community initially focused on legal education. Initial contacts with the refugees and with the social service delivery agents serving the refugee commu-

nity revealed that in the area of legal matters (from traffic regulations to growing marijuana), the Indochinese were consistently
confused and frustrated.

This simple observation developed further into a dual
premise for our research endeavor: If refugee assimilation were to
be facilitated, then we would have to both find a way to communicate essential civic processes that guide our daily lives, and access
the refugee community and articulate its perspective. It is the latter of these two premises that is fundamental to the possibility and
utility of the former. That is to say, our goal was to understand the
social situation of the refugee community in its own terms in order
to know how to articulate those invisible and yet essential civic
processes. To paraphrase the collective reflections of the various
refugee communities with whom we worked, membership in a
community in no way guarantees participation in community life.

Thus, we would characterize our research methodology as
community-based. This chapter reflects the expanding focus of our
research agenda, from the creation of a legal education project, to
a summarization of our observations regarding critical factors
affecting social integration, leading us to a consideration of the
role of community organizations in the development of fledgling
groups-to-communities. More specific factors revealed through our
research that we believe affect Indochinese community development are summarized, and conclude the chapter by making some
observations regarding the implications of utilizing a community-
based approach for social scientific investigation and its potential
policy effects.

REFUGEE LEGAL EDUCATION AND
COMMUNITY PARTICIPATION

The impetus for developing legal education targeted to the
Indochinese (Vietnamese, Lao, Cambodian, Hmong) refugee population came originally from the local refugee task force. The task
force is a coordinating body consisting of voluntary resettlement
agencies (VOLAGs), health and human service providers, municipal and state agency representatives, and refugee mutual assistance organizations. When a series of minor incidents occurred
indicating that refugees were encountering problems in understanding the legal and criminal justice system, as well as dealing
with the legal system's confusing mixture of administrative organs,
the task force commissioned the creation of a law committee to
review the situation and to take some steps toward implementing
appropriate remedies.

The law committee's initial efforts were directed toward identifying the principal obstacles to refugee "legal integration" and to formulating a legal education program that was informative, effective, and attractive. The program's stated goals were:

1. Educating refugees about their rights and responsibilities.
2. Encouraging refugee participation in the legal justice system.
3. Promoting trust between the refugee communities and law enforcement and justice officials.
4. Enhancing the awareness and sensitivity of law enforcement and legal service deliverers to refugee needs and cultural norms.

Within the law committee's framework, a research and technical assistance team created a legal education project entitled "Legal Education through Cultural Dialogue" (LETCD). The goal of LETCD was twofold: to establish a legal education program that both *informs* the relevant public, in this case the Indochinese community, and *enables* that public to participate meaningfully in the legal process.

Over 30 months, the LETCD project conducted extensive interviews with refugee community members; approximately 25 hours of these interviews were tape-recorded. The project initiated ongoing cooperative relationships with refugee community organizations, established linkages between the communities and legal service and enforcement service deliverers, designed a series of educational community events, provided technical assistance to legal and enforcement officials, and implemented a first-step cultural education program employing the local public access television channel.

A crucial research component was a series of meetings with leaders of the Vietnamese, Lao, and Cambodian communities. During these meetings, the researchers were exposed to a litany of frustrations and confusions that are relatively commonplace for Indochinese resettlement practitioners. In Southeast Asia, many criminal and civil disputes are resolved using informal means. For example, as many of our key citizens explained, bribery is an acceptable dispute resolution practice employed to avoid public embarrassment, and one that has been reinforced by decades of social and legal strains caused by the political turmoil in their countries of origin. Crimes go unreported because of mistrust of law enforcement officials and a general fear of authority. Extended experience with martial law in their homelands and the apparent irrational arbitrariness of refugee camp administration had made them wary about law-related institutions and insecure about their standing in their adopted country.

Subsequent discussions led to invitations to the homes of the refugees. The interviews and discussions conducted in these more familiar and sometimes festive surroundings produced a more complete picture of the real and perceived obstacles the Indochinese experienced in the resettlement and acculturation process.

We discovered the existence of a great deal of insecurity about their "social place." This insecurity goes beyond, albeit in part is certainly generated by, the incompatibilities between the "traditional" more personal societies of their homelands and the "modern" more complexly differentiated, more formal social organization characterizing the "American way of life." This insecurity was linked in their minds to a feeling of exclusion from important choices affecting their lives, and to the inability to control their social environment. The perception was one of nonparticipation and isolation, stemming not simply from their being strangers but from a sense that they had been placed in a position of dependency on a highly abstract social service system.

In her volume on church-related sponsors of Indochinese refugees, Fein (1987) describes the problem as follows:

> But refugees do not live by bread alone. The need for community and to re-create the institutions of daily life that requires some ethnic concentration is a need most refugees . . . have shown. One must also ask whether personal dignity is enhanced or diminished by the processes of resettlement and relationships with sponsors and/or agencies involved. (p. 123)

A sense of community and autonomy are essential characteristics of genuine participation in social life. The problem, as Fein phrased it, is that American sponsors may unintentionally reinforce the dependency of the Indochinese refugees.

Queries about legal knowledge soon enough spilled over into political questions, and articulations of the political process led to even broader discussions about "finding a way to get a handle on" the civic and economic stratagems so crucial to the life chances of individuals and communities within American culture. As one Vietnamese participant explained, the experience of the Indochinese refugee in the United States is like that of someone who has been invited to a dinner party; he or she is welcomed warmly and graciously by the host and generously encouraged by everyone present to make him or herself at home. Yet, this guest is not invited to enter the kitchen, where all of the interesting discussions take place. In other words, the baseline issues are not simply matters of services and education but also of enablement; it is not only a question of encouraging participation, but of empowering incentives that generate a real stake in the civic life of the community.

GENERAL FACTORS AFFECTING INDOCHINESE SOCIAL INTEGRATION

On the whole, this refugee population remains ill-prepared in many areas directly affecting the stated goal of refugee resettlement established by Congress and entrusted to the Office of Refugee Resettlement. This goal is self-sufficiency through resettlement assistance (Public Law 96-212: Refugee Act of 1980). These "new Americans" remain socially isolated and unable to comprehend or successfully manipulate the many demands placed on them by the various social, legal, political, and cultural taken-for-granteds of everyday American life. Refugees cease being refugees as soon as they are resettled in this country; appreciating this social fact and preparing these new Americans for the transition to a permanent cultural and demographic subpopulation within the United States constitute key policy issues affecting resettlement practices and a central intercultural communication task affecting many urban communities across the country.

The limits to social integration are the limits set by accessibility and understandability (Schutz, 1967). Functional integration presupposes access to actual and possible communicative actions; self-sufficiency promotes social integration by establishing enabling skills with respect to the physical and social environment. Society is a system of reciprocally accessible communicative actions. The boundaries of a society are the boundaries of possible meaningful communication. A democratic system that offers rights and responsibilities but does not also furnish the social means to effect those rights or fulfill those responsibilities is nominally, rather than functionally, democratic. Restated in another way, the extent to which a society is not integrated and does not permit actual self-sufficiency is the extent to which all people are equal; some people are more equal than others.

From our perspective, problems related to self-help have important consequences in five primary areas, each of which is of immediate concern, both from the standpoint of public policy as well as from that of the "new Americans" themselves.

Chronic Dependency. Initial resettlement assistance and subsequent assistance structures (Cash Assistance [CA], Aid to Families with Dependent Children [AFDC], etc.) can produce a quasi-permanent pattern of public maintenance and therewith a long-term condition of dependency on human service support systems. Chronic dependency stems in part from the social disablement associated *a fortiori* with limited benefaction-oriented service provision attitudes toward refugee resettlement (Office of Refugee Resettlement, 1983).

Increased emphasis on the acquisition and the exercise of the skills necessary for social and communicative competence can counteract the oftentimes substantial pressure placed on refugees to become acculturated only to the intricacies of private sector subvention and public welfare mechanisms by enabling refugee communities to genuinely participate in the American social process (Etzioni, 1981).

Stabilization of "New Americans." The passage of time has created and will continue to encourage the gradual stabilization of "new American" East Asian subpopulation clusters in urban areas. At this point, a new phase in the refugee transition experience has commenced, namely, the transition from refugee to urban subpopulation status. As has historically been the case with other immigrant and refugee groups, the new refugee cultural groups will attempt to establish and to articulate their own identities in relation to the larger context of the urban environment. Moreover, they will endeavor as part of this process to be acknowledged for their cultural self-definition by American institutions and American society as a whole (Fein, 1987).

The potential for social disaffection as well as for factional and intergenerational tension within these cultural groups can be reduced by developing and implementing initiatives whose chief purpose is the social enablement of the refugee population encouraging its integration into American society. The function of these initiatives should be promoting an external orientation within these groups in a manner that protects their cultural integrity by making the American social process at once comprehensible and accessible to them.

Meaningful Social Participation. The social and economic prospects of these populations to a great extent depend upon how much and how capably they perceive themselves to be participating in American society in comparison with other subpopulations (Monterro, 1980). Unfortunately, even (and perhaps most especially) in agencies and organizations involved in refugee resettlement, a review of the number of refugees having leadership responsibilities at the local and the state levels produces a dismal conclusion.

The perception of meaningful social participation and social recognition requires both familiarity and trust on the part of refugees with respect to American social and economic institutions. The "new Americans" must have the opportunity to control their own futures. The degree to which they are comfortable in their knowledge of the American social process and have confidence in this knowledge will in no small measure dictate the pace at which they relinquish their self-attributed refugee and/or newcomer status and begin to perceive themselves as Americans (Etzioni, 1981; Fein, 1987).

Employability. From the standpoint of the individual refugee, the employment, and particularly the underemployment, histories of many refugees are directly and significantly affected by a sense of intimidation and social incapacitation. For the refugee population, the perception of belonging and effectuality, which grows out of social enablement, positively influences employability and economic initiative in ways that certainly complement and may even compensate for some deficiencies in specific job-related and language-related skills (Stein, 1979). (For example, one Laotian participant in the legal education project has gone on to become a deputy sheriff.)

For these reasons especially, our research has led to the conclusion that greater attention needs to be given to acculturation and social enablement skills. These skills promote individual self-sufficiency and community self-reliance in lieu of a narrow social maintenance orientation that encourages social isolation and economic dependence (Starr & Roberts, 1982).

Technical Assistance. There exists one additional problem that impacts broadly on public policy as well as management practices in almost all areas of Indochinese refugee resettlement assistance. Growing uncertainty about funding agendas, as well as legislative disenchantment with current resettlement strategies and operations as are reflected, for example, in amended work registration requirements and in more restrictive "nonprivileged" public assistance categorization for the Indochinese, indicated leaner fiscal times for refugee resettlement providers and certainly indicated diminishing public interest in Indochinese refugee assistance (Public Law 97-363: Refugee Assistance Amendment of 1982).

In such a situation, it is particularly important that technical assistance initiatives take into account the particular needs and expectations of the community. Technical assistance should be designed, delivered, and evaluated in a manner that is sensitive and responsive to the particular social environment and cultural understanding of the community as a whole. To be effective, such assistance needs to be congruent with the capabilities and priorities of the communities and community organizations themselves (Patton, 1980). The actual translation of knowledge and skills into effective community participation presupposes the incorporation of the community itself into the delivery of the knowledge and skills. Social and cultural factors do comprise key communication process variables in the provision of organizational and community development assistance to ethnic organizations.

Even where this assistance does take root, it can actually promote the creation of an organizational style that is out of touch with the community it represents. In any case, generic technical assistance does not take into account either the individual cultural characteristics or the unique social history of the recipient community.

The technical assistance program developed for the legal education of refugees employed a community-based approach to organizational development. This community-based perspective seeks to achieve sustained effects by carefully attending to these basic realities of the Indochinese community organizations: (a) the social, economic, and educational condition of the recipient community; (b) significant cultural variables as they impact on leadership, management opportunities, and local priorities; and (c) realistic expectations about their service capacity and ability to influence the community as a whole.

THE LESSONS OF COMMUNITY SELF-HELP

Community organizations in urban ethnic environments typically provide many tangible support services within their communities, supplementing such regular service delivery systems in areas like housing, referral, counseling, language assistance, and employment. In addition, they often serve as sole providers for a variety of important community needs. In this latter role, community organizations furnish valuable services in establishing emotional, social, cultural, and political support networks (Patton, 1980).

Because of their versatility and because they are part of the communities they serve, these community organizations can offer natural and highly credible mechanisms for supporting the general ethic population. Consequently, it is in the best interest of regular service providers, including social service, health, education, mental health, and law enforcement, to encourage and strengthen these indigenous community self-help associations.

Historically, self-help organizations have developed among various ethnic groups for the purpose of enhancing the delivery of essential services, because of concern over injustices, or in response to genuine dissatisfaction or even disenfranchisement with respect to established institutions. Duo (1973) presents an illustration of the development of a community-based institution in response to disaffection with regular institutions in his study of the history of Chinese-American dispute resolution processes. In the late 19th and early 20th centuries, Chinese immigrants experienced severe discrimination on the part of U.S. legal and legislative institutions. As a result, the Chinese community withdrew from the American culture and its institutions and substituted traditional Chinese values and methods of social control. Primary among these values was the emphasis on consensus methods of dispute resolution, that is, mediation by members of the community, a system still emphasized in many Eastern cultures (Cohen, 1967; Lubman, 1967; and O'Connor, 1981).

In the Chinese-American culture, associations were formed based on family, occupation, or geographic location. These associations provided an internal structure for the community and made possible thereby a functional alternative to the "alien" legal institutions. The associations handled the resolution of interpersonal and community conflicts through mediation, or they served as conciliators between disputing factions. These associations emphasized the involvement of community members in the creation and operation of an alternative dispute resolution structure. As time passed, and the Chinese-American community became more accepted in American society, its reliance on these alternative means of dispute resolution decreased. As perceptions of the American system became more favorable, and as assimilation into the American culture progressed, the community also adopted the premises governing mainstream American legal institutions. By the end of World War II, the associations' services had been supplanted by the use of adversarial litigation techniques. The transformation of the social organization of Chinese community and the history of its interaction with a nonresponsive system demonstrates Duo's (1973) central thesis, "As changing laws reflect changing mores, so changing institutions and functions of law reflect the changing needs of the community creating them" (p. 629).

The example of the Chinese-American community highlights the problematic nature of creating responsive law and policy in the presence of nonresponsive ones. Basically, the strength of a community is to some degree predicated on the persistence of a contrary dysfunctional law that promotes a shared sense of mutual need and vulnerability. The general concern for group self-interest which is so important to the development of self-help organizations, results in many groups because of the recognition of community needs that are *not* being met. This is an important lesson to learn regarding the promotion of self-sufficiency among new immigrant populations in the United States.

Our experience with the Indochinese has revealed that they are, to a great extent, incapable of recognizing the pervasiveness of their integration into social welfare service delivery mechanisms. This lack of social self-awareness breeds dependence and enervation by inhibiting the development of a sense of social context and of a critical social perspective. As a result, an important first step toward Indochinese self-sufficiency and eventual integration may actually entail demonstrating to them their paradoxical social position; they are simultaneously annexed by and isolated from the greater social system.

FACTORS AFFECTING INDOCHINESE COMMUNITY DEVELOPMENT

Our research also disclosed a set of social, cultural, and communication variables that directly impacts upon organizational development among Indochinese:

1. The homogeneity of the refugee population has been exaggerated. Refugees come from quite divergent educational and social strata. These class distinctions (most pronounced among the Vietnamese and less so among Cambodians and the Hmong) create natural segregation points, much as they do in mainstream society. These distinctions militate against cohesive communal association.
2. Refugees tend to associate on the basis of religion, class, and vocation. In areas with very large Indochinese populations (e.g., California), this natural segregation has not prevented successful community organization; in states with smaller populations, this can pose substantial obstacles to effective community cohesiveness.
3. The American concepts of self-help and community-based service organizations have no clear equivalent in East Asia. In that part of the world, associations have primarily social and ceremonial functions (e.g., matrimonial or holiday celebrations). Moreover, these associations are ordinarily utilized by the upper strata of society.
4. In East Asia, civil governmental structures historically provide primary support systems. As a consequence, individuals have been socialized to seek assistance through formal structures. This orientation has been transferred by the refugees and encouraged by resettlement practices, both private and public, to this country. This condition diminishes the apparent relevance of community organizations for many refugees.
5. Traditionally, authority is acknowledged and obeyed. Consequently, there is a limited tradition of self-help organizations advocating and negotiating with public and private institutions. Activities not provided or permitted by civil institutions are traditionally conducted informally, out of the sight of authority. Hence, the willingness to access channels of authority and to work within a system of legitimate authority must be instilled.

6. Owing to the recent political history of their homelands, there is a general fear and mistrust of authority, often including figures of authority within their own communities.

7. Refugee Mutual Assistance Associations (MAAs) can find themselves in competition with public and private service providers for the same client population. To be sure, many refugees who provide services as part of their MAA are also employed by VOLAGs, or public agencies.

8. Although individuals with organizational and management experience do exist within Indochinese communities, particularly in the Vietnamese community, they often lack the experience and political skills suited to the creation of self-help organizations and to the mobilization of the community for the purpose of self-help. Many of their technical skills are not directly transferable to community service organizations, which must rely heavily on consensus and volunteers.

9. There is lack of self-confidence on the part of refugee leaders in their ability to negotiate with officials in U.S. service delivery structures. This impairs their effectiveness and reduces the relevance of the community organization for the community members.

10. In many of the communities, the "Americanization" of youth has reduced the authority of parents and elder members. Consequently, a very substantial portion of the general refugee population, which is demographically quite young, has not become involved in MAAs, which are typically ruled by older members of these groups.

Each of these conditions and attitudes interacts with and reinforces the others. The various communities and ethnic subgroups within the general Indochinese refugee population are affected differentially by these factors. Different types of information and training must be delivered as appropriate to the social dynamics of the community and its organization. In some cases, organizations must actually be constructed from the ground up; in other cases, only limited guidance is required. Some MAAs exist in name only; others constitute functional entities providing useful services, but may be virtually anonymous and almost completely informal, and are consequently unable to attract recognition from mainstream institutions.

Because community-initiated action is at the heart of self-help organizations, policymakers and service providers must take care that the means employed to gather information or to deliver services and training are sensitive to this essential phenomenon.

Human community expresses collective human action. Refugee communities require a collective self-awareness as the precondition for purposively manipulating their social environment and directing and articulating the collective expression of community needs and aspirations.

CONCLUSION

Our efforts on behalf of Indochinese legal education quickly expanded into a more general examination of the factors affecting the pace of Indochinese integration into American society. From the standpoint of legal education, the explanation for this is apparent: Most especially in dealing with the legal and criminal justice systems, the responsibility for initiating, advocating, and negotiating a course of action is placed upon the individual. Consequently, the individual's self-confidence and capacity to "make the system work" are presupposed for participation in the legal system to a much greater degree than they are, for example, in the economic system. But the more remarkable reason for this situation is the extent to which the individual refugee has been kept in the dark about the essential processes of civic life and the disposition of the refugee's own life-choices.

Having premised our work on a community-based point of view, our research placed strong emphasis on discovering and assessing the views and concerns of the refugees themselves, both as individuals and as members of particular communities. In our view, the first principle of community-based research is that community members know best their own life situations and that requires the research process be ratified as having value to the life situation of the community. As we have found, most especially in the case of the Indochinese groups, the social welfare as well as social scientific exclusion of the relevant population is a significant problem. These practices effectively seek to disqualify the refugee from choosing his or her own position and role within the social and civic life of his or her own community and mainstream society. In our research, "letting the refugees speak" emerged as the central theme. But it was not merely the opportunity to speak as such, but rather the invitation to speak about something "in particular" and "for some end" that generated a kind of meaning-core around which various concerns came to be articulated and analyzed. In the conduct of such a research orientation, valuable, accurate, and privileged information is shared because refugees perceive that researchers are doing something, and therefore must know how things really are. In short, "needing to know," "being willing to listen," and "in order to do" modes of operation become experientially interdependent.

Community-based research starts with the recognition of community members' self-knowledge, requiring the ratification of research as valuable to the community. In order to spur meaningful action, popular participation must be socially and culturally particularized so that the population can be drawn into the process of inquiry and assessment. This viewpoint acknowledges social action as a legitimate component within the research design and seeks to *empower* the community by assisting it with *articulating* and *comprehending* the relevant structures fashioning the meaning and unity of the social action environment. Policymakers and service providers can begin by understanding the community on its own terms and by trying to grasp the idiosyncratic logic of the community. When approached in this way, the community can realistically benefit from the knowledge generated. The process of technical assistance can act as an incentive to extend to and sustain a networking process both internal and external to the community. In so doing, the interaction should lead to results that are recognizable as potentially useful to the entire community.

Community self-help organizations form around indigenous desires for control over and within their communities. Whatever their explicit theme, the underlying motive that spans the efforts of a community is the desire to achieve greater control over their life-situations. The prospects for increased cohesion offer a number of advantages to community members who suffer under undesirable social conditions:

- Active concern about community self-image can be mobilized into purposeful participation.
- A more positive community self-image can be transformed into a desire to improve the quality of community life.
- Collective action increases the legitimacy of requests and demands directed to public officials.
- Concerted community requests and demands tend to have a greater impact on decision makers, thereby increasing the community's own perception of its effectiveness.

An emphasis on social enablement fosters self-help, self-esteem, and self-actualization at both the collective and individual levels. Effective community organization can draw refugee communities into the American social mainstream as full participants, as well as provide a much needed escape route from their chronic marginalization at the recipient end of the service delivery process.

EPILOGUE

An interview guide (see Appendix) was developed cooperatively with the Lao community. It was based on our research practice and utilized by the Lao community in order to develop its own organization. The interview guide is a general model for facilitating refugee enablement and proved to be viable in addressing civic integration.

APPENDIX: REFERENCE MANUAL FOR INTERVIEWS

LAO COMMUNITY LIAISON

GENERAL INSTRUCTIONS:

For each interview you should return the following material to Dr. Pilotta:

1. completed General Information Form
2. completed Topic Questions Interview Response Form

Legal Education Through Cultural Dialogue

The project for Legal Education Through Cultural Dialogue (LETCD) is being conducted by a research team from Ohio State University and is under the leadership of Professor Joseph Pilotta of the OSU Department of Communication.

This project has the full support of the Columbus Area Refugee Task Force, but the research team and its director are *not employed* by any federal, state, or local justice or social service agency. As a result, the researchers are completely independent and can serve as channels for communication between the Indochinese community and government or social service agencies.

The project's goal is to promote *legal self-reliance* within the Indochinese community and to encourage the *full and equal participation* of the Indochinese community in American society. In order to accomplish this goal, the project is developing a model legal education program through continuing discussion with the Columbus area Indochinese population.

Indochinese legal education through cultural dialogue will be accomplished in the following ways:

1. Creating written translated material and audio tape recordings designed to provide the Indochinese with important legal information that answers their questions about the U.S. legal system. This information will be created in a way that is *relevant to the expressed needs of the Indochinese community* and will be distributed to them.
2. Gathering information that will help the Indochinese understand the U.S. legal system and will help Americans understand the Indochinese.
3. Educating the legal and social service system about the Indochinese culture in order to improve trust between the legal and social service system and the Indochinese.
4. Collecting narrative historical material containing the stories of the Indochinese refugee experience and documenting the major concerns of the Indochinese about their adjustment to a new life in American society.

In order to participate fully and equally in American society, the Indochinese must make their voices heard. They can do this by sharing in this project for legal education through cultural dialogue.

Research Objectives

The goal of this research project is to discover the major needs and concerns of the Indochinese living in the Columbus area. The Indochinese must tell us about their needs and explain their problems in order for us to write legal education materials that will be useful to members of the Indochinese community.

Because the U.S. legal system is very complicated and often confusing, and because the legal system in the United States influences the lives of people in many different ways, we need to learn as much as possible from the Indochinese community about the many different aspects of their lives.

In order for this legal education project to be successful, we must find out what is on the minds of the Indochinese people who are living in the Columbus area. The Indochinese must teach us about their lives, their culture, their experiences, and their concerns about their lives in the United States.

Project Plan

The development of legal education begins with the community and ends with the community, but it has three major steps in-between: information collection, analysis, and production of legal education materials.

1. Information collection is the gathering of the questions about the law and learning about the Indochinese cultures and the lives of the refugees in the United States through conducting interviews with Vietnamese, Laotian, and Cambodian community members. This is the step that the Lao Community Liaison is participating in with us at this point.
2. Analysis involves reviewing all the information collected in order to discover what the crucial needs and concerns of the Indochinese are. Analysis leads to the development of legal education material that is needed by the community.
3. Production of legal educational material involves writing and translating documents that answer the questions the Indochinese have about the law. It also includes placing this educational material on tape-recordings for the community's use. This written and tape-recorded material will then be distributed to the community through the community liaisons and relevant agencies.

Each step in this process is equally important; only when all three steps have been completed will the development of relevant legal education for the Indochinese be accomplished.

Interviewing Principles

We obey two principles when conducting interviews: the principle of comparative differences, and the principle of relevance.

The Principle of Comparative Differences. Few Americans know very much about the Indochinese. Because Americans know so little, it is often difficult for them to understand the Indochinese people. Because they do not understand the Indochinese, the legal system and the social service system frequently do not know how to deal with their problems. Consequently, it is very important that the Indochinese teach Americans about the differences between life in the United States and life in Indochina. Although the Indochinese know there are differences, many Americans do not. Understanding how life in the United States differs from life in Indochina will better enable us to assist the Indochinese with their adjustment to life in the United States and with becoming legally self-reliant.

Therefore, *interviewers* must ask the people they interview to tell them about *how life in this country is different from their life in Indochina.* Interviewers should do the following:

- Ask refugees to compare life in the United States with life in their homelands.
- Determine in what ways the legal, social, and educational systems in the United States differ from the legal, social, and educational systems in Indochina.
- Determine in what ways are they similar.
- Determine what Indochinese people do not understand about the legal, social, and educational systems in the United States.
- Determine what things in the United States confuse or worry them.

THE INDOCHINESE NEED TO TEACH AMERICANS ABOUT THEIR LIVES

Encourage the people you interview to explain how their lives have changed, what they do not understand about the United States, what things about the United States they want to learn more about, and what Americans do not understand about the Indochinese people.

The Principle of Relevance. In order for us to provide useful educational material for the Indochinese, we need to know what is on the minds of the Indochinese people. We need to know what the Indochinese think about the social service and assistance system, the legal system, and the educational system. We need their ideas about their problems and their concerns. The Indochinese need to have their voices heard; participating in this project is one way to do this. We need to know what worries the Indochinese people. We need to know what kinds of information they want and need. We need to know how this project can serve them.

THE INDOCHINESE NEED TO HAVE THEIR VOICES HEARD

Because our goal is to create educational material that is based on what is relevant to the Indochinese community, it is important that the Indochinese tell us about their experiences. They need to explain what life has been like for them in the past and what life is like for them in the present. They need to tell us how they were treated in their homelands and how they are now being treated in the United States. In other words, it is important that the Indochinese tell us their story.

What Makes a Good Interview? Everyone who is interviewed must have the chance to tell his or her story completely and to have his or her opinions heard with regard to the problems and the needs of the Indochinese community. Interviewees should be encouraged to share their ideas, concerns, problems, and complaints.

If an interviewee wants to talk about a topic that is not listed among the interview questions, *he or she should be allowed to do so.* Interviewers can simply record this information under the category labeled "other" on the response form.

Interviewers must encourage interviewees to speak honestly, frankly, and openly about their experiences and beliefs. They should not be afraid to state their criticisms or complaints about their lives in the United States. They must state their true feelings. Only by participating fully and freely stating their opinions can legal education material be developed that will be useful to them. Their help will enable the success of this project.

Those people interviewed should be told that the information they depart is confidential unless they provide written permission for it to be used in the oral history collection being developed for Asian American Services. Only Dr. Pilotta and his assistants, Mr. Widman and Ms. Jasko, will have access to the interview information. In short, we guarantee the anonymity of all people who participate and help us with this project.

ALL INTERVIEWS ARE CONFIDENTIAL

Finally, it is very important that interviewers accurately write down the opinions of the people to whom they talk. We need to know what the people who are interviewed think, not what the interviewers think. It is a primary responsibility of the interviewers to accurately report the views stated by the people interviewed. In order to do this, interviewers must be careful not to let their own opinions influence the written summaries of the interview.

If these guidelines are followed, the interviews will greatly contribute to the success of this research project.

Interview Procedures

Interviewers should work in teams of two people. The main responsibility of one interviewer is to ask the interview topic questions. The main responsibility of the second interviewer is to take accurate notes about the responses of the people interviewed.

In addition, both interviewers should ask the people they interview to clarify or explain their statements and to give examples. Just as in any ordinary conversation, interviewers should ask additional questions whenever necessary and request the information they need to understand what is being said by the interviewee. Interviewers must be certain that they understand what the person interviewed *means* when he or she responds to a question. In this way, both interviewers work together in order to reach a complete understanding of the beliefs and the opinions stated by the people they interview.

Although it is not necessary that the topics be discussed in the exact order that they appear on the topic questions interview response form, interviewers should attempt to make certain that every topic question on the list is discussed at some point during the interview. The interviewing method that is being used is called *directed conversation*. Interviewers seek to cover all of the topics on the list while allowing the conversation to take place in a natural way.

The topic question interview response form can be used in two ways:

1. Interview notes can be taken on a separate sheet of paper and then both interviewers can work together to write a summary for each topic in the space provided on the form. This is especially valuable if the interview is conducted in the Lao language.
2. If the interviewers use a tape recorder, they should fill out the form after they have listened to the tape-recordings. (It is a good idea to take notes during the interview, even when using a tape recorder.)

Three Additional Interview Procedures

First, interviewers should work to make certain they are accurately reporting the opinions stated by the people they interview. In short, interviewers must avoid distorting the interview summaries by including their own personal opinions.

Second, the interviewers should fill out the "Interviewer Evaluation" part of the form after the interview. Four kinds of information that can be included there are:

1. What the *interviewers think* about what was said during the interview and how the *interviewers interpret* it.
2. Any additional information the interviewers think we should know.
3. Any problem they had with the interview.
4. Any disagreements between the two team members about the information reported on the topic questions interview response form.

Third, interviewers should ask the people they interview for the names of other community members who should be contacted for an interview.

Summary of Interview Procedures

1. Interviewers should work in teams of two people. One interviewer should be asking the topic questions; the other interviewer should be taking notes.
2. Both interviewers should raise questions requesting clarification and examples from the people they interview whenever it is necessary to do so.
3. Interviewers should try to cover all the topic questions on their list while attempting to carry on a normal conversation.
4. Interviewers should fill out the topic questions interview response form completely.
5. Both interviewers should look over the written summaries on the form in order to check for accuracy and completeness.
6. Interviewers should attempt to report the opinions of the people they interview, not the personal opinions of the interviewers.
7. Interviewers should complete the "Interviewer Evaluation" section of the topic questions interview response form.

GENERAL INFORMATION FORM

Return completed form to Dr. Pilotta

INTERVIEWERS' NAMES: DATE:

LOCATION OF INTERVIEW:

INTERVIEW LENGTH: TIME BEGUN   TIME ENDED

Background Information about the Household(s):
1. Names, addresses, and telephone numbers:

2. Number of people in the family, their sexes, ages, and relationships:

3. How many people live together in the same house or apartment?

4. Do they rent or own their own home?

5. How many family members are attending school, including the adults? Which schools and what kinds (vocational, etc.)?

6. How many family members speak English? How many are attending English as a Second Language (ESL) classes? Where are they attending?

7. How long have you lived in the United States?

8. Where did you live in the United States before you moved to Columbus? How long? Why did you move to Columbus?

9. Where did you live while in Laos? What region or province? In the city or in a rural area?

10. What kind of education or special (vocational) training did you receive in Laos? Did you receive any job training in the refugee camp?

11. What kind of jobs did you have while in Laos? How did you earn a living?

12.   What jobs have you held in the United States? Are you
        presently unemployed? Does your spouse have a job?

13.   Does any member of your family have health problems?

14.   How many of your relatives are still living in Laos or in
        Indochina? Where? What is their relationship to you?

15.   Do you have any relatives living somewhere else in the
        United States or living in some other country? Where?
        What is their relationship to you?

16.   Who or what agency is your sponsor?

17.   What religion do you profess?

Comments:

INTERVIEWER TOPIC QUESTIONS

Employment and Public Assistance:
  1.   Are you aware of the differences between working and
        living off public assistance?
  2.   What do you know about (a) workmen's compensation,
        (b) unemployment, (c) insurance benefits, and (d) equal
        opportunity regulations?
  3.   What has been the greatest obstacle to your getting a job?
  4.   Do you know where and how to find a job?
  5.   What do you feel could be done to help you get a job?
  6.   Are you aware of the rules and regulations governing
        public assistance?
  7.   Have you ever had difficulty with public assistance? What
        happened?

Police and Perception of Authority:
  1.   Do you know the different types of law enforcement agen-
        cies and the differences between them? City, County, State,
        Federal?
  2.   Do you know what the duties of a police officer are?
        Explain them.
  3.   What do you think you should do if you are stopped by a
        policeman or if a policeman comes to your home?
  4.   If you do not cooperate with a policeman, what do you
        think will happen to you?
  5.   Do you know how to contact a policeman if you need one?

6. Have you ever talked with a policeman? If not, why?
7. Do you think the police can help you or protect you? Why or why not?
8. What do you think the police ought to learn about the Laotian culture?
9. How do you feel about American agencies and social workers? Do you think that they help you?
10. Which agency workers are the most helpful? Why?
11. Which agency workers are the least helpful? Why?
12. What do you think agency workers and social workers ought to learn about the Laotian culture?
13. Does the mutual assistance association help you?

Neighborhood Conditions:

1. Are you happy with where you are living? Why or why not?
2. Are you happy with your neighborhood? Why or why not?
3. What do you think could be done to reduce the amount of crime or trouble in your neighborhood?
4. If a city authority were to come to your neighborhood to teach you how to protect yourself or how to improve your neighborhood, would you go to listen and ask questions?

Domestic Law:

1. What do you think are the major differences between the family customs and laws in this country and family customs and laws in Laos?
2. If you had a question, do you know whom to ask?
3. What do you know about the laws governing marriage, divorce, and children's rights in this country?
4. Are you aware of the American law that children under the age of 12 cannot be left at home alone without supervision?

Youth:

1. Are you worried that your children will get into trouble with the law?
2. Are you aware that there are different laws for children and teenagers (under 18) in this country than for adults? If yes, what are the differences?
3. What worries you the most about your children?

Education:

1. Do you understand the American law that requires all children to go to school until they are 16 years old?
2. Are your children having any trouble in school? If yes, what kind?
3. Are you happy with what your children are learning in school? If not, why?

Housing:
1. What do you think your rights and responsibilities are as a tenant?
2. Can you tell me why tenants sign leases with landlords? Explain.
3. Can you tell me some reasons for calling the landlord?
4. What would you do if you had a question or if you had something wrong with your house?
5. Have you ever had any trouble with your landlord or your house? If yes, what happened?

Weapons:
1. Can you tell me what the laws are with respect to owning weapons, for example, knives and guns?
2. Do you think that many people in this country own weapons?
3. Do you think that many people in your neighborhood own weapons?
4. Do you think that people should or need to own and carry weapons? Why?

Drugs:
1. Do you think that it is against the law to have or to grow marijuana in this country?
2. Can you tell me what "controlled substance" means? Explain.
3. Is it against the law to use drugs like marijuana or opium in your food or as medicine?
4. Do you think that many people in your neighborhood use drugs? Explain.
5. Do you think that many Laotians use drugs? Explain.
6. Who would you call for help and what would you do if someone got sick from taking drugs?

Taxation System:
1. Do you understand why the government takes money from your paycheck? Explain.
2. What do you know about the taxation system in this country?
3. Will you get into trouble if you do not pay your taxes?
4. Do you know how to pay your taxes?

Court System:
1. Does going to court frighten you? Why?
2. Do you feel that you will get fair treatment and justice when you go to court? Why or why not?
3. What would you do if you had to go to court?

4.   Do you know how to get a lawyer?
5.   Can you tell me what the Public Defender's Office and the Columbus Legal Aide Society are?
6.   Do people who go to court always go to jail? Why or why not?
7.   What does it mean to pay bail?
8.   If you pay bail, do you still have to go to court?
9.   Do you understand what will happen to you if you do not go to court when you are required to?
10. What does it mean to be on parole?
11. Can you tell me what a judge does?
12. Why do police gather evidence and why are people called as witnesses to testify in court?
13. Do you think that a judge, a lawyer, or a policeman can be put in jail, if they break the law? Why or why not?

Constitutional Rights:

1.   Is everybody who goes to court entitled to a lawyer? Why or why not?
2.   What do you do if you have to go to court but you do not speak English?
3.   What do you think the phrase "innocent until proven guilty" means?
4.   What happens if you are in a car accident and you do not have car insurance?

Contracts and Credit:

1.   What should you do before you sign a contract? Explain.
2.   Have you ever signed a contract before you understood clearly what it said? Explain.
3.   Do you know what happens if you sign a contract and then you later change your mind? Explain.
4.   Can you tell me what a credit card is and how it works? Explain.
5.   Can you tell me what a "credit history" is?
6.   Have you ever had any problems paying a bill or with a collection agency? What happened?

Insurance:

1.   Tell me the kinds of insurance you know about and what they do.
2.   Have you ever had any trouble with an insurance company or an insurance salesman? What happened?

General Questions:

1.   What has been the most difficult part of your adjustment to living in this country?

2.   What do Americans <u>not</u> understand about Laotians?
3.   What did you expect to find when you came to the United
      States?
4.   What do you like the most about living in the United
      States?
5.   What has disappointed you about the United States?
6.   What thing most confuses or worries you about the United
      States?
7.   Do you like living in Columbus, Ohio? Why or why not?
8.   What things can be done to help you?

TOPIC QUESTIONS INTERVIEW RESPONSE FORM

Interviewers should use the space provided on this form to summarize what was said about each topic discussed during the interview. (See page 7 of the manual.)

Interviewers' Names:

Date of Interview:

Return completed form to Dr. Pilotta

(Not included in this appendix are the sheets headed by each group of topic-related questions followed by additional blank sheets for answers/responses.)

ການສຶກສາກົດໝາຍໂດຍຜ່ານການຝຶກຫະນາວັທນະທັມ

ທ່ານ ທຣັກແລະນັບຯ:

ປຊາຊຸນຜົນເມືອງອາດຊ້າແລະຫນຸນທ່ຍໃນສຫະຣັຖອະເມຣິກາ ຈະໄດ້ຮັບການປະກັນໄພແລະການປ້ອງກັນ
ສິດຜົນປະໂຍດໂດຍເທົ່າທຽມກັນ ພາຍໃຕ້ກົດໝາຍຂອງປະເທດ. ແຕ່ວ່າກົດໝາຍຈະສາມາດປ້ອງກັນທ່ານໄດ້
ກົດເໝວ່າ ທ່ານຮູ້ວ່າ ກົດໝາຍຫມບຫຍ່ຽງ ແລະຈະມີວິທີໃຊ້ມັນແນວໃດ. ທຸກວ່ຄົນຄວນຈະຮູ້ກົດໝາຍ.

ໂຄວການ ການສຶກສາກົດໝາຍໂດຍຜ່ານການຝຶກຫະນາວັທນະທັມ ໄດ້ຖຶກຈັດຂຶ້ນແລະນຳພາໂດຍ ຄນະຄຶນ
ຄວ້າຈາກມຫາວິທຍາໄລ ໂຮໂຍໂອ ແລະພາຍໃຕ້ການນຳຂອງ ທ່ານສາສຄາຈານ ໂຈເຊັຟ ຜົນອຄຕ່າ ຜູ້ຊົ່ວຊ່
ກົດຍຸ ແຜນກ ຄມະນາຄຶນ ຂອງມຫາວິທຍາໄລຄັ່ງກ່າວ. ເມື່ອວັນທີ ໒໔ ມັກຮາ ໑໙໘໕, ພວກຂ້າພະເຈົ້າໄດ້
ເປັນຜູ້ຄຸ່ມຄຸ່ມ ການສັມນາວ່າດ້ວຍກົດໝາຍຄົວຕົ້ນຕົວຂອງເມືອງ ຂອງ ແລະໃນວັນດຽວກ່າວ ໄດ້ມີຄພຍຸຈາ໌າ ອຊຕໝານ,
ລາວ ແລະຂເມນ ປະມານ ໕໐໐ ຄົນ ເຂົ້າຮ່ວມການສັມນາ ແຜ່ອສັກສາຣະຫຽບຣ້ວຖັຍກົດໝາຍອະເມຣິກາ
ທີໂຮງການສາມາກ້າຜ່ວມຄອມຂອງເມືອງ໌ປຸຖົ່ມ. ການສັມນາຄ້ວນນີ້ນອາເປັນຄ້ວທາ໌ຈົດທ່ຈະພັທນາໂຄງການ
ຄົວຢ່າງການສຶກສາຄານກົດໝາຍສຳລັບຊຸາ໌ວໍພຍຸ ອຊຕນາມ, ລາວ ແລະຂເມນ.

ພວກຂ້າພະເຈົ້າຂາຍວ່າມັຕລາຍໆທ່ານບໍ່ສາມາດເຂົ້າຮ່ວມການສັມນາຄ້ອມນມ. ພວກຂ້າພະເຈົ້າຍຸ໌ຈາຍອຶກ
ວ່າ ມັຕລາຍທ່ານທຶເຂົ້າຮ່ວມການສັມນາ ມີຄວາມຂອງໃຈຢ່າງຫຍຸ໌ຜູ້ຍ້ນມະຍາຍ ແຕ່ນໍ່ໂອກາດໄດ້ຖາມ ເພາະ
ພວກຂ້າພະເຈົ້າມໍເວລານ້ອຍຫລາຍ ພວກຂ້າພະເຈົ້າສຶ່ນໃຈຢາກຂາຍຄວາມຂອງໃຈຂອງພວກທ່ານ ແລະຄວາມ
ກ້ວວມສຶ່ນໃຈກ່ຽວຄຽອງກົດໝາຍໃນສຫະຣັຖອະເມຣິກາ. ດ້ວມນບພວກຂ້າພະເຈົ້າຈຶ່ງຍາກຈະມາຍ້ຣົມຢ່າມຖານ
ຂາວພວກທ່ານຄຈ໌ຮ໌ເຮຶ່ອມຂອງທ່ານ ທຶສຖານທີໃດ໌ກໍ່ໄດ້ ຫຖ່ານເຕ໌ມວ່າເຫມາະສົມແລະສຄວກຫຂວກທ່ານ
ເພຫ່ຈະໄດ້ສຶມຫະນາກັຍທ່ານໂດຍກຶວ.

ຖ້າຫາກເມື່ອໃດໃຄພວກຂ້າພະເຈົ້າໄດ້ມໍໂອກາດອອກຢ່ຣົມຢາມພວກທ່ານໃນຄມ໌ວຸນ ພວກຂ້າພະເຈົ້າຢາກໃຫ້
ພວກທ່ານແຈ໌ງໃຫ້ພວກຂ້າພະເຈົ້າຂາຍເຣ໌ອງ ຄວາມກ້ວວມສຶ່ນໃຈກ່ຽວກັຍກົດໝາຍອະເມຣິກາ. ພວກຂ້າພະເຈົ້າ
ປະສົງຢ່າກລົມກັຍພວກທ່ານກຶ່ວກັຍ ອຊຕກາມ, ປະຈາສຸ໌ເຄາະ, ຄ້າເວຈ, ຄວາມສັມພັນະຕລາ໌ງຜູ້ເຊ໌າ
ແລະເຈົ້າຂອງເຮ໌ອນ, ຄະຄ໌ວຄຍາ, ຣະຍໍຍສານ, ການສຶກສາ, ຣະຍໍຍການຄໍຍພາສັ ແລະຕໍ໌ວຂອມ໌ງ ທ່ານ
ຄວາມຜໍວພັນກັຍກົດໝາຍຫຂວກທ່ານເຕ໌ມວາສ໌ຄ໌ມ. ພວກຂ້າພະເຈົ້າຈະໃຈຂາວສາມຕຕາມໃຫມາະເພຫ່ຈະເປັນ
ມຸນຖານໃນການຈັດທ່ຳ໌ອຄສາ໌ວຄ້ວຍກົດໝາຍສຳລັບຂາວອໍນຄຸຈໍມ.

ເນ໌ວງຈາກວ່າໂຄງການນມປ່າໝາຍຫຈະສາວ ອອກສາມການສຶກສາກົດໝາຍ <u>ຂ້ວອງຄາມສ໌ວຍ໌ມຄວາມ
ຜຸກຍ໌ນແລະມໍຄວາມສຳ໌ຄັນຕ໌ຂຸມຊຸ໌ນອໍນຄຸຈໍມ</u>. ການເຈ໌າເຮ໌ວງກຣ໌ວຄັຍປ໌ຍການຂອງຂາວອໍນຄຸຈໍມໃຫພວກຂາຍະ
ເຈົ້າຟ໌ວກັ໌ມໍຄວາມສຳ໌ຄັນຫລາຍ. ພວກຂາຍະເຈົ້າຈໍ໌ເປັນຕ໌ວງຮູ້ວ່າຂາວອໍນຄຸຈໍມຄວາມນໍຄວາມບັຄຕ໌ຂມໍ໌ໃກໍ໌ແກ. ເຜ໌ວ
ຫຈະະເຣ໌ກໃຕ໌ໂຄວການນມ ໂດຍປ໌ະສໍຄປະສາຄຄວາມຮູ້ຄານກົດໝາຍຫຶສ໌ຄັຍຕາ໌ທທ່ານຄອ໌ງການ ແຜ່ຄຈະະເຣ໌ກ
ໃຕ໌ພວກທ່ານມໍສໍຄຄສຣິພາຍຄຂ໌ຫທ່ານທ໌ວມຂຸ໌ມຊຸ໌ນອະເມຣິກາ, ພວກຂາຍະເຈົ້າຈ໌ຳ໌ເປັນກໍ໌ມ໌ຄວຂາຍ໌ລໍຖາ໌ມແລະຄວາມ

ກ້ວງວົມຂອງທ່ານກໍຣ້ອງກັບກິດຕະມາຍ. ພຽວແຕ່ການໃຕ້ຂາວສານທ່ຈໍເປັນແກ່ພວກຂ້າພະເຈົ້າ ມັນກໍຈະເຮັດໃຫ້ໂຄງ
ການມີບົນລຸເປົ້າຕມາຍໃນການຊ່ວຍເຕລືອຊາວອົມດູຈົມ ຊວນ ວຽຕນາມ, ລາວ ແລະ ຂເມນ.

ໂຄງການມີໄດ້ຮັບການສັບຍສນຸນຈາກ ອົງການກໍຕັຍອົພຍົບເຂຕໂຄລົມບັສ, ແຕ່ວ່າຄມະຄົມລວ່າ ແລະ ຜູ້ອຳນວຍ
ການບັນມມລູກຈ້າງຂອງ ຣົຖບານ ພາວ, ຣົຖບານທ້ອງຖົມ, ສາມ ຕລິ ອົງການປະຈຳສິ່ງ ເຄາະຕລິ ວົ ການໃດໃຊ່
ການຕມວ. ຄມະຄົມດວ່າເປັນ ຄມະ ອອກ ຈາກ ແລະ ເຮັດວຽກເປັນ ສ້ງ ກຮວ ການຄົມ ຕະ ຕ ອ ຊາວ ອົມດູຈົມ ແລະ
ອົງ ການ ຈົດ ຕົວ ຂອງ ຣົຖບານ ຕລ ອົງ ການ ສ່ ງ ເຄາະ ອມ ງ.

ຈຸດ ປະ ສ ວ ຂອງ ໂຄງ ການ ມ ກິ ຕິ ການ ຍົກ ຣະ ດັຍ __ການ ກຸ້ມ ຕົມ ຂອງ ດ້ານ ກິດ ຕມາຍ__ ໃນ ຊຸມ ຊຸມ ອົມ ດູ ຈົມ ແລະ ຜ ອ
ຊຸກ ຍູ້ __ການ ເຂ້າ ຮ່ວມ ຢ່າງ ເຕົມ ສ່ວມ ແລະ ສ ນ ຕ ນ ພາຍ__ ຂອງ ຊຸມ ຊຸມ ອົມ ດູ ຈົມ ໃນ ວົ ສ ວ ຄົມ ອະ ເມ ຣິ ກ ນ ແລະ ດ້ານ ກິດ
ຕມາຍ. ຜ ອ ທ ຈະ ເຮັດ ໃຫ້ ເປົ້າ ຕມາຍ ບັນ ສ ຳ ເຣົ ຈ ຍົ້ມ, ພວກ ຂ້າ ພະ ເຈົ້າ ກໍ ລ້ວ ທ ຳ ການ ຜົດ ບາ ຕ ຜ ມ ການ ສຶກ ສາ ດ້ານ
ກິດ ຕມາຍ ໂດຍ ການ ອອກ ຍ ມ ຍາມ ແລະ ສົມ ຕະ ນາ ກັຍ ຊາວ ວຽຕ ນາມ, ຂເມນ ແລະ ລາວ ທ ອ າ ໃສ ຢູ່ ໃບ ຍ ຣ ຄອມ
ເມ ອ ງ ໂຄ ລົມ ບັສ. ໂຄງ ການ ມ ຍ ເປັນ ໂຄງ ການ ມ ຍ ສ ຣ ສ: ຍ ມ ໂຄງ ການ ກ ນ ສຶກ ສາ ດ້ານ ກິດ ຕມາຍ ໃຄ ຄ ຄ ສ ຳ ລັຍ ຊາວ
ອົມ ດູ ຈົມ ໃບ ທ້ອງ ປະ ເທຄ ສຕະ ຣ ຖ ອະ ເມ ຣິ ກ. ດ້ວ ມ, ການ ຊ່ວຍ ເຕລ ອ ແລະ ການ ຣ່ວມ ຂອງ ພວກ ທ່ານ ກໍ ໂຄງ ການ ມ
ສາ ມາດ ໃຫ້ ບ ມ ປະ ໂຍດ ແກ່ ຊາວ ອົມ ດູ ຈົມ ໃບ ທ້ອງ ສຕະ ຣ ຖ ອະ ເມ ຣິ ກ.

ຜົມ ສຸດ ທ້າຍ, ໂຄງ ການ ມ ຈະ ສ ຳ ວ ອອກ ສາມ ເປັນ ລາຍ ລ ກ ອ ກ ສອມ, ເຫ ຍ ອັດ ສ ວ ທ ບ ມ ທຸກ ຄວາມ ຣ ຕ ຳ ວ ວ ທ
ຕ ອ ຍ ລ ຳ ຖາມ ແລະ ຄວາມ ຂອງ ໃຈ ຂອງ ຊາວ ອົມ ດູ ຈົມ ຊວ ກ ລ ອ ກ ຳ ຕມາຍ ໃບ ປະ ເ ທ ຄ ນ. ພວກ ຂ້າ ພະ ເຈົ້າ ຍ ວ ມ
ຈຸດ ປະ ສ ວ ຈະ ຣ ອ ຍ ຣ ວ ມ ຊາວ ສາມ ຕ່າງ ງ ທ ຈະ ສາ ມາດ ເຮັດ ໃຫ້ ຕົມ ອະ ເມ ຣ ກ ນ ເຂ້າ ໃຈ ປ ມ ຕາ ຕ່າງ ງ ທ ຊາ ອອ ຕ
ມາ ງ, ຂເມນ ແລະ ລາວ ກ ລ ວ ປະ ສ ຍ ຢ ໃບ ຣະ ຕ ວ າ ງ ຕ ເຂ້າ ເຈົ້າ ກ ລ ວ ປ ຍ ໂ ຕ ຂອງ ເຂ້າ ກັຍ ຊຸ ຄ ໃ ມ ໃບ ສ ວ ຄົມ
ອະ ເມ ຣິ ກ ນ ມ. ໂດຍ ການ ຣ ອ ຍ ຣ ວ ມ ເຣ ອ ງ ຣາ ວ ຕ່າງ ງ ຈາກ ປະ ສ ຍ ການ ຂອງ ຊາວ ອົມ ດູ ຈົມ ແລະ ໂດຍ ການ ສ ມ ຕະ ນາ
ກັຍ ເຂ້າ ເຈົ້າ ໃບ ສ ວ ຕ ເຂ້າ ເຈົ້າ ມ ຄວາມ ກັ ວ ວ ມ ສ ຍ ໃຈ, ພວກ ຂ້າ ພະ ເຈົ້າ ກ ຈະ ສາ ມາ ດ ສ ຳ ວ ແ ຜ ນ ການ ການ ສຶກ ສາ
ດ້ານ ກິດ ຕມາຍ ຕມ ສອມ ຜູ ກ ຜ ມ ໃບ ຄວາມ ຕ ອ ງ ການ ອົມ ຍ ຍ ກ ອ ມ ຂອງ ຊຸ ມ ຊຸ ມ ຊາ ວ ອົມ ດູ ຈົມ ດ ວ ຍ ຣ ອ ກ ກັຍ ທ ກ ການ ຊ ວ ຍ ຝ່າຍ
ກິດ ຕມາຍ ແລະ ຝ່າຍ ສ ວ ລ ມ ສ ວ ເຄາະ ໃຫ້ ເຂ້າ ໃຈ ຄວາມ ຈ ຳ ເປັນ ແລະ ຄວາມ ກ ວ ວ ມ ຂອງ ຊາວ ວຽຕ ມາ ງ, ຂເມນ
ແລະ ລາວ.

ພວກ ຂ້າ ພະ ເຈົ້າ ປະ ສ ວ ຍາກ ໃຫ້ ທ່ານ ເຂ້າ ຣ ວ ມ ໃບ ໂຄງ ການ ມ ຍ ຜ ອ ຍ ມ ປະ ໂຍ ດ ຂອງ ຕ ຕ ທ່ານ ຂອງ ແລະ ຕ ມ ຍ ຜ ອ ຍ.
ຍຸກ ຄ ມ ຕ ຈະ ອອກ ມາ ລ ມ ກັຍ ທ່ານ ຈະ ແມ ນ ຕ ມ ລາວ ຂອງ ຜູ້ ຊ ວ ໃຄ ຣ ວ ມ ເຮັດ ວ ງ ກ ກັ ຍ ພວກ ຂ້າ ພະ ເຈົ້າ ໃບ ໂຄງ ການ ມ. ກຣຸ
ມາ ຕ ອ ຍ ລ ຳ ຖາມ ທຸ ກ ຍ ຜ ມ ມາ ຍ ຢ່າງ ລະ ອ ງ ຄ ຜ ອ ວ າ ພວກ ຂ້າ ພະ ເຈົ້າ ຈະ ໄດ້ ຕິດ ຕ ກັຍ ທ່ານ ແລະ ຈ ດ ຕ ມ ມາ ຄວາ ມ ລາ
ອອກ ມາ ພົບ ກັຍ ທ່ານ. ພວກ ຂ້າ ພະ ເຈົ້າ ຍ ນ ດ ອອກ ມາ ພົບ ທ່ານ ຕ ຄ ອມ ຂອງ ທ່ານ ຕາມ ວົ ມ ເວ ລາ ທ ທ່ານ ຕ ມ ສະ ດ ວກ
ຈະ ເປັນ ເວ ລາ ຄ ອມ ແລ ງ ຕລ ວ ມ ເສ ້ າ - ອາ ທິດ ກ ໄດ້. ການ ສ ມ ຕະ ນາ ຈະ ຕ ຍ ເປັນ __ຄວາມ ລ ຍ ຍ ຢ່າງ ຕ ວ ດ ຍ ດ__.

ຖາ ຍາກ ຊາ ຍ ລາຍ ລະ ອ ງ ຕ ມ ກໍ ຣ້ອງ ກັຍ ໂຄງ ການ ການ ສຶກ ສາ ດ້ານ ກິດ ຕມາຍ ມ ພາ ຍາ ຕິ ດ ສາ ສ ດາ ຈາ ນ ໂຈ ຊ ຍ
ຜ ລ ອ ຕ ຕ າ ຕລ ອາ ຈາ ນ ຕ ມ ວົດ ແມນ ໂທຣ: ໘໘໘-໐໓໕໐໐. ຕ ຈະ ຕິ ດ ຕ ເຈົ້າ ຕມາ ຍ ຕ ຕ ດ ຝ່າ ຍ ລາ ວ ກໍ ໄດ້ ຊວ ມ
ຍຸ ດ ສ ຍ ຍົດ ຕ ອມ : ໘໘໔-໐໑໘໑ ຕລ ຕ ຳ ຮ ຊ ວ ຍາ ຊຸ ມ ບດ ຕ: ໘໘໔-໑໑໔໑, ໘໑໘-ກ໐໘໘໔ ຕລ ທ ອ ງ ທ ມ ຣ ຕ ມ ະ
ວົ ໂ ລ: ໘໔໔-໐໐ກ ງ.

ດ້ວຍ ຄວາມ ນ ຍ ຕ ແລະ ຣ ກ ແ ພ ງ

ກຣຸນາກຽກຂໍ້ຄວາມລຸ່ມນີ້ ແລ້ວສົ່ງໄປຕາມຢອກຢ່າງພະເຈົ້າຫນາຍໃນ ສອງ ອາທິດ.

ຊື່ : _____

ທີ່ຢູ່: _____

ໂທຣະສັບ: _____

ວັນ ເວລາ ທີ່ສະດວກໃນການອອກມາພິບທ່ານ : ວັນທີ_____ເດືອນ_____ຈຸຊປີ

ເວລາ:_____ໂມງ

ສຖານທີ:_____

ສິ່ງຟອຣ໌ມນຫງາ :

SEVEN

Windsor Terrace Profile

It was the initial goal of the research presented in this chapter to employ community-based, qualitative research techniques to assess the "root causes" of social stress within the Windsor Terrace community at the Columbus Metropolitan Housing Authority (CMHA). To complete this research task, interviews were set with Windsor managers, VISTA volunteers, and residents to review their perceptions of services and what they thought needed to be done to improve service delivery at Windsor Terrace. Soon after beginning the actual interviews in the late summer of 1988, it became clear that the broader question needing to be answered was simply: What do people think is going on at Windsor Terrace? (See Appendix A for a statistical summary of our findings.)

In any case, there are two different ways of framing the same basic question. Windsor Terrace is a stress-filled environment by ordinary standards. But it is nonetheless an environment to which the residents have adapted reasonably well, perhaps too well. To be sure, Windsor Terrace residents are often regarded by outsiders, and sometimes viewed by one another, as apathetic, complacent, and docile. Windsor Terrace is not governed by "ordinary" social rules, and its residents tend not to arrange their lives or direct the upbringing of their children according to the usual logic of education, employment, acquisition, and attainment. The indisputable and most uncompromising fact of everyday life at Windsor Terrace is that Windsor is a social setting governed by its own extraordinary rules and social practices, and further that residing at Windsor entails a lifestyle and a way of thinking that sets it apart and effectively segregates it from "'ordinary," "expected," "normal," in short, mainstream attitudes and practices.

It took some time to develop trust between the researchers and Windsor residents. Trust—especially in the case of outsiders, managers, and White folks—is a comparably scarce commodity at Windsor. The first introduction to Windsor in conversations with the residents was ordinarily that people come and people go, programs start up and they disappear, promises get made and quietly get forgotten. And more importantly, the whole process was mysterious to the average resident. Researchers, services, and programs dropped out of thin air one day, and then disappeared from sight the next. At Windsor, this is a kind of popular wisdom that militates against even the best intentions.

Nevertheless, between approximately mid-August 1988 and May 1989, a pattern of recurring themes did emerge from a series of casual conversations, telephone calls, observations, and actual interviews. The organization of this chapter reflects the themes and echoes the most recurrent contexts in which they took shape, were discussed and were revealed.

The research yielded a rich texture of conversations, ideas, and evaluations coming directly from the principals in the Windsor Terrace community. This information has been evaluated as well as collected, confirmed and discussed as well as reported. This is possible only because the research is linked publicly as well as programmatically with actual community development activity. On this basis, the researchers gradually shifted the relationship with the researched from interrogation toward working cooperation. In this light, over time, it became possible to distinguish the themes that are the most relevant to the researchers from those that are the most salient to the researched, and thereby to gain greater confidence in the researchers' ability to reconstruct intelligently and systematically the actual concerns and interests of the research population.

METHOD

The research method employed was a community-based, qualitative technique. This approach was employed and refined for research attached to the Urban Consortium for Human Services Development (UCHSD) over a period of approximately 8 years. Although the technique is not unique to the UCHSD, it is nonetheless a consistently practiced and elaborated approach by UCHSD researchers during consecutive years of research with minority, inner-city, and low- to moderate-income populations in Columbus.

Between August 1988 and May 1989, 75 interviews were conducted with individuals and small groups (two to three individuals), as well as more than 250 hours of observations, meetings, and informal discussions. (These figures do not include the time devoted to additional items including literature review, curricula development, leadership training, technically assisting the Windsor Concerned Moms/Resident Council [CM/RC], data analysis, and report preparation.) All interviews and discussions about perceptions, policies, programs, and people were conducted under the pledge of confidentiality. Neither interviews nor informal discussions were tape-recorded.

Interview solicitations and the evolution of research features were guided by referrals, networks, and the gradual disclosure of common themes. Copies of the standard interview questions have been included in Appendix B. These questions were used as guideposts for actual interviews, but as the situation warranted, discussions frequently expanded into related and sometimes unexpected topics.

Regular evaluation of the progress of the research and the direction of both the content and the targets for further interviews were undertaken by the principal researchers. In addition, evaluations and assessments of the key themes were regular topics of discussion between the principal researchers and the project director. Finally, an assortment of tentative evaluations and "trial balloons" were reviewed by key participants through the process of re-contacting them for follow-up discussion in order to confirm the researchers' assessment of important themes and dominant viewpoints. Additional information was gathered through simple direct observation of activities at Windsor Terrace, including happenings in the Community Affairs office, the activities of various service providers, and the relationships evident between tenants and service providers and between themselves.

The rationale for this procedure is to identify multiple avenues of confirmation–disconfirmation of informant proposals and researcher assessments. Furthermore, the aim is to accomplish these tasks in a way that is not entirely constrained by the performance expectations that regularly accompany the interview setting. The underlying conceptual justification and mechanism for establishing the credibility of the research activity in the community is provided by the assumption that the research activity is geared to generate a focus for community development. The social action setting enables the researcher to move beyond reporting strategies and response expectations toward a setting where cooperation and informal confidence improve access to much needed information.

This chapter summarizes the major themes, ideas, and opinions identified during the research process. As possible, the chapter recreates the major elements of the contexts in which these perceptions were stated. The chapter also summarizes the researchers' assessment of the linkages between and among the various themes we identified.

PERCEPTIONS OF THE ENVIRONMENT

Not surprisingly, residents' perceptions of their physical environment reflect the rather stark and drab atmosphere created by buildings that are so obviously public housing. More specifically, residents wished for many of the same home improvements any tenant in low- to moderate-rent housing might wish for: the installation of showers, new carpeting, updated kitchen appliances, and changes in the exterior appearance of the units, including the creation of secured garden spaces and a way to clean up the dumpster areas. Some residents also expressed concern over a lack of supervised and secured recreational facilities for young children (e.g., playground equipment, sports equipment, and the like).

The psychological environment is best summarized as one of great distrust and social isolation. There was also a sense of isolation from the greater surrounding Linden community and an outright sense of alienation from the city as a whole. These two themes played out in a variety of ways.

Distrust was widespread and nearly global. There was distrust of CMHA personnel, of social service personnel, of neighbors, and of all White people. The net result was that each person, or perhaps each friendship group, had to encounter and seek solutions to problems that in fact were common to the community as a whole and that someone in the community likely had already encountered. In other words, there was little informal warehousing or pooling of information such that the community might have come to view itself as its own resource.

The distrust of neighbors also appeared to manifest itself in the male–female relationships, which tended to be transitory and sexually oriented. Although this is neither unique to this group nor even inherently negative, in the Windsor setting it fed a pattern of economic and psychological dependency among the female heads of households. The dependence was not on males as providers or as contributors to the household, but on a system that rewards reproduction economically. We suspected that at some time during early adolescence, females opted for pregnancy as a declaration of independence and as a sort of economically based career choice.

The pattern we heard about from the residents can be summarized in the following way: Young female adolescents became mothers, dropped out of school, and lived with their own mothers (who in some cases treated their grandchildren as their own children) until they reached the legal age at which they could apply for their own apartments.[1] Adolescent males, on the other hand, opted for impregnating young women but remaining socially bonded with other *young men*, be it to hustle drugs, acquire temporary marginal employment, or just hang out.

The point here is that adolescent females tended to grow up to become single heads of households who were economically dependent on the social welfare system. Adolescent males, on the other hand, grew up to live on the periphery of the system that supported them in their childhood, and that subsequently supported the mothers of their children. The "ordinary" composition of a household (i.e., two married parents with children), as a basic economic unit was discouraged. On the other hand, the conditions for a self-sufficient household headed by a single (female) parent did not exist: Crucial employability skills, home management skills, and role models for independent living were not present.

Given these circumstances, the marriage bond in the ordinary sense did not offer a solution to the cycle of dependency; indeed the traditional nuclear family does not in general offer a very useful model for understanding the practical day-to-day lives of Windsor residents. The organization of the social welfare system, in its consequences if not its design, provided incentives to single (female) parent households. Low educational attainment combined with the lack of economic opportunity militates against two-parent households. The preponderance of single female heads of households makes sense under such social and economic conditions.

One of the significant ramifications of being socialized into a familial system of this sort is that it stands in contrast to the still predominant custom of males and females (adults) forming a primary bond. For example, it is still a controversial topic among the (predominantly) White middle class of this country for a single, economically self-sufficient female (adult) to bear and/or rear a child alone. However, it is neither controversial nor uncommon to the residents of public housing across this country. At the same time that single parenting is an accepted, taken-for-granted social practice in public housing communities like Windsor Terrace, the role models for single parenting and the support system for rearing children are not geared toward the independence of the household but to meeting the

[1]There is abundant literature on teenage childbearing and on Black female heads of households. Some representative examples include: Battle (1987), Dash (1989), hooks (1989), Moore (1986), Simms (1986), U.S. Congress (1986), and Wilson (1987).

qualifications for entitlement benefits and to generations of economic and social dependence on the entitlement system. This sort of social dissonance makes transitions from welfare to economic self-sufficiency all the more problematic, even for the youth.

The residents viewed their environment as unattractive, unfriendly, and suspicious. They felt that their community was isolated and only tangentially related (by way of social service agencies) to the larger social structure in which they were embedded. As a consequence, residents lived in a world that had only limited horizons. That is, their sense of future was abbreviated because they saw their possibilities defined by services delivered to them through government agencies and a few social service or church-related groups. The parents' sense of future (or the lack thereof) had been passed on to their children and then to the following generation. Similarly, mothers seemed to focus on what they did not wish for their children, and not (as is common among working and middle-class parents) on the child's possibilities. Many women expressed a dread of the very real possibility of seeing a male child begin selling or running drugs in order to obtain income. However, they did not talk much about the future of their children in terms of education and/or careers. The closest expression to a similar sentiment was made by the one young woman who said she hoped her children might "get a good job and maybe move out of here."

Some final summary points about the environment are evident from 1980 Census Data. In South Linden (where Windsor Terrace is located), the poverty rate was 25.4% for Whites and 33.2% for Blacks. Of the number of families living below the poverty level, 68.9% were single female heads of households. Concurrently, only 50.3% of the Black adults 25 years of age or older were high school graduates; an estimated 22.9% of the youth (ages 16–19) were deemed high school dropouts.

This handful of figures from South Linden provides simple measures for some of the more salient features of Windsor Terrace: low income, single female households with high unemployment and limited educational attainment. Windsor Terrace (1988) demographic information extends the overall picture: The average tenant had completed 9 years of school, depended on public assistance, and had an approximately 30% likelihood of being involved in substance abuse.

Perceptions about the environment appeared to be strongly colored by the average cycle of publicly subsidized family life: namely, women with multiple children and truncated educations who are preoccupied with the everyday requirements of coping within the system that maintains them.

SELF-PERCEPTION AND SELF-ESTEEM

The Women

The women were most commonly single and the heads of households, and therefore were the organizing force in the home. Yet, one of their most striking characteristics was that individually they lacked confidence, especially in speaking to outsiders. Their reticence in interacting with others was clearly related to both a general lack of confidence and more directly to their poor verbal skills. It needs to be noted that these women did not appear to experience any difficulty speaking with family or friends, and our judgment about their verbal skills was made in the context of their interaction with people from outside of this community or social circle.

More specifically, the kind of "poor verbal skills" to which we refer centers on a common inability to articulate and clearly convey thoughts, feelings, and attitudes. They frequently were at a loss for an appropriate word or expression and so spoke in an abbreviated and elliptical manner. Moreover, they were clearly uncomfortable with their attempts to express themselves, for they became embarrassed and flustered and quickly aborted their attempt. They were also quick to accept any attempt to paraphrase their partially articulated thoughts instead of feeling free to modify that paraphrasing.

The simplest illustration of this verbal incapacity was the willingness to accept an interviewer's paraphrase. As an interviewer, one regularly rephrases or summarizes what has just been said in order to obtain confirmation or clarify information. With the respondents at Windsor, we noted seldom attempts on the part of the women to defend or explain their own phrasing of a situation. This happened to such an extent that it became relatively easy to put words into their mouths; the impression was created by the respondent that they were willing to say what they thought the interviewer wanted to hear. Furthermore, in a number of instances, where respondents were asked to elaborate or expand on a particular statement, they tended to simply repeat what they had just said. Neither a vocabulary, conceptual sophistication, nor confidence was apparent.

This verbal awkwardness appeared to affect the self-esteem of these individuals in the form of self-consciousness about their public self-presentation. As one woman put it: "I have . . . trouble . . . getting out, saying it right . . . finding words . . . to say what I mean." She also acknowledged that speaking to us caused her significant anxiety, and that the thought of speaking to a group composed even partially of strangers, evoked great stage fright. Although she did not actually appear to be as inarticulate as she feared, it took 20 to 25 minutes of dialogue to elicit this information.

Although this was not a universal trait among the residents we talked to at Windsor Terrace, a general lack of self-confidence regarding their self-perception and verbal skills was common enough among the women to prompt our recognition that improved self-confidence is linked to the improvement of communication skills.

It is possible to disagree about how genuinely effective or ineffective these women were in their actual communication with one another, with service providers, or even with prospective employers. It is, in fact, the judgment of the researchers that their skills were limited. That assessment is detailed later. What is important at this point is that the individuals perceived themselves to be limited in their ability to communicate, and this self-evaluation was linked in their eyes with a lack of confidence in dealing with people outside of the community. (*Community* was defined by the residents as other people "like themselves," and further as "people in housing.")

More than a few women expressed dissatisfaction with their physical being, most commonly due to being overweight. Their physical appearance, they acknowledged, discouraged them from venturing out. Combined with their awkward verbal skills, the net result was a group of individuals who were afraid to be seen or heard outside of their (likely narrow) circle of relatives and friends (which uncomfortably and unfortunately coincides with a folk wisdom regarding children's place in public settings: "Children should be seen and not heard").

Beyond their awkwardness and discomfort, some of the women we interviewed expressed a clear desire to learn marketable skills and to tackle that undertaking with the knowledge that they would be concurrently required to develop their self-confidence and their self-presentation.

There was an additional element contributing to the low self-esteem and general lack of self-confidence evidenced in these women. It can be best summarized as a lack of home management skills. Some of the women interviewed noted that they lacked even a rudimentary understanding of good nutrition, and also felt that they had limited and boring diets. They also felt their knowledge of food preparation techniques was similarly limited.

Obviously, home management entails a good deal more than food selection and preparation. It also entails fiscal management and performing or securing maintenance services. Although these women functioned as single heads of households, they had little, if any, experience in budgeting and otherwise managing money. This included a lack of familiarity with ordinary but essential mechanisms for fiscal management, such as balancing a checking account, developing fiscal assets, securing bank loans, and purchasing insurance. And although this inexperience is the logical result of growing up and living in a welfare economy, it posed for them a large and significant obstacle to both escaping welfare for employment, and to the development of their self-esteem, self-confidence, and self-sufficiency.

The Men

The adult males at Windsor did not appear to play visible social roles. Our observations of males at Windsor were limited to three settings. First, teenage males who could be observed "hanging around" and were quick to seek female attention. When we spoke with them, they talked about sports, a lack of activities, no meaningful commitment to education, made wistful remarks about money and purchasing things, and exhibited few realistic expectations about future plans and economic options.

Second, adult males requesting information or apparent favors from their wives or cohabitants. The striking feature of these interactions—we witnessed several brief ones—was that the males were addressed abruptly, given or denied what they requested, and then just as abruptly dismissed by their female counterparts.

Third, young male children appeared always in the company of their mothers only, except in the case of a couple of Asian families. Mothers, without exception, referred to their children as "my" or "mine," never as "ours." Women did not volunteer information about their spouses or cohabitants. When asked, they were reluctant to speak about them, and were most nondisclosive. Younger males appeared to look up to the teenagers; we could not find evidence of adult male role models.

The most prominent characteristic of the males at Windsor Terrace was their virtual invisibility. We knew, of course, that adult males were present; during warm weather they could be seen about the neighborhood. When we spoke with the adolescents, they had little if anything to say about their fathers. Teenage males were more willing to speak about how the "White man" prevented them from getting what they wanted. By appearances or, at any rate, by what was disclosed in the interviews, the adult male did not seem to play a strong role in the community; instead, the household, and by extension the community, was dominated by women and children.

COMMUNICATION SKILLS

A deficit in communication skills certainly added to the impression of apathy on the part of the residents. A general inability to express themselves combined with a self-consciousness of that inability yielded a pronounced reticence that seemed to confirm the suspicion of apathy.

Our research and interactions with the residents led us to believe that the issue at hand was not "indifference" as a personal attitude, but rather (in part) was a deficiency in some basic skills. What we are addressing is an ability, or lack thereof, to have at one's disposal a vocabulary and a general linguistic sophistication that cuts across the boundaries of socio-economic class. That is, individuals first need the ability to decide that the colloquialisms they employ at home or among peers are not necessarily appropriate for use during an employment interview, or when dealing with bank representatives, or with their children's grade-school teachers; more importantly, individuals also need the linguistic resources to respond differently to various situations verbally.

Linguistic resources and *linguistic sophistication* refer to the flexibility to use, at one's discretion, an assortment of grammatical and syntactic constructions. This selection of grammatical constructions is not value-driven (i.e., made on the basis of correctness), but rather is made on the basis of appropriateness in regard to one's audience or listener. To employ a simple illustration, a different vocabulary and sentence structure would be used when explaining the workings of an internal combustion engine to a 7-year-old than to an adult, and yet another vocabulary would be used when speaking with a mechanic. The ability to choose and employ these differently constructed explanations is what we mean by linguistic sophistication, which results in the skill of linguistic flexibility.

Such linguistic flexibility may include selecting from among various regionalisms, colloquialisms, dialects, and even languages. Such selection does not imply or require that any particular value be attributed to any single one of these linguistic variations. We are not advocating nor judging the debate around the labeling of "Black English" in relationship to "Standard American English." This debate lies outside of the topic discussed here. From our perspective, it is unfortunate that too often such labels carry value judgments. Instead, our focus here is on an individual's ability to communicate successfully and confidently, not only with his or her cohorts, but also with those outside of his or her typical and immediate community.

Indeed, there is some research indicating that this sort of linguistic flexibility marks the "upwardly mobile" among working-

and middle-class populations. Research also indicates that class distinctions based on economic realities are reflected in educational and linguistic differences. To the extent that this is true, it stands to reason that a pronounced lack of linguistic flexibility marks an individual as not likely to be a member of the upwardly mobile segment of the population. And, the individual is frequently treated differently because of this.

Many people are shy and awkward about self-expression. But many Windsor residents appeared to be verbally uncomfortable to the point of being literally incapable of getting their point across (verbally) without resorting to tremendous effort and reliance on much repetition and the listener's ability to paraphrase and fill in gaps. They lacked both self-confidence and skills. These skills included: (a) a vocabulary sufficiently large and not entirely colloquial in nature, enabling one to rephrase the same thought differently as seems appropriate to help listener understanding; (b) an ability to assess one's listeners and adjust one's presentation accordingly (i.e., to assume as a speaker a significant part of the burden of establishing mutual understanding); (c) the ability to develop different modes of expression (involving both vocabulary and grammatical distinctions); and (d) the ability to selectively and smoothly employ differing modes of expression. Additional related, but less essential, skills included: public speaking, participating in and/or leading a small group discussion, and interviewing.

As a good portion of this chapter is devoted to detailing our research findings, it is clear that many of the residents had something to say. It is our belief that the individuals we interviewed, and very likely most of the Windsor residents, had even more to say than they themselves knew. The more capable (and confident) a person is in expressing him or herself, the more he or she finds to say.

Clearly, these kinds of communication skills are closely aligned with literacy and with the relative success of grammar school and secondary school education. The development of vocabulary and grammatical sophistication (and hence, of linguistic flexibility) is most often facilitated by exposure to books and to other well-read individuals. Successful literacy programs deliver not only a vital skill, but also simultaneously provide the means for individuals to enrich their lives and to augment their self-presentation and their self-esteem.

For this reason, of all the social service programs attempted or in place at Windsor Terrace, the literacy program was the most important. Active participation in the mainstream working-class or middle-class culture requires literacy. As a tool, literacy provides access to information, understanding, and self-development.

What is important is that these skills can help to counteract social isolation, most especially to the extent that it is *self-imposed*.

It is a truism of social science that human beings are the most secure in the company of other individuals like themselves. In the case of Windsor Terrace, and perhaps of public housing communities in general, this quite ordinary tendency created a problematic situation because some or many of the characteristics of the setting were deemed undesirable by the general public. And, individuals (in this case, the residents at Windsor) who relied on the security of this natural aggregation themselves voiced dissatisfaction with their situation. Clearly, substance abuse, low educational attainment, and economic dependency are not generally desirable social characteristics. Equally important, Windsor residents themselves stated their dissatisfaction with their quality of life.

Social isolation and low self-esteem are a part of a larger socio-emotional system that also includes poor or partially developed communication skills. Linguistic (and more broadly communication) patterns serve simultaneously to mark some people as insiders and others as outsiders. When these same patterns function only as barriers marking borders and not as bridges, they reinforce social isolation. Of course, sometimes such patterns also reinforce both collective and individual elitism; at Windsor they served instead to reinforce negative self-images, weakening individual self-esteem, and fueling collective dissatisfaction with the quality of life.

APATHY

One theme that was stated repeatedly in different ways by Windsor tenants and management is that the general population was "apathetic," or hard to motivate, or nearly impossible to get involved in most anything. As one individual stated: "I have been here more than 10 years, and these people don't get involved in anything unless you are giving something away or taking something away."

It is easy enough to conclude that the people living at Windsor were lazy, unmotivated, and indifferent to what happened around them or to them. But at the same time, when we spoke with individuals or small groups of tenants, they often provided lists of things that they did care about (e.g., physical facilities, drugs, difficulty with transportation, lack of input into the system, services, not enough money, and no place for the children to play).

When we spoke with Windsor tenants, we repeatedly encountered a discrepancy between what they said they cared about and what they were willing to do to act on those concerns. Apathy, as it turns out, actually describes a relationship between the residents and the environment more than it represents how any particular individual thought or felt.

There did not appear to be any tradition of self-help at Windsor or at least not in recent memory. Instead, Windsor tenants tended to act like tenants anywhere: When something is broken they complained to the manager. But there is one crucial difference: The environment in which they lived was one that they felt they could not leave. They lived in public housing because they "had to" live there, not because they chose to live there. Making requests and initiating changes in their own lives or in the environment were not meaningful options. The tenants were fully dependent on the complex social maintenance system that supported them. Welfare, AFDC, and CMHA were all part of the same package. What were the incentives to make changes? And where could they possibly have gone?

One striking consequence of this situation was the tendency to assume that "management" was responsible for almost everything. The tenants exhibited only an ambiguous sense of personal or collective responsibility for the physical and social conditions at Windsor. The property they occupied was "not theirs," therefore, the physical look of the environment was something for management to deal with. Of course, to a great extent, even if the tenants had wished to invest in the maintenance of the property, they lacked the resources to do so. But, more important was the lack of initiative and skills to deal with the social environment. An assortment of issues excited people (drugs, kids, safety, noise, garbage), but the tendency was to talk in terms of getting CMHA to do something. When it came to what they themselves could do, it became a matter of explaining that people did not appear interested, and if they were, that they were not clear about how to take action.

A look at the phenomena of individual tenants acting as social isolates coping daily with elaborate service, housing, and financial support systems, reveals that the individuals were not apathetic as individuals (coping is most certainly an activity), but only as a group. This is an important contradiction that is influenced by a second theme discussed later, namely, the absence of a community consciousness.

There was a clear sense that "the system"—welfare system, educational system, CMHA—presented an unending series of obstacles. But, what is worse, these were obstacles in a path that led nowhere. There were only obstacles and annoyances that form part of coping in an environment that did not appear to offer a chance for mobility—economic mobility, social mobility, educational mobility, or personal mobility.

Achievement was not part of the system. If achievement was anywhere, it was part of the underground economy. Making money on the side, which was of course unreported, purchasing objects that one's neighbor did not have, involving oneself in often questionable and sometimes illegal activities: These were the ways to get social status, the only ways to stand out in the crowd.

Apathy, in such a situation, becomes an acceptable "public posture" that needs to be maintained. The alternative would be to adopt "failure" as a public posture. Indeed, this is the enigma; by definition, the entire population of Windsor were failures, otherwise they would not have been "forced" to live in public housing.

We have reviewed some of the individual manifestations of this situation in the section on self-perception and self-esteem, and we have seen that deficient communication skills can create self-imposed limits on personal effectiveness on the environment, so for present purposes we need to look at the social (external) characteristics of apathy.

What we discovered regularly was a conviction that there was no way out of the present situation. From an objective point of view, there is good reason to accept this judgment as a rational assessment of the situation. First, we encountered a number of cases in which two or even three generations of residents had lived in public housing. (We even encountered one mother who claimed that her grandmother had lived at Windsor Terrace.) Second, the majority of the "official" tenants at Windsor were female heads of households with multiple children, less than a high school education, few (if any) marketable skills, and a thin or nonexistent employment history. Third, children were socialized from an early age that they may want a lot of things, but that they live at Windsor, are supported by public dollars, and should be cynical about the reality of the "system" giving them—much less allowing them to earn—what they want.

Fourth, if a resident initiated changes (perhaps by finding employment), he or she had to deal with a series of bureaucratic intrusions into his or her life and perhaps "suffer" penalties—higher rent, reduction or loss of benefits. Fifth, residents may not have liked themselves or the "system," but at least living "this way" at Windsor and being part of the entitlement system had some rules and a reward schedule with which they were familiar, and that appeared to be solid and reliable. It was a support system that in its own way was safe. The world of work, insurance, budgets, social status, and education is complicated, unfamiliar, and very threatening. Sadly, the educational system, rather than functioning as a stepping stone to a wider world, appeared to be only a round-about way back to public housing. The drop-out rate supported this conclusion, as did the teen pregnancy rate, the typically poor school performance situation, and the youth unemployment rate.

In summary, what we are suggesting is that apathy is a very reasonable response to such an environment. It is a powerful coping mechanism and a functional antidote to the apparent lack of socially legitimate forms of opportunity. These people were not indifferent. The setting was deadening, shot-through with disincentives to step out of the system; people seemed apathetic because there was nothing reasonable for them to care about. Apathy was a characteristic of the system.

There were many constraints to what could reasonably be done to counteract the complacency that seemed to overwhelm individual initiative and to militate against organized programs aimed at promoting self-improvement among the Windsor Terrace residents. In our view, the necessary remedies involved promoting status differences and opportunities for personal achievement within the community and, where feasible, between the different public housing complexes.

In a subsequent section of this chapter, we discuss Windsor Terrace from an economic point of view. Therefore, for the present, we discuss social status and the opportunity for achievement without considering economic factors.

To a great extent, competition, or more precisely, socially legitimate forms of competition were absent from the Windsor environment. As we discuss later, one most prominent avenue to social status, to "be somebody" in the community, came through participation in the illegitimate drug economy. But with that exception, the brutal truth, for the most part, was that most everyone was the same at Windsor, and that they were merely treading water. As we have already suggested, Windsor tenants tended to view themselves as existing at the bottom rung of the social hierarchy, and they did not talk or act as if they were genuinely convinced that they could move "up and out." The only effective reward schedule, as is discussed in the next section, was established by the entitlement economy.

The problem for management and community leaders thus became how to go about finding avenues to stimulate healthy competition and a sense of pride among the residents. In such situations, it is necessary to find many little ways to achieve that end, but it should be kept in mind that it is precisely through these small steps that successful persuasive campaigns are mounted and learning takes place. In general, it is a question of developing an agenda consisting of feasible activities and desired aims—and then of employing these aims to create competition for status recognition. A sense of self-importance should be stressed and, for reasons detailed in subsequent sections, monetary rewards should always be the last resort. Community activism of all kinds needs to be recognized and supported. Children who are doing well in school need to be identified and recognized. Individuals who have "moved up and out" of public housing need to be held up as role models. Community organizations need to be supported.

For example, the Windsor Terrace CM/RC spent too much time raising what was, in effect, pocket change through bake sales, car washes, or selling items at sporting events, especially since the funds raised were spent on consumables, like taking children to the movies. This is not to say that underwriting outings for the children is unimportant. Rather, the problem is that these activities strain the limited organizational resources and attention span of an organization, and reduce its ability to deal with other community needs. The CMHA would have been better served by setting aside a small amount of funds, establishing a rudimentary Request for Proposal system exclusively for its recognized organizations at the housing complexes, and encouraging the different residents' organizations to develop projects competitively. Other areas for competition or recognition could include sports, academics, arts, and improving the environment (a couple of Windsor residents created small flower gardens in their yards).

In addition, the CMHA could have reviewed the feasibility of devoting some of its public relations dollars to create its own newspaper specifically for tenants. As needed, these dollars might have generated better pay-offs than those gained by using local public print and broadcast media. Such a vehicle would serve three aims. First, it would help disseminate important information. Second, it would highlight positive images about public housing to public housing residents. Finally, it would provide an in-house organ to acknowledge accomplishments by individual tenants. Distribution of such an organ would be vastly simplified by the segregated nature of the housing complexes. Repeatedly Windsor tenants stated that people did not know what was going on within Windsor—programs, activities, and so on. They also did not know what was happening with or at other CMHA complexes.

Regardless of the specific mechanisms developed to promote these aims, the formula we recommended was a simple one: Competition for recognition; being different, being better than one's peers is desirable. Because the "system" seems inherently psychologically desensitizing, it is necessary to introduce socially legitimate means for recognizing individual human talents and individual human accomplishments. In short, giving pride in one's personal achievements a concrete, specific, and tangible presence in the community.

ENTITLEMENT ECONOMY

As a general proposition, the primary socializing mechanism for Windsor Terrace residents was entitlement-related incentives and disincentives. Approximately 90% of the tenants received AFDC, welfare, and/or an assortment of public assistance and human service provisions. As the consequence, the principal power holders and most visible role models in this environment are human service functionaries. The role of the human service or public assistance providers is to dispense entitlements; the role of entitlement recipients is to exhibit behaviors and perform social welfare functions that ensure the uninterrupted flow of entitlement benefits.

The entitlement economy was one of the two real, effective economies at Windsor Terrace. The other economy, the illegitimate one, was the drug economy. Despite presenting a kind of a parody of the work economy, the entitlement economy works in very much the same way as the work economy, only substituting entitlements for capital. Entitlement recipients are expected to live up to a set of expectations in exchange for goods and services. Entitlements thus become an occupation, and the entitlement lifestyle a way of life.

A striking example of how the entitlement mentality pervaded the fabric of Windsor Terrace is provided by the Windsor Terrace Community Affairs office. The office was established, according to Community Affairs VISTA staff, to identify and "bring in" human services for the Windsor community and/or to "advocate for the poor." From our own observations, Windsor Community Affairs was a reasonably well-run coordination office and conduit for service deliverers and a nascent, informal outreach office for social networking. Community Affairs staff provided crucial support for service deliverers, principally in the form of coordinating services, supplying "insider" information, and creating credibility for them within the population. Windsor Community Affairs also took on the role of providing much-needed moral support and some technical assistance for the CM/RC. Beyond these functions, its role was undefined.

When we spoke with tenants, although some did not know that the office existed, the consensus was that the job of Community Affairs was to deliver services and to solve problems. In the case of the latter, we did observe that Community Affairs was being used by tenants as a one-stop crisis intervention center. When someone had a problem with assistance, or a family emergency, or a personal problem, a call was placed to Community Affairs for either direct assistance or for a referral. In this situation, whether as a service deliverer or as an in-house site to deal with emergencies, Community Affairs played an important social maintenance function. Where it provided a central information center and support for the CM/RC, it became a starting point for the creating of a legitimate formal infrastructure.

But behind these real benefits, there remained the problem that Windsor Community Affairs had been defined operationally by the general population as part of the service provision network. In other words, the tenants who availed themselves of Community Affairs used it as another outlet to get things done for themselves. But "having things done for" had become such a part of their lives that Windsor Community Affairs ended up reinforcing the role of CMHA tenants as the *recipients* of entitlement goods and services.

The example of Windsor Community Affairs is a microcosm of the social paradox created by entitlements. On the one hand, Community Affairs was making genuine progress in coordinating and improving the delivery of much needed social and human services to a depressed community. On the other hand, the more services that became available, the higher the expectations of the tenants became, and the less impetus among the tenants for change or relocation was generated.

But, what is perhaps most important of all, among tenants the assumption was—and we think it was true in fact—that the initiative for the various programs either in place or starting up at Windsor Terrace, including literacy, child care, parenting, drug counseling, and so on, were initiated by the CMHA central office. This does not mean that these programs were not important or that they did not service genuine needs in the community, but only that these initiatives did not come from the community. In other words, even where programs created improvements, the community remained nonetheless passive and subordinate.

Another way of looking at the social-psychology we encountered at Windsor is characterized by the expression "welfare rights." Putting the politics and policy management aspect of this notion aside, what welfare rights meant in concrete day-to-day economic terms was the right to be poor. Thematically and frequently, the issues and perceptions disclosed and discussed by individual Windsor tenants fell into two general categories: (a) what and how much they needed to have done for them, and (b) how it would be pleasant to have money.

The first category was discussed extensively: environmental improvements, activities for children, drug-related problems, inadequate medical services, and so on. But these discussions did not generate in the listener any confidence that the entitlement recipients had a sense of being in control of their own lives, nor did they indicate that for they could someday assert control. The second category of topics was accompanied by unreal expectations. We did not encounter individuals who aspired to working-class status. Their aspirations were shot through with fantasy: annual incomes of $30,000 to $50,000 and more were cited. Economic attitudes were not being shaped by working-class expectations, but by images mediated by television. The most common references were to TV game shows, sports and entertainment celebrities, TV soap operas, and the Ohio Lottery.

Windsor Terrace tenants were not regularly exposed to the working class or their neighborhoods. The entitlement economy fosters a social structure that differs significantly from the mainstream social structure. Entitlement encourages dependency of single female heads of households, and offers males (from puberty onward) no meaningful way to contribute or otherwise participate in the family or the greater community. Virtually all of the responsibilities typically associated with the male role in mainstream society are provided by social service delivery systems in such situations.

Although working culture individuals trade their labor, knowledge, skills, and time for income, welfare recipients trade their time, energy, and incapacities or underutilized abilities for social support. Furthermore, employed persons enjoy the privilege of deploying their incomes at their own discretion within the constraints established by income level and credit rating. But welfare recipients have marginal discretionary freedom in deciding how their (legal and reported) income is to be allocated among basic needs and luxuries. This creates two related conditions: (a) entitlement recipients feel powerless to control virtually any aspect of their economic existence, and (b) entitlement recipients do not develop a sense of responsibility for the direction of their own present, much less their own future. What is important is that the missing element that could have given the social and human service programs at Windsor Terrace direction and coherence was the underlying trajectory set by motivation for securing and building economic opportunity and achieving security for oneself and one's family.

The ability to manage their day-to-day affairs while working to build a future for themselves and their families is a skill learned and developed or, in the case of public housing residents, not learned and developed. The rules and regulations of the entitlement economy do not allow for the opportunity to assume and manage individual responsibility. Instead, entitlement requires passivity and subordination, and demands incapacity (real or apparent) as the qualification for receiving economic rewards from society. The net result is a group of individuals—not a genuine community—who are segregated from mainstream society and who are largely or wholly unprepared to succeed at the task of making a life for themselves and their families in a work culture. Therefore, although providing employment opportunities is the necessary precondition for mainstreaming this population, employment alone is far from a sufficient condition. Dropping these people into jobs without providing auxiliary support and supervision is much the same as placing third-world refugees into jobs without social support; although they are not incapable of successfully acclimating to working-class culture, they cannot reasonably be expected to succeed without supportive resocialization.

Learning to appreciate, accept, and cope with responsibility is a lesson that is ordinarily part of a series of experiences that each child goes through as he or she matures. When this happens, responsibility can reasonably be expected to be integrated into a mature adult's world view and perception of self. As such, it is intrinsically motivating. That is, having been reared to embrace a work culture, an individual sees the world as a composite of opportunities and obstacles for individual achievement. But the child reared in the entitlement social order does not see the same set of obstacles and opportunities. In the entitlement economy, self-reliance is not a function of individual economic action, but of adhering to the expectations established by the social support system. Earning income is something others (or other kids' parents) do, and is not a genuinely viable option. That is, unless individuals turn to a mechanism outside of the entitlement mainstream, because, in effect, the socially legitimate avenues for mobility appear and, to a great extent, effectively are, blocked in the entitlement economy. Consequently, many individuals with creativity, the ability to learn quickly, and entrepreneurial drive turn to the only genuine avenue for assuming responsibility for their livelihood that is available in their community—the underworld economy of drugs.

A final observation about the entitlement economy, although while not an explicit topic of conversation in our interviews with residents, nevertheless played an unmistakable role in the overall social organization of Windsor Terrace: It is a nearly pure case of a flow-through consumer economy. Dollars and entitlement vouchers, food stamps, eligibilities, and the like were not generating wealth for the Windsor Terrace residents. Windsor residents constituted little more than middlemen for public dollars that actually supported human service providers, physicians, public service employees, business establishments located at the borders of Windsor, farmers, and community centers.

It is important to recognize that neither economic wealth nor vital social attitudes like honesty, industriousness, or trust are encouraged in a community by entitlement incentives. Because purchasing power was being spent entirely with outsiders, the Windsor community was completely subject to external economic interests. This real fact of everyday life, and not logistical or management obstacles, probably more fully explains in the long term the absence of any visible form of economic cooperation among Windsor tenants. We could identify neither awareness of the potential economic clout possessed by the collective to negotiate or to create mechanisms to improve living conditions, nor consumer awareness.

The dollars did not turn over in Windsor Terrace, they merely passed through the community. This simple fact was evident everywhere, and an awareness of the economic role of

Windsor residents in the larger system was not appreciated by the residents and, we suspect, was probably taken for granted by the merchants and service providers who were truly benefitting from these consumer dollars.

RACE AND TRUST

In speaking with Windsor Terrace residents, allusions were regularly made, most always negatively, to "the man," the "system," or simply to "they/them." It was furthermore quite clear from the context that these labels are code for "White man" and the "White system." On a couple of occasions, however, it was also stated that these labels can apply to Blacks who work for and/or represent the "White system."

"White" encompasses more than race; it refers to a set of institutions; these institutions stand for authority, influence, economic achievement, and education (knowledge). In general, their statements took the form of "they can, do, know, . . ." but "we can't, don't, don't know how to . . ."

Certainly, race did make a difference to the residents of Windsor Terrace, but primarily as it represents "access" or "opportunity." In our interviews, we noted that racial differences were more likely to be cited as the reason for lack of economic opportunity and for differences in material wealth, than for differential treatment at the hands of law officers, which the residents seemed to attribute to their very residency at a public housing complex.

Residents were cynical and cautious about any activity or interaction with individuals or programs that were a part of "the system," and were most willing to participate only in the case that such participation resulted in direct material benefit—or entitlement. At the level of this sort of program or activity participation, trust in the system, in the intention of the provider, in intangible benefits, in a future in which change and growth is likely or possible appears to be absent. Instead, the formula appears to be: "If I get something now, then I am interested." In such a situation, this is not trust but only an exchange of commodities. Stated in more abstract terminology: It is as though a significant part of the worldview and hence reality of the Windsor residents included the assumption that for them, there was no American dream, no future, no inclusion in social progress. And that is because participation resulted always in the same end: passive entitlement to a static quality of life.

Residents expressed the feeling that they (as public subsidy recipients and, for some, as Blacks in a "White world") were constantly being channeled to the periphery of society by a set of institutions that conversely also served as their means of daily support. Given that the society on whose periphery they existed is so proudly based on "inalienable rights," it is easy to see how entitlements could come to be understood as "welfare rights"—these are the rights that exist at the periphery. And to the extent that social welfare institutions themselves employ the very same linguistic/social presumption, these very institutions can be seen as reinforcing the social marginality of the very people such institutions were designed to aid in the form of enabling their (the recipients') socio-economic self-sufficiency.

For some social analysts, this phenomenon is known as "institutional racism" and has as an extension an entire history of oppression. It is a kind of racism that partially entails the color of an individual's skin, or the place of birth, or their cultural heritage, but more importantly reflects misapplied social assumptions or, more properly, myths about "equal opportunity," success based wholly on hard work and sincerity, and luck or fortune (most of the time, most people get what they deserve, or a person's life circumstance reflects the quality of personhood). In this way, institutional racism includes sexism, doubling (at the very least) the difficulties confronted by women locked into social marginality.

Like all other forms of racism, institutional racism may actually be a product of "good intentions" gone awry; protection can shield a person and thereby enable his or her growth and future self-sufficiency, or it can serve to subordinate an individual and thwart his or her potential growth, thereby precluding any independence and self-sufficiency. Unfortunately, it requires less oversight, thought, and effort (in some regards) to "protect" or "provide for" or "administer" someone than it does to systematically provide both protection and enable autonomy.

But our actual conversations with Windsor Terrace residents did not consist of discussions about abstract issues like institutional racism or oppression. Instead, the conversations used the much more concrete language of controlling what happens to them as individuals and to their children. When we conclude that there was a widespread lack of trust in management, service providers, and outsiders (Whites), we are specifically referring to two omnipresent factors in the lives of Windsor residents:

1. The residents did not feel that they could control, make choices about, or influence the quality of their lives.
2. The residents claimed not to understand (in some meaningful degree) the system that controlled them, and felt at a loss to influence how that system operated.

Regardless of how much it can be said to have been actually perpetuated, the lack of trust was nonetheless symbolized by racial differences. What residents talked about was a lack of access, a lack of opportunity, of what they needed, and that "this is how things are." Race, entitlement, and low self-esteem combined to create a simultaneously complacent and dissatisfied population.

CONCEPT OF A COMMUNITY

The concept of a *community* implies a sense of interdependence and a sense of shared investment or resources, as well as mutual recognition of each other as members of the same communal entity. Most social scientists recognize that modern society houses two types of communities: one is distinguished by the addition to the definition just given of members also sharing geographic proximity (e.g., that they are all physically located within specific boundaries such that each lives next door to other members); and the second sort of community also fits the aforementioned definition, but its members need not share immediate geographic proximity, nor any semblance of geographic proximity (i.e., they may live tens, hundreds, or even thousands of miles apart and maintain their sense of community by means of telephone conversations, visits, and other means).

In fact, our discussions with the residents led us to believe that the Windsor community was a community primarily on the basis of geographic proximity only, and seemed to be lacking much of a sense for interdependence and shared resources. Among the residents of Windsor Terrace, the sense of community expressed revolved around two main elements of their collective self-perception: having the same landlord, and an awareness of the quality of the media image currently attached to the area.

They clearly stated that "Earl," as manager, was the focus of their complaints/maintenance problems (as is appropriate) and was also an object of some amount of distrust and hostility. This is evidenced in the story told to us by several of the residents about a third party, whom they felt was unfairly treated by Earl in connection with a conflict surrounding improper unit maintenance. One striking aspect of this retelling is that it did not include even an implicit understanding that Earl was a part of a much larger system that bound his actions as well as those of the residents. They therefore seemed unaware of the fact that they stood to gain more by depersonalizing any such conflicts and responding to such a situation at a more strategic (systemic) level.

Another significant aspect of the way this incident was retold is that, although the incident's details had made the circuit among a group of residents, none of them considered the option of joining forces and mobilizing their collective resources (e.g., to form an advocacy group). Although they recognized that they were collectively bound by system (CMHA) rules, they did not seem to recognize that there was power in this very collectivity. This sense of powerlessness had been reinforced by previous residents' councils that—in the residents' recent memory—lacked a member with even a modicum of organizational knowledge or with an ability to see the larger picture. Consequently, resident meetings quickly degenerated into gripe sessions. Organizational leadership skills would be crucial to any development of a residents' council or some similar group.

The second main aspect of their sense of community revolved around an awareness of a highly negative media image. This negative image was the result of the fact that the major media focussed attention on this area only when something sufficiently "newsworthy" occurred. In this case, newsworthiness was determined by the degree of violence involved in any given incident or event. Most frequently, the media coverage was of drug-related violence (e.g., shootings, raids on crack houses, etc.). Although it is generally true that a good deal of news coverage is devoted to negative events, it is also true within the Columbus viewing area that the major media (especially the local television stations) have made an effort to focus at least some attention on positive aspects of the greater community. Unfortunately, such alternative focusing did not include Windsor Terrace or only rarely any of the other public housing or other economically depressed neighborhoods—at least according to Windsor tenants.

As a result, the residents clearly expressed their cognizance of this negative image and were concerned that some residents were coming to accept this image as the true and complete reality. We can confirm that for some of the residents, their fearfulness of violence in the neighborhood had indeed been heightened by the media coverage, in one case even though the individual had never had any firsthand experience with local crime. This fear presented an obstacle to the development of a genuine and productive sense of community among the residents, which in turn hindered the development of a meaningful and productive residents' council. On the other hand, some of the other residents expressed strongly their opinion that the media coverage was both inaccurate and unfair, and they expressed an interest in developing activities or events that might counterbalance the negativity of the community's image.

It needs to be noted that the fear on the part of the residents was far from unfounded because a substantial and powerful underworld economy based on illegal drug trafficking was in place within the community. Its presence and the violence attached to it were also significant obstacles to the development of a positive sense of community among the residents. Fear, realistic or exaggerated, compounded the difficulty. There was genuine danger in proposing activities that overtly and directly opposed the drug culture. And it is clear to us that no residents were willing to jeopardize their safety in the name of community development. Our research conclusions and recommendations clearly reflect this reality.

In order for a community organization to successfully develop, two criteria must be met. The residents must come to feel that participation does not jeopardize their health and well-being, and that there are some social and material benefits attached to participation. In order for a community organization to become self-sustaining and self-perpetuating, residents must be introduced to the notions of self-determination, responsibility, and interdependence. That is, they must be encouraged to see themselves as active in controlling their own lives, responsible for their present and future state of material and psychological being, and as interdependent on their fellow community members.

Equally essential to the eventual success of community revitalization and the development of a community organization are communication and leadership skills. These are the mechanisms that ensure that the net result of information sharing is the formation of enduring bonds that eventually become a powerful network. But first, residents need to develop a larger perspective on their lives and social situation. This ability is closely aligned with literacy, which simultaneously serves as a tool for accessing and delivering relevant information and services, selected and applied by the individuals directly impacted—the residents themselves.

THE DRUG ECONOMY

The stark reality is that the quasi-underworld economy of dealing illegal substances, especially "crack," is a potent and well-entrenched force in the public housing community. It is also the only genuinely stable and readily accessible alternative means of securing an income exclusive of public support. This is true, in part, because the current welfare system penalizes even partial or low-paying employment by reducing benefits. Income that goes unreported is neither taxable nor reduces public support entitlements.

Successful drug trafficking requires intelligent planning, creativity, and initiative. It contains a significant element of risk, rewards know-how, and yields lucrative benefits. It is no accident that the armed forces use television advertisements that paint very much the same picture of a career in the services; they are hoping to attract bright, ambitious, energetic, and risk-taking individuals. Indeed, many of the same personality characteristics and social skills that make for a successful drug dealer also make for success on Wall Street or for a career in the corporate world.

Windsor residents either implicitly or explicitly acknowledged the illegal drug economy as a taken-for-granted aspect of their environment. This is not to suggest that the residents were undisturbed by this situation. Quite the contrary; one young mother told us that she was anxious about the possibility that her young son, who had begun hanging around the local gas station to earn money by offering to pump gasoline for motorists, would soon discover that aiding the sale of drugs was far more profitable. The story is especially poignant because the boy's announced goal for earning money was to purchase gifts for his mother.

Through this and similar discussions with other residents, it became clear to us that adolescent males in particular had little or no opportunity to earn disposable income. Transportation was scarce, and there were few businesses in the immediate vicinity to provide employment; as a result these adolescents gravitated toward drug trafficking as a source of economic opportunity.

Of course, not all or even most of the Windsor population were actively participating in the drug trade. And as ethically or morally opposed to such activities as these residents may have been, they were all too aware of the genuine dangers associated with any anti-drug or anti-crime (for in their eyes, these are the same thing) activity. Drug trafficking is often a violent business. Partially because of this, past efforts to galvanize the community around anti-drug campaigns failed and, in our opinion, must continue to fail. As more than one resident expressed it, the community was well aware of the dangers associated with drugs, but what they needed was not more anti-drug education (propaganda) but personal security and economic alternatives, in particular for the youth.

It became clear to us that if a robust sense of community and a community organization were to be developed at Windsor, it could not be organized around an anti-drug or even an anti-crime theme, but instead could only be fostered by positive and productive alternatives to drug involvement of any kind. In other words, community development would need to focus on potential, not on threats. Instead of telling residents "*don't* use drugs" (as they have already heard repeatedly), the message should be "*do* these things . . .": for example, finish high school, learn a trade, develop a talent, help the elderly, fix up the physical environment, play a sport, or plan a future. The residents would need to develop a much more convincing vision of an alternative lifestyle that helps make real the sense of the anti-drug messages to which they have been constantly exposed at school or through mass media. It is important for everyone that the message becomes more than "don't do drugs—do nothing." "Don't congregate in large groups because it makes White folks nervous." "Don't leave the neighborhoods because you don't have any money, and no one wants you loitering around." For in real terms, that is precisely how the anti-drug slogans have translated at Windsor. Alternatives are needed that offer, or have the potential to offer, meaningful personal and social identities, and control over one's own life, while being at the same time socially legitimate and socially acceptable alternatives.

We can summarize the attitudes about the drug problem we encountered as follows:

1. Drugs, however reprehensible, were simply a part of the environment in much the same way that the possibility of contracting a deadly disease, like cancer, is much to be feared but is a part of life.
2. Even though they were not quick to express fear or a sense of feeling personally threatened, most every Windsor resident we talked to was clearly intimidated by drug traffickers. As a group, Windsor residents have been quite unwilling to cooperate openly with law enforcement authorities.
3. Mothers, although eager to have their children educated about the hazards of drugs, did not exhibit much confidence that there was any strong connection between drug education and a drug-free lifestyle.
4. The presence of the drug culture contributed to social disunity by creating suspicions between residents and reducing their willingness to confide in or depend on one another. The drug dealers' organization has inhibited other forms of social organization.
5. Drug dollars are real disposable dollars. Disposable dollars translate into social status.
6. Drug enforcement and law enforcement officials are not really serious about forcing out the drug dealers. (Or if they are serious, they are incompetent.)

In light of this situation, a direct assault on the drug economy that depended in any large measure on public or even implicit cooperation from Windsor residents would not be practical. The low morale, lack of self-confidence, social disunity, absence of economic alternatives, and the physical environment in evidence at Windsor Terrace—one might generalize to public housing as a whole—have made Windsor a highly conducive setting for drug trafficking.

It would simply not be feasible, or even fair, to expect Windsor residents to shoulder any major burden for ridding the community of the drug menace. Of course, ultimately the responsibility for making successful inroads against a drug economy inevitably does depend on each individual and upon the collective initiative of the community. But, although acknowledging this truism, it is most important to bear in mind that the problem was much more complicated than simply Windsor Terrace residents "saying no" to drugs. It was much more complicated because the social economics of the environment provided fertile soil for illegal (cash-generating) activities, and because the population was suspicious about drug enforcement pronouncements made by public authorities. In the final analysis, no "outsider" could solve the drug problem for the community, but what outsiders can do is take steps to improve both economic opportunity and the credibility of drug enforcement.

The drug economy appeared to be as much a natural part of the public housing environment as generations of single female heads of households with multiple children. Of course, the difference is that substance abuse is illegal and punishable. What appeared to be needed was a *vigorous* and *aggressive* drug *enforcement* initiative mounted by forces from outside of Windsor Terrace. Such an initiative, if it could be made visible and appear to be a semipermanent or at least long-term commitment, would receive the tacit approval of many or most of the Windsor residents. Programs aimed at drug education and community crime prevention could have a chance to make an impact at Windsor, only if Windsor residents could be spared the uncertainty and potential for social ostracism that accompanies self-policing. The social fabric at Windsor Terrace was much too fragile to hold up under the strain of law enforcement obligations. The assumption of (or wager made by) law enforcement officials was that what is at first presumed to be tolerated or implicitly welcomed will eventually become publicly embraced and openly supported.

It is important to appreciate that Windsor tenants were not indifferent to the drug problem, much less supportive of the drug culture. What they felt is that they had been abandoned by the system. Lacking social resources and policing capabilities, they were made the targets of anti-drug proclamations and public policy rhetoric. If there was one case where we encountered cold, deep-seated, and realistic cynicism among Windsor residents, it was in the area of the drug trade and drug enforcement. Simply stated, we know of no law enforcement personnel who lived at Windsor Terrace. Consequently, it must be kept in mind that Windsor residents would "wait out" any anti-drug initiative to see if it were real or only an apparent and short-lived effort.

On the other hand, what needed to be done in a way that publicly and systematically involved Windsor tenants was the creation of activities, programs, and social practices that excluded drugs; excluded drug money, excluded drug users, and excluded drug talk. At the same time, an alternative economy needed to be stimulated—an economy that not only excluded drug use, but also encouraged attitudes and values in which drugs do not have a place. Economic activity that creates wealth in the community would offer a genuinely anti-drug social antidote and an alternative form of social differentiation.

Despite many differences of opinion about how anti-drug initiatives are to be achieved, the root causes of the drug economy lie elsewhere. Hundreds of research projects have established that we have the know-how to affect change. What is lacking is not know-how and programs but a clarity of purpose, of motive, and of intention. What do we want to do, why do we want to do it, and how much are we willing to pay for it?—and not so much in monetary terms as in basic changes in the class and racial structure of our society. These are the largely unanswered questions.

The issue is the culture of poverty and the entitlement economy. Drugs seem to be the answer to the question "What does the system think of me?"

CONCLUSIONS

The public investment in public housing is immense in sheer dollar terms, but this investment pales in comparison to the social and personal investment of public housing residents in coping with life in public housing. It is tempting to conclude that Windsor Terrace has constituted a kind of reservation or holding facility for the permanently disenfranchised segment of society. Disenfranchisement in the political sense of the term, if it applied at all, did not have much meaning in Windsor Terrace. Windsor tenants were not political, and it does not appear likely that they will become so. Rather, they have been disenfranchised or disqualified from participation in mainstream society.

To the degree that they have been disqualified, they are without access to meaningful participation in mainstream society. They have become a passive "cared for," "tolerated," and "managed" community. As the consequence, Windsor residents simply have not played by the same rules as the majority culture. Social programs that have been satisfied to merely maintain an acceptable quality of impoverished existence, a marginally humane standard of living, could not at the same time offer a way "up and out" of public housing, much less out of the cycle of dependency they themselves have fostered. Social programs by themselves perpetuate passivity and dependence. At Windsor, we encountered a cycle of poverty and public housing occupancy that spanned in some cases three generations. The answer to the question "What is going on at Windsor Terrace?" is actually quite simple: poverty, dependency, and illiteracy. Combine these elements, and the further conclusion is patent: Windsor Terrace is a community apparently without hope.

It is in light of this situation that we believe that the primary aim of CMHA initiatives must be to instill a sense of hope in the population. Creating aspirations is the first step to engendering social mobility.

SUMMARY OF CONCLUSIONS

There were 12 principal conclusions. They are as follows:

1. Distrust of authority and isolation from the social mainstream generally characterized the Windsor Terrace environment.
2. Female heads of households lacked confidence in their own ability to deal effectively with people from outside of the community.
3. There were not enough legitimate male role models (i.e., individuals with skills/education and employment).
4. Inadequate language and literacy skills, both written and oral, limit and lower self-esteem and have functioned as a barrier reinforcing social isolation.
5. Tenant apathy and lack of individual motivation appeared to be an adaptive strategy to a "system" that offered no apparent interest in the social and economic betterment of the residents.
6. For Windsor residents, dependence on a system of entitlements had become a way of life that was regularly reinforced by social welfare and service deliverers.
7. Dependence on a system of entitlements discouraged individual responsibility and self-reliance.
8. Race differences functioned symbolically to stand for socio-economic, educational, and opportunity differences.
9. Residents did not feel they could influence the "system" that appeared to control their lives.
10. Social cooperation and social unity between and among Windsor Terrace residents were hindered by inadequate communication, over emphasis on negative factors in the community, limited participation and understanding by

residents about CMHA management policies and practices, and dependence on immediate gratifications reinforced by the entitlement system.

11. Drug use has been a function of a number of factors, including most especially availability, economics, social prestige needs, and peer pressure.

12. Although drugs have not been welcome in the community, grass roots drug prevention and drug elimination efforts in Windsor Terrace have been impeded by cynicism about the sincere intentions of drug prevention initiators, insufficient social and economic alternatives, and social disunity.

RECOMMENDATIONS

First, economic activity and economic opportunity need to be stimulated at Windsor Terrace. Beginning to find a solution to economic despair is the bedrock for meaningful social reorganization and individual improvements.

Second, economic initiatives should concentrate on two segments of the Windsor population: young adult female heads of households and adolescents. In the case of young adult females (mothers with school-aged children), they (a) constitute a significantly large proportion of Windsor households, (b) cope with household management, (c) are principal role models in the home and so a potentially powerful socializing influence, and (d) are still at an employable age. In the case of adolescents, employment and disposable income are clearly connected in modern youth culture—if they don't find the money one way, then they will find it another. The socially acceptable avenue would be the culture of work.

Third, human and social service programs need to be organized in a way that encourages individual responsibility and rewards self-reliance; programs that (inadvertently or not) reward dependence and compliance need to be reconsidered.

Fourth, literacy is equally vital to individual economic viability and individual self-worth. A strong literacy program is perhaps the single most important social program that can be made available at Windsor Terrace. Staying in school and getting something out of school also need to be stressed. "Earn-and-learn" approaches that reinforce the connection between education and economics deserve some attention.

Fifth, community organization—as in the case of the Windsor CM/RC—needs to be stimulated, nurtured, rewarded and, if need be, goaded. Community organizations, particularly given the impoverished social cohesiveness of Windsor Terrace, make self-sufficiency manifest and collective initiative tangible in the eyes of the general population.

Sixth, genuine alternatives to the preponderance of negative and proscriptive admonitions need to be created at Windsor Terrace. In too many cases, if a Windsor resident does not in fact do what he or she is told not to do, he or she is left with little to do. Positive social activities for youth need to be supported—sports and scouting at Windsor are a start.

Seventh, drug enforcement and activities aimed at improving personal security are needed to complement crime prevention and drug prevention activities that emanate from within the community.

Eighth, Windsor Terrace is a large and densely populated housing complex. The South Linden area, where Windsor is located, offers limited economic or social mobility. When a densely populated enclave made up of largely impoverished individuals is combined with an already clearly underclass surrounding neighborhood, the resulting economic stagnation and potential for antisocial behaviors should come as a surprise to no one. Consequently, one possible partial remedy that, although it falls outside the scope of this study, still merits consideration is to reduce the size of Windsor Terrace complex and to disperse part of the population to alternative subsidized housing sites.

SUMMARY OF RECOMMENDATIONS

1. Economic opportunity, jobs, and job skills need to be stimulated at Windsor Terrace. Economic opportunity should be a priority concern.
2. The literacy program needs to be supported, strengthened, and expanded.
3. Economic initiatives should be targeted to benefit young female adults and adolescents.
4. Educational attainment of any kind needs to be encouraged and recognized. Most especially needed are "earn and learn" strategies that use economic rewards as incentives both to keep adolescents and young adults in school and to push them toward achievement.
5. Human and social service programs need to be organized in a way that encourages tenant responsibility and tenant self-reliance. Programs that reward only compliance need to be reconsidered.
6. Tenant and/or tenant organizations need to be actively involved in the planning, implementation, and evaluation of social and human service programs.

7. Tenant organizations need to be encouraged, supported, rewarded, and consulted.
8. Drug prevention and drug elimination programs need to combine a serious initiative from outside the community, complemented by strengthening social organization and personal security within the community.
9. Positive options (programs, activities, opportunities) need to be created as alternatives for those behaviors currently being discouraged. Residents already know what they cannot or should not do; they need to know more about what they can or should do.
10. Internal communication within the communities about events, people, and activities needs to be improved in order to clarify information and encourage social cohesion.
11. The public image of the community needs to be improved in order to encourage a more positive and confident attitude within the community.
12. Windsor Terrace is a large and densely populated housing complex. The South Linden area, where Windsor is located, offers limited economic or social mobility. When a densely populated enclave made up of largely impoverished individuals is combined with an already clearly underclass surrounding neighborhood, the resulting economic stagnation and potential for antisocial behaviors should not be a surprise. Consequently, one possible partial remedy which, although it falls outside of the scope of this study still merits consideration: to reduce the size of the Windsor Terrace complex and to disperse part of the population to alternative subsidized housing sites.

APPENDIX A: SUMMARY STATISTICAL SUPPLEMENT TO THE WINDSOR TERRACE PROFILE

In order for this supplement to be a useful and reliable guide to the Windsor Terrace profile, it is important to understand the methods employed in composing this document and their relationship to the original methods employed in conducting the research.

We employed qualitative interview and participation observation techniques to develop the information and assessments included in the Windsor Terrace profile. A set of interview topics were employed to guide our conversations with Windsor residents and staff; these items have been included in Appendix B. We formally interviewed 75 people ($n = 75$) of which 10 were teenagers (n

= 6 male and 4 female), and 4 were staff. In addition to the formal interviews, we held discussions with 17 other individuals who were not otherwise interviewed on a formal basis, and accumulated more than 250 hours aggregately of discussions and observations on site. The 17 informal interviews are included in our observational data set. A description of the original research techniques can be found in the Windsor Terrace profile.

Because we did not employ a survey questionnaire but instead an interview protocol, we have submitted our interview data to a simple content analysis in order to arrive at the weights and percentages that are reported in the supplement. It is important to understand that information and conclusions that are based primarily on observations are not part of the database for this supplement. Instead, we used only the interview notes. There are two exceptions to this rule: the sections addressing self-perception and self-esteem and the section on communication skills employ a heavy ingredient of observational information. They have been written-up in this supplement in a way that reminds the reader how they were so derived.

The supplement is organized into individual summaries that reflect the section-by-section organization of the original Windsor Terrace profile. Reported percentage weights have been rounded and, with the exceptions just indicated, are based on 75 interviews. The subheadings contained within each section are the content categories employed to sort, weight, and organize the interview data.

Perceptions of the Environment

Physical Appearance of the Facility. Everyone interviewed had something critical to say about some feature of the physical environment. Approximately 60% stated a desire for some physical improvement or maintenance in their own dwelling unit. Showers, carpeting, painting, window screens, plumbing, and kitchen improvements were mentioned most frequently.

A large majority of the sample, approximately 80%, talked about the general appearance of the grounds and the appearance of the neighborhood as a whole. When it came to specifics, trash and the clean up of the dumpster areas, along with the need for safe play areas for young children, are at the top of the list (about 50%).

More than 90% believed that "in general" the Windsor Terrace neighborhood appeared run down or unattractive or depressed or unsafe. The wrought-iron fencing around the commons areas was cited as unattractive and unfriendly. Comments also cited the need for painting, curbs, and sidewalks.

Approximately 70%, believed that the appearance of the neighborhood was attractive to criminal elements, encouraged irresponsibility among the teenagers, and/or negatively impacted "pride" in the community. In general, the sentiment was that Windsor Terrace needed to be "cleaned up."

Isolation and Distrust. Subsequent sections of the summary provide detail about these factors: at this point only some general characterizations are provided.

All respondents regarded Windsor Terrace as an enclave of its own with reasonably demarcated "turf." Churches, stores, and some essential services were the reasons to leave Windsor. We did not find anyone who believed that there was "much" cooperation or "much" participation with the surrounding Linden area.

Residents regarded the on-site facility management as either the place to go when something was wrong with a unit or as the office that enforces rules and rejects requests. All those interviewed espoused one or both of these attitudes. Some of the residents liked the manager, some of the residents did not like the manager; we did not encounter strong feelings one way or another.

Residents did not frequently cooperate with one another. Lack of cooperation and trust among residents was directly cited by about 50% of the sample, and indirectly cited by about another 10% to 15% of the remainder. The residents were as likely to blame one another as they were to blame CMHA for the run-down physical appearance of the neighborhood. And they were also as likely to indicate that they did not know how to or have much hope for the possibility of building cooperation among residents, as they were to believe that (somehow) CMHA could do something to get people to work together.

Stated simply, the residents believed that social service personnel—whether on site or off—were people who gave services to the residents because that was their job. This message was stated in many different ways, but the attitude was unmistakable.

With regard to CMHA as an institution: CMHA is (a) a landlord pure and simple, (b) an (abstract) bureaucratic decision maker/power broker, (c) someone to blame, (d) irresponsible and insensitive, and (e) undependable because it would start activities/programs and would not stand behind them very long. Some combination of these categories characterize the attitudes of the entire sample.

Single parenting. All but one of the females in the sample either was or had been a single female parent of one or more children—in 40% of these cases they acknowledged bearing one or more children out of wedlock. In all cases, they reported that they felt that they themselves were primarily responsible for their children.

In five of these cases, women reported they had raised children who were actually their grandchildren. Four others indicated that they as children had lived in public housing with their grandmothers for a period of time. In all of these cases, and in another six cases where this situation was discussed, no one found this arrangement particularly remarkable.

The cycle of children having children was either directly addressed or taken as the assumption in discussion of some other topic by more than 80% of the sample. In these cases, it was either stated or simply taken for granted that the support of these children involved some form of public subsidy.

More than 70% of the adult females admitted that they had truncated educations, lacked job skills, and/or were not acquainted with any friends who lived for very long without some sort of public subsidy.

Self-Perception and Self-Esteem

Observed Self-Confidence. Approximately 95% of the women appeared to lack confidence in regard to interacting with people from outside their normal social circle. All of the women had noticeably weak verbal skills. An example of this was their willingness to accept an interviewer's paraphrase. A limited and constraining vocabulary was the second most common difficulty exhibited.

This verbal awkwardness appeared to affect the self-esteem of these individuals by making them self-conscious about their public presentation. In nearly all of the cases, the individual's perception of herself appeared to be limited in her own eyes by a lack of confidence in dealing with people from outside of the community.

Educational needs. Most of the women we interviewed (60%) stated their desire to learn marketable skills, including improvement in their communication skills. Many of the women (80%) also felt that they lacked home management skills of one kind or another (ranging from nutrition to finances) and this appeared to contribute to their generally low self-esteem.

Communication Skills

Observed Skill Levels. There was a general and common lack of verbal and linguistic skills among the Windsor Terrace residents.

Overall, there was an impoverished vocabulary and general lack of linguistic sophistication of the sort that cuts across the barriers of socio-economic class. The very large majority (upward of 90%) of the residents interviewed displayed insufficient verbal resources to respond flexibly and strategically to all but a few verbal situations. This restricted flexibility marks an individual, or more likely "stigmatizes" an individual, as not likely to be a member of the mobile segment of the population.

Most of the Windsor residents (75%) we interviewed appeared to be verbally uncomfortable to the point of experiencing significant difficulties in getting their points across verbally. The verbal skill lacks include a large and reasonably diversified vocabulary (85%), an ability to assess one's auditor and adjust one's presentation accordingly (80%), and the ability to develop different modes of expression by punctuating a statement with varied grammatical and vocabulary distinctions (80%).

Verbal difficulties notwithstanding, it is our belief that the individuals we interviewed, and very likely most of the Windsor residents, had even more to say than they themselves knew. The more capable and confident individuals are, the more they find to say.

These verbal skills are clearly aligned with literacy education. A literacy program not only could provide a vital skill but also could offer the means for these individuals to enrich their lives and to augment their self-presentation and self-esteem.

It is important to notice that literacy education can help to counteract the social isolation of public housing residents—most especially to the extent that such isolation is self-imposed.

Linguistic and, more broadly, communication patterns serve to distinguish insiders and outsiders in a community. When these patterns function primarily as barriers, they reinforce social isolation and restrict mobility of all kinds. This is very much the case at Windsor Terrace, where language restrictions reinforce negative self-images, weaken individual self-esteem, and fuel collective dissatisfaction with the quality of life.

Apathy

Residents Were Unmotivated and Indifferent. The overwhelming sentiment among the interviewees, in the range of 70% to 80%, was that the population was highly resistant to "getting involved." This opinion was stated in different ways: the repeated failure to get residents to turn out for an event, the view that residents or small groups of residents only looked out for themselves, management complaints and resident observations that one had to give people something or feed them or threaten to take something away in order to get people to a meeting, remarks to the effect that many people had gripes but no one was getting organized to effect action, the observation that CMHA did not seem to care much about what the residents thought, or that CMHA did not support people who tried to get involved in the community. An important factor is that the residents themselves were aware of the situation.

The dominant explanation for this indifference varied depending on whom one asked. Individuals responsible for facility management or for services or some other form of leadership indicated that "people want something for nothing" or that no one had resources to get activities moving. The more mature adult residents (approximately ages 35 and up) said that people kept to themselves and did not get involved in CMHA business. The younger adult females (women in their 20s and early 30s) stated that they were concerned about their children but that "everyone is too busy to come out" or that "they promise to help but do not show up."

Responsibility for Community Involvement. When we asked the resident population who should take responsibility for involving them more in the community either by identifying the needs in the community or initiating activities that responded to the community's needs, more than 75% felt that CMHA should be taking the leadership role. Approximately 50% felt that CMHA and the community needed to work together. About 25% felt the responsibility primarily fell on the residents. Only about 15% expressed much optimism about the potential for community initiative, and only about 30% thought that CMHA was likely to be very supportive.

In about 40% of the sample, respondents either directly referred to some past CMHA initiative or spoke generally about CMHA "services" as being undependable and said services would probably be discontinued if not work successfully over the short term. In one way or another, more than 55% of the sample indicated that CMHA is (our word) arbitrary and (our word) unpredictable. Finally, as stated earlier, blame for lack of cooperation among residents was attributed almost evenly to CMHA and the residents themselves.

Individual or Collective Initiative. In discussing achievement, mobility, and positive change either in terms of one's personal finances or the community collective, adult residents always alluded in some way to the obstacles and disabilities they faced or to the "penalties" they were likely to incur in terms of the loss of some benefit.

Windsor Terrace Concerned Moms. With respect specifically to the Windsor Terrace Concerned Moms/Residents Council (CM/RC), it should be noted that a great deal of the group's time was devoted to fundraising activities (e.g., flea markets, garage sales, and food sales). In 1988, an estimated $300 was raised by these activities. But a great deal of volunteer time and good will was expended to raise this money. This was the case to such an extent that the organization tended to use up its limited people resources without being able to mount activities that would build visible benefits for the community and so give it an opportunity to expand its constituency.

Internal Communications. Finally, communication within the community or between CMHA and/or service providers and the community was a tremendous problem. Approximately 50% of the respondents cited a lack of information about activities in the community and about CMHA policy. Moreover, in every interview conducted, there was at least one example of misunderstanding or insufficient information about either CMHA policies or about some activity or program at Windsor Terrace.

Entitlement Economy

Community Affairs Office. Sixty-five percent of all the residents queried believed that the Community Affairs Office was a source of services. Of the residents we interviewed, 75% had some contact with Community Affairs. Of the residents who had some experience with Community Affairs, 90% had come in contact with it through youth activities (e.g., scouts, sleep-overs, socials, and especially through a community member, Marvin Johnson). Of those in contact, 90% believed that Community Affairs was "important," and that they were making progress in the community. The remaining 10% had no opinion.

Entitlements. Invariably, the need for services or better (more) benefits came up in our interviews with the residents. Everyone talked about the need for more health benefits, child care, transportation services, training, or about difficulties in coping with their subsidy levels. In this context, their limited purchasing power was the principal topic—the residents simply felt more money was needed to cope. (Needless to say, no one claimed to be doing well financially.)

Earning Income. As just indicated, the residents stated that when they did earn money, they were penalized through loss of benefits. Approximately 50% acknowledged that "some" residents did earn unreported income. Only two individuals acknowledged that they had personally at some time earned unreported income.

About 30% of the mothers stated that spending money for their children presented a problem. Of the teenagers 50% ($n = 10$) said they earned some income. All of the teenagers talked about earning "big" [fantasy] incomes "someday."

The majority of the younger mothers, approximately 65%, indicated that they would be interested in training that would help them get steady employment. At the same time, they expressed disdain about low-level jobs (e.g., "washing someone else's floor").

When asked if they would move out of Windsor Terrace if they found a "good job," the responses were divided almost evenly into positive, negative, and uncertain. In all cases, however, there was uncertainty and confusion about items like loss of benefits, how to manage living expenses when they were responsible to pay for everything themselves, and leaving the neighborhood where they knew people.

Race and Trust

People Living in Public Housing Are "Different" from Outsiders. There was a generally held assumption that Windsor and other public housing residents were different because they have no money, are on welfare, do not have influence, depend on others, and so on. The assumption or the explicit opinion in all of our interviews was that public housing residents were stigmatized by (our word) "inferiority" of one kind or another. Add to this the fact that overwhelmingly the population of Windsor Terrace, and our entire sample, consisted of African Americans. In this situation, race, socio-economics, and public housing residency were confounded.

The adults used the language of "them and us," and meant by that clearly the difference between "haves and have nots." The language of racism was not used by the adults. The teenagers did, however, refer to "Whites," and all of the male teenagers ($n = 6$) alluded quite plainly to differences based on race.

Dependency. In every interview, some allusion to dependency surfaced. In about 35% of the cases, being dependent on (and unable to influence) CMHA was cited. In more than 70%, being dependent on service providers and entitlement administrators was discussed. Sometimes these references were reasonably positive (e.g., this or that agency is helpful); sometimes they were negative (e.g., misunderstandings, ineligibilities, and the like), but the residents do clearly understand that someone else makes the decisions. More than 50% indicated they did not understand how decisions were made. Approximately 25% thought it was possible to contest the system, but only if they had "help" of some kind.

Concept of Community

Negative Image in the Public Media. Approximately 45% of the residents volunteered that newspapers and television had negative things to say about the Windsor community, namely, its rate of crime and violence. Respondents agreed that the media portrayed a negative image of Windsor. About 20%, however, indicated that they thought this image was fair. About 50% thought the media needed to portray positive aspects of Windsor, but about 40% did not think that positive media coverage would make much of a difference in the public perception. Of those who did not think that positive media coverage would affect the public perception of Windsor, 90% also believed that no one really believes anything except bad news about poor Black people anyway. About 70% of the residents believed that negative media coverage encourages the Windsor residents themselves to feel endangered or threatened or discouraged. (Drug- and crime-related perceptions are discussed in the next section.)

Windsor Terrace Community Organization. The only community-based organization in place at the time, at least nominally, at Windsor Terrace was the CM/RC. Approximately 50% of the respondents said that they had heard of the CM/RC, and 75% of these knew (only vaguely in most cases) that the CM/RC "represents the tenants at CMHA." The remaining 25% did not claim to know what CM/RC does. Approximately 45% thought that CM/RC was part of Community Affairs.

When CM/RC was explained to the respondents, 65% thought that CM/RC was a "good idea," but only 20% expressed confidence in CM/RC's potential to make improvements in the community. Only 15% of the sample had attended at least one CM/RC meeting.

The Drug Economy

Perception of the Nature of Criminal Activity. When asked about "crime," 90% of the respondents said that drugs and crack houses were the chief issues. Approximately 35% of the sample used the words "drugs" and "crime" synonymously. The remaining 10% referred to petty thievery, vandalism, noise, and assaults—especially regarding male teenagers.

Approximately 40% admitted to knowledge of some individual who had used or been involved in drugs at some time. And 80% of the mothers said that drug involvement, whether as users or dealers, was the thing that concerned them the most about their children.

Personal Security. Only approximately 30% of the sample thought that Windsor Terrace was a dangerous place personally. Of the remaining 70%, approximately 75% believed that Windsor was not dangerous as long as they were careful. But 50% acknowledged that they worried about the safety of their children. Only 10% admitted to being crime victims, but 70% said they knew someone or had heard of someone who had been a victim of crime.

Of the sample, 55% said the best policy was to "mind your own business." Of the remaining 45%, only about 15% said that they personally "might" get involved if they saw someone committing a crime or being harmed. Of the entire sample, about 50% said they might call the police.

Perception of Drug Dealers. Three quarters of the sample admitted to being frightened or intimidated by drug dealers because they are dangerous and organized. Sixty percent explained that the dealers had a "system" of signals, intelligence, and look-outs—50% of this group said they had learned about these arrangements primarily from their children. Nearly two thirds indicated that drug dealers are influential because they have ready cash.

Reasons for Involvement in Drugs. Mothers indicated that children became involved in the drug trade because they wanted money (65%), there was not much for children, and especially teenagers, to do at Windsor (60%), they are pressured by peers or are being approached by someone older (50%). When we asked teenagers why teens get involved, 60% cited money as the chief reason, and the remainder cited "boredom" and money.

Interestingly enough, 35% of the sample indicated that "gangs" were not as much of a problem as they used to be because the drug dealers had taken over. Sixty percent said they thought people came from the "outside" to purchase drugs at Windsor. (At Canonby Court, we heard that the parking lot was full all night long at certain times of the month—and that they "knew" these people were not from the Sullivant/Canonby area.)

One half of the sample said they either knew of or suspected certain units in the Windsor complex to be either "houses" or vendor locations. When asked if they would report these units, only 15% said they would; the remainder were uncertain.

Drug enforcement. Of the sample, 65% regarded the Columbus Police Department as ineffective, saying they either really did not care or did not know enough. When asked if they would cooperate with the police, only 35% said that under the current conditions they would cooperate if they felt it would make a difference. In general, 70% of the sample said they would cooperate with authorities if they could remain anonymous or safe, and if their cooperation would lead to a positive result.

Eighty percent agreed that CMHA needed to do something about the drug problem. Opinion was fairly evenly divided over whether the police or CMHA was the most responsible for inadequate drug enforcement.

Only 20% of the sample believed they could trust the police department, and only 15% believed that they could count on the police department to do something about drugs when they were called on to take action.

Three quarters of the mothers said that drug education in the schools was important, and 75% said the most important goal at Windsor Terrace should be to remove drug dealers from the community.

When asked if the community should work together to rid itself of drugs, 60% said that they did not know what they could do on a personal level because of few resources and concern about security. However, 70% agreed that they "might" help if they thought CMHA and/or the police department were seriously enforcing the drug laws.

APPENDIX B: INTERVIEW QUESTIONS

These items were employed to create consistency from one interview to the next. These topics were regularly expanded on, modified, and additional information was offered or requested in the course of the interviews.

For Tenants:

1. How long have you been living at this facility?
2. How would you describe the physical condition of the facility?
3. Explain what steps need to be taken to improve the physical condition of this facility.
4. When something goes wrong in your apartment, how quickly does the maintenance department respond to your request for repairs?
5. Do you feel safe living at this facility? Why or why not?
6. Would you be willing to participate in a block-watch or neighborhood crime prevention program?
7. Do you think that "crime" and "violence" are major problems at this facility?

8.   In what social programs provided by this facility do you participate? Are they useful? What changes would you suggest?
9.   What kind of social programs are needed that are not currently available at this facility?
10.   Do your neighbors ever get together to discuss improvements at this facility?

For Staff:

1.   How long have you worked at this facility?
2.   How long have you worked in public housing?
3.   What do you feel the role of public housing is in serving its tenants?
4.   How would you describe the physical condition of this facility?
5.   How would you characterize the quality of the relationships between manager and tenants?
6.   In what way(s) does this facility differ from other CMHA facilities either in physical environment or tenant/manager relationships?
7.   As a manager, what do you think are the priority items that need to be addressed to improve this facility?
8.   What social programs are available at this facility? Describe them. Assess their relevance or effectiveness from your standpoint.
9.   CMHA facilities are frequently associated by the local press with criminal activities. Is this a fair assessment?
10.   What steps or programs would improve the "perception" of CMHA facilities in the local public arena?
11.   What programs at this facility are targeted specifically at youth?
12.   From your standpoint, is "violence" a problem at this facility?
13.   Are there any additional questions I should have asked, or any topics that you feel should be included?

EIGHT

The Politics of "Social Difference": Consequences of Socially Conditioned Inactivism

It is the politics of "social difference" that can provide the analytic orientation sufficiently comprehensive to make sense of the otherwise discrete case studies presented in chapters 5, 6, and 7. We need to examine the unique aspects of "social distinction," "social difference," and "minority" (racial, ethnic, and therefore social) in order to fully elaborate and finally explicate the socio-political and theoretical significance of the politics of social difference forming the basis of critical politics.

The meanings of *difference* and *minority* first need to be contextualized within the framework of social organization. That is, we must understand difference/minority within the principles of modern social organization. Traditionally, social organizing is understood as a set of elements whose interrelationships are best characterized as hierarchical. The notion of hierarchy implies a particular pattern of interrelating: that these relationships can be placed on an abstract continuum (like complexity or power) and thus, each element stands in place on this scale and can be understood and identified by its position on the scale in relation to the position of other elements on the scale and to each other. Consequently, each element must be identifiable in at least two ways: by its distinctiveness and by its connectedness/interrelatedness (see chapter 9).

So, we can say that the individual element must be marked by both distinction and connection. Social distinction becomes essential to having a social place or position. But if distinctiveness is essential to position or place, the connectivity is essential to social mobility, for motion or movement within the framework of social organization requires the coordination (cooperation) of or with other elements. Mobility without such coordination places individuals at risk of exclusion from the system. Social distinction and connection, then, form opposite faces of the same coin: The former providing the means to anchor in a kind of (social) harbor, and the latter providing the sail of social and economic mobility.

Social difference, taken to the extreme of minority, however, marks a place in the social order without co-temporaneously providing genuine connectivity. Without social connectivity, there is no real possibility of social mobility. To (socially) institutionalize difference as minority is to have created an intranscendant social category. Acceptance into this category is tantamount to entering a room with no exits.

In the case of a central city community's self-identification as a social and racial minority, the perception of this kind of intranscendant difference (self-identifying as a minority community) is often combined with an acceptance of broad cultural goals, and a rejection of the traditional methods of achieving such goals. It is a particular and contemporary form of social and economic disenfranchisement, an attitude, if you will, unfortunately reinforced by both popular culture forms and by the socio-economic realities of most minority neighborhoods. There is a difference between, for example, wanting attainment or acquisition and wanting achievement; in the first case one wants to be famous, win the lottery, and so on, and in the second, one hopes for a level of skill warranting reward and recognition. For a large part of the central city community, socio-economic disenfranchisement means having no access, understanding, or acceptance of the socially approved means (mechanisms, channels, vehicles) of goal achievement. This mixture of wanting materially but not apprehending a means of attainment leads to a displaced sense of agency. The means of social success are tied up in the rules of a game biased against minority participants—only the rule-makers have power or agency. In this case, the rule-makers are White members of the social system. And because cultural values and goals are common currency, and because American mythology still contains the empty promise of equal and ample opportunity for all, a curious sense of entitlement has evolved among minority members. But it is entitlement to what others already have, and not to the means of that attainment. If one believes that agency lies external to oneself (because the system treats one as without agency), then one is unlikely to value access to the means of attainment, for only agents can transform means into ends. Indeed, even minority members who gain access to an attainment means such as higher education will frequently manage the opportunity as a chance to manipulate the system and not as a chance to develop and hone new skills. This is to suggest neither that scamming the system is tied in any way to racial or ethnic membership, nor that this is an unreasonable or ineffective strategy. Rather, this is to point out a difference in manner of participation between what is socially prescribed and what is (sometimes) enacted.

To continue, the sense of agency seems to be displaced into a sense of identification as a minority, as though enacting an identity as a minority were both a means and an end. Although most socio-cultural acts of identification are certainly ends in themselves, the particular nature of central city community identification as a minority has at least two qualities that render it significantly different as a subcultural identity from many other minority (subcultural) identities. The first of these is the displaced and abbreviated sense of agency previously described, and the second is a cultural (systemic) characteristic described in the anthropological literature as *liminality*.

In socio-cultural terms, that which is liminal is that element or group whose identity is sufficiently ambiguous as to contain at least one set of paradoxical conditions, such that its members are disenabled from participating in the larger social system in a meaningful, productive, adult way. So, what are the paradoxes comprising the label *minority* in application to central city communities? To begin at the most general (and pervasive level), to be Black is to be not White (or some other color binary). If to be White is to be successful by working inside of the system, then to be Black is to be successful by working against or at least outside of the system. The problem this appears to create is that for a Black to succeed in a WASP society by following conventional (White) means, is to simultaneously reject one's minority membership or identity: a crippling paradox.

For example, the educational system is viewed as oppressive of Black historical experience and repressive of Black cultural expression. This is an identity based not on some particular cultural articulation, but rather on difference, if not opposition to mainstream (White) culture.

This stands in contrast to some other minority groups, who embrace much about mainstream culture (goals, values, etc.) and who demarcate difference or subgroup membership by the use of primarily ritualistic events (i.e., specific marriage customs and costumes, religious displays, food preparation, rites of passage, jewelry, emblems, and organized community activities or events). However, each of these cultural demarcations, although emphasizing unique subcultural features and a sense of community and identity, occurs while individual members participate in general and on a daily basis within the structure of the (White) socio-cultural hegemony.

It is beyond the scope of this chapter to comment on or evaluate the gains and losses of such acculturations, except to note that both parties are affected by the process. The exact nature, extent, significance, value, and meaning of these changes is a difficult and elusive topic. Rather than seek to assess such a process, our intent here is simply to observe and partially characterize it as it relates to the issues at hand, and in doing so assist in illuminating system characteristics and processes relevant here. The point is to make note of the fact that ethnicity need not be equivalent to social and economic marginality.

Clearly, this conclusion flies in the face of the partially articulated perspective underlying many of the comments and explanations offered by "minorities," many of whom have voiced the sentiment that they are denied success as well as access by virtue of their race. At this point, the question seems to be: Is their lack of access and success the result of self-imposed minority identification or the result of socio-cultural racism? In fact, both perspectives are partially valid because the social system and the subgroup each participate in the articulation of minority membership as agentless and liminal. Each participates in the communication code that articulates "Blackness, Brownness or Yellowness," as specifically evident in the Driving Park and Windsor Terrace studies. And this code binds its participants in a kind of reciprocity that perpetuates the code and the social system.

One of the key consequences of this code is the lack of consistent economic cohesiveness. What does not occur is the sort of economic solidarity that would take the form of central city Blacks purchasing primarily from other Black business owners, which would generally mean patronizing neighborhood businesses. For instance, as one respondent noted, Jews living in the far northwest corner of the city commonly travel to the east side, a 20- to 30-minute trip, to patronize Jewish-owned businesses, whereas Blacks living only several blocks away make no effort to patronize Black-owned businesses. In short, as a group, they seem not to display economic solidarity.

And yet, this is not to suggest that as a minority group central city Blacks lack a sense of community, but rather to make note of the manner in which "community" is articulated: It is an interpersonal phenomenon, and not a socio-economic one, with one obvious exception—the case of neighborhood organized drug dealing. In Windsor Terrace, the money generated by such endeavors was not being funneled back into the area and local businesses, and most certainly it was not the neighborhood that gained in any respect from drug trafficking.

Adapting how we can understand this theoretical and practical theory of communication codes has an intellectual and political benefit in that such codes are posited to operate throughout a system (e.g., society) without distinguishing among cultural variations. These codes reduce contingencies that might overwhelm an individual, and thereby enable great amounts of social differentiation along economic lines, while enabling the now differentiated segments to interact predictably. Thus, the codes provide the means to relatively stable system ends by providing or perhaps "enlisting" a kind of compliance on the part of all individuals. Because the codes remain out of conscious consideration of most system participants, compliance does not require consenting cooperation on the part of these same individuals. Because their behavior is compliant only in terms of the system's needs, and not in terms of the needs of an individual's psyche, it is not necessary to resort to either personality characteristics nor to hypothetical genetic or cultural predispositions to explain and understand the behavior of individuals and groups. In short, in applying this theoretical construct, it is not necessary to blame individuals in order to explain social phenomena.

Communication codes are characterized by both reducing the field of alternatives, and reciprocity. Communication codes are complexity-reducing mechanisms that are accomplished through the management of fields of contingency. In a social system, the fields of contingency are the alternatives (action and meaning) available to individuals. One way to define *meaning* is as a reduction of these alternatives through the mutual acknowledgment of the participants. In this way, meaning is created by the increase in the probability of the selection of some very limited actions on the part of the participants. The net result is that each participant can be said to understand the situation in the sense that it is predicable to a large degree for the participant. This is, of course, a limited and specific way of defining *meaning*, and is not meant to deny or invalidate other ways of defining the term. It is also not to suggest that alternative or additional kinds of meaning both actually occur and are possible to discern given the same parameters as are utilized here. The point, instead, is to sharpen the focus of this theoretic discussion in a way that will enable us to more clearly understand the detail and application of communication codes to minoritization.

The first step is to determine whether any set of transactions can be said to be constitutive of, or at least indicative of, a communication code. We can judge communication processes for clues to the existence and enactment of codes by looking for the following pattern in the exchange: participants who complete their own action selections and know this from each other. Immediately, the participants are linked because both the selection choices and their completion require confirmation by the other. Once this takes place, the participants become bound because their future exchanges and action selections are predicated upon confirmation on the part of the other. It is, in part, this particular kind of interdependence which earmarks the formulation of a communication code.

Communication codes seen as mechanisms, as catalysts that guide transactions, the specifics of the selections, are not as important as is the motivating quality of the selecting process. It is motivating in terms of the selections made by the other. That is to say that, when the manner of one partner's selections serves simultaneously as a motivating structure for the other, a communication code can be said to be formulated. Clearly, if it is the manner, and not the content of the selections that is the compelling or conditioning aspect of the transactions, then a code is formulated because it can be said to be both abstract and ahistorical in nature. By encoding the manner of the selecting, a code is freed from the boundaries of the here and now and can operate out of consciousness, because, in fact, it is the code which now orders the situation and not the situation that determines the encoding.

One of the benefits of employing the concept of communication codes is that it provides a way of specifying how that which communication scholars call *context* affects human interaction. Thus, we can operationalize the variable context as the presence of a specific code or set of codes that co-condition the selections of the actors, so that the interpretation or meaning created is wholly a product of a highly reduced field of contingencies perceived by the participants. Contingencies are further ordered by a code so that some specific combinations of selections are rendered highly probable. Because probability (determined by codes) greatly enhances predictability, and predictability constitutes one basis of/for meaning, context operationalized as communication code(s) directly affects the range of possible and likely meanings available to the participants.

Because codes manage complexity by reducing contingency, they not only reduce the number of action alternatives available to the participants, but they simultaneously order those contingencies, the remaining preferred alternatives, and in so doing, significantly increase the probability of a few of those remaining selections. (This sequence of contingency reduces "motivation" because of the net effect: the high probability of the selection of some few alternatives by the participants.) For a participant, the field of options appears to be intrinsically limited, that is, limited due to the nature of the world or of the situation, not as the consequence of the operation of codes. Two results follow from this apprehension: limited and narrow changes seem possible, if any do; and, the actors do not see themselves as participating in the mechanism responsible for the curtailment of their options.

This net effect is further reinforced by the fact that codes are ahistorical and atemporal in nature, and these qualities render them invisible to social participants. When a mechanism is invisible and only the effects of it are manifest, it is easy to conclude that either some completely different mechanism is at work, or that nothing in particular is at work; that the effects merely constitute "reality." In this respect, codes gain potency and efficacy by being ahistorical and atemporal, in contrast to the more typical assumptions communication researchers make about the nature of context: that it is very much a product of the specific histories of both the parties involved and their joint history (their relational history) in addition to immediate situational variables.

Reciprocity, the second key characteristic of codes, is crucial to both the success of the social system and to the ability of the individual to participate in the system. It is a marker of inclusion. It is also, in principle, the characteristic responsible for exclusion from system processes. Without the reciprocation of the other during interaction, the field of selection remains relatively unpredictable, which is to say that compliance of any kind is not a likely result. The other is not responsive to the individual's manner of selecting alternatives, so that the individual cannot seem to influence the selection of alternatives (the behavior) of the other: a situation of relatively high contingency and low predictability. Given the potency and efficacy of codes when enacted, being unable to enact a code would cause an individual to feel excluded and ineffective, and over time, possibly impotent and/or helpless.

It is the reciprocity that serves as boundary marker for the system participants. Not that it demarcates members from nonmembers, but rather, it indicates points of differentiation within the system. That is, the failure to engage reciprocity of the code (any code) occurs as a means of distinguishing subsystems within the larger social system. In fact, it is exactly because codes, as atemporal and ahistorical phenomena, possess the potential for guiding communication processes throughout the entire system that the points at which there is a failure of reciprocity are functionally equivalent to actual physical borders. From a system perspective, it is highly efficacious to utilize a mechanism that simultaneously serves to cohere the system elements and to differentiate among subsystems.

THE ENCODING OF THE CENTRAL CITY:
"MINORITIZING" A POPULATION

One way to distinguish between *cooperation* and *compliance* is to observe the presence or absence of a sense of proactivity on the part of an individual or group of individuals. Compliance is behavior directed and determined by another, whereas cooperation is self-directed behavior influenced by another. For the social actor, the difference lies in one's understanding of possible alternatives available for selection. For the social observer, the difference lies in his or her alignment with implicitly or explicitly specified outcomes or goals embedded in the presumption of a perspective. The same observable behavior may be judged either compliant or cooperative depending on whether the attribution of proactivity is made and to which party or parties. But if we instead adopt a system perspective, it is possible to evaluate the behavior of social actors as *adaptive*, that is, as responses to system conditions.

Minorities find themselves facing conditions of scarcity in terms of all types of resources. As the behavior of any interactant can be said to condition the behavior of other interactants, the conditions of the social and physical environment can be understood as expressing a set of expectations on the part of the system in regard to the actors. In the absence of any other mitigating circumstances, such conditions translate as expectations which serve to limit the field of possible responses. That is to say, if those inadequate resources are experienced as not only characteristics of the environment, but also as a kind of social and communicative code, then those conditions become the encoded expectations of possible selections on the part of those actors. Those conditions are transformed into symbolic media, and as a social actor, I read them as the answer to the question "What does the system expect of me?"

Although the studies presented in chapters 5, 6, and 7 are too exploratory to provide sufficient data to allow us to hypothesize that the social and environmental conditions combine to formulate a hitherto unidentified and unnamed communication code, it is not beyond the scope of this research effort to suggest that, because communication codes are such potent and efficacious mechanisms (as previously discussed), their characteristics operate as a kind of blueprint for the creation and interpretation of much of social reality. As a functioning member of this social system, I implicitly abstract the general pattern of communication codes and then typically utilize that pattern to deconstruct (if you will) many or most aspects of my experience in the social world.

From a system perspective, this makes pragmatic sense. If, in fact, communication codes have evolved as a response to increasing levels of complexity, and so are mechanisms for reducing complexity by limiting contingencies—and they seem to be doubly effective because they both cohere elements while allowing for subsystem differentiation—it would be counterproductive for many different mechanisms to evolve because complexity would then reappear only at a higher level of abstraction. In short, such a development would constitute a failure to reduce complexity. Put more succinctly, the development of more than one pattern for reducing complexity would not be mere redundancy, it would be another form of complexity. Redundancy within a pattern (or mechanism) would increase its overall information value; a multiplicity of patterns for reducing complexity in terms of guiding behavior alternatives is not redundancy, but diversity.

It is consistent within a system perspective to conclude that any pattern or mechanism successful at reducing complexity is likely to be employed with great frequency. Although this conclusion is not to suggest that such a strategy does not also have its drawbacks, it nonetheless serves to enable the continuation of the system because of the self-replicating nature of the mechanism (the codes). Not only can specific codes be replicated, but the duplication of the general pattern helps to ensure the potential for the formulation of new codes as they might be needed. The abstract and ahistorical nature of codes renders them the ideal sort of mechanism from a system perspective because, as such, they are both generically and specifically replicable and are therefore both triply efficacious and yet versatile. Their versatility resides in their potency in transforming any and all actual and potential contingencies into a set of preferred and manageable alternatives.

The desirability of those alternatives is entirely relative to one's perspective. The perspective from which desirability is most likely assured is that of the system itself, and it is probable that social systems operate on general system theory principles.

Most relevant here is the fact that evolution does not proceed on the basis of optimization of alternatives. That is to say that changes in an organism need not be optimal in order to endure, but merely functional at some historical period of time. Similarly, the utility of some development may fade, leaving the change in place. As a consequence, it is not always a simple matter to determine the function or appropriateness of some entity's current state of evolution. Lacking sufficient information or understanding of the original context, it is all too easy to draw erroneous conclusions. It is easy to forget that developments are often originally adaptive, although it might not be clear that they are now adaptive, nor clear in exactly what ways they were originally adaptive.

What appears to be most applicable to the case of evaluating the response of social actors to system demands is that such

responses need to be carefully examined in light of both their original
context and from the perspective of the actors. This highlights the difference between the sensibility of the system and that of the actor:
What is functional for one is not necessarily optimal for the other.
From a system perspective, the need for self-replication may consistently override the option of optimization for/of system elements.

At strategic points, the deployment of a code (maybe "socio-
economic mobility") or codes minus the component of reciprocity
creates the economic marginalization of the inner-city regions of
urban areas through the replication of subsystem divisions that, in
turn, maintain a particular simplification or balancing of a host of
symbolic and material contingencies. This, in turn, enables the
continuation of a particular pattern of resource allocation while
minimizing both the likelihood of and potential success of any
challenge to that pattern. By encoding specific behavioral expectations into variations of communication media across the spectrum
of social differentiation, and by the selective engagement of code
reciprocity, the system induces replication of itself, including a
segment characterized by economic and social marginalization.

From the perspective of the social actor, such marginalization is certainly not experienced as anything nearing optimal.
Nonetheless, from a system perspective, such a component serves
various functions, and because system elements are interdependent,
altering this component is difficult and implicitly threatening to the
future of the system which is biased in favor of actualizing any
future state as a replication, if not near duplication, of its present
state. In other words, the system itself, although potentially adapt-
able, is inherently conservative, favoring preservation of the status
quo. Replication more commonly wins out over optimization.

In offering up greatly reduced alternatives and in favoring
the selection of one or several of those alternatives over others,
codes provide the sort of information on which individuals predi-
cate their understanding of self, of the world, and of the relationship between the self and the world. In so orienting the individual
to the world, codes influence the ability of individuals to generate
new or different perspectives. Because one can only ask questions
about what one understands (or believes oneself to understand: I
must be able to articulate what it is I know that I don't know in
order to formulate a question), one can limit the extent and range
of questions an individual might raise. Put differently, that people
often don't know that they don't know is, to some extent, a by-
product of the nature of communication codes. The net result is
that they don't know what questions to ask because they don't
understand the relationships that constitute the encryption
scheme for locating the information they need but don't know they
need.

These are precisely two of the problems that emerged as thematics in the interview data: asking the right questions to get at relevant information and determining that one does in fact know what one believes one knows. The way a social actor knows virtually anything is from engagement with the social system (e.g., with other actors and/or institutions). Here again, reciprocity is a key to the communication process and its social consequences. If successful engagement is characterized by the articulation of code reciprocity, then disconfirmation would be characterized by a lack of reciprocity. If a communication encounter does not activate reciprocity as anticipated by a social actor, then there is only disconfirmation of the assumptions and understanding that predicated the interaction. The result is that the actor must conclude that he or she does not know what he or she thought he or she knew or understood. And without the engagement of the reciprocity, there is a sudden and steep rise in contingencies and therefore a complexity accompanied by a parallel drop in predictability. The interaction is now characterized by uncertainty, and the actors experience discomfort and possible dissatisfaction.

Furthermore, without the engagement of reciprocity of the code, the linking and binding functions of communicative transactions are not accomplished, or at least not in the ordinary sense in which connectivity is recognized and understood as a positive force in the sense that it is the presence of some relationship. In a backhanded sort of way, the failure of reciprocity links individuals in the sense that it firmly establishes the absence of connectivity, but in the context of a social system, demarcation of relational boundaries (exclusion as well as inclusion) is still acknowledging a relationship in terms of the larger system. That this negative linking is still a form of social relating reflects on the need of the system to replicate itself, and on the idea of socio-economic competency and mobility. In terms of the system, it may be necessary, or at least desirable, for certain elements to remain, in socio-economic terms, immobile, in which case it is inaccurate to label those elements as socio-economically incompetent. For, from a system perspective, such immobility is really a form of competency, of accurately enacting the expectations of the system.

It is clear that codes must, in fact, order the social situation and constitute the context of an interaction, what Luhmann (1995) so elliptically refers to as "code-guided communication processes." Minorities attempting to deal with bank loan officers clearly illustrate an example of the effect of code-limited alternatives restricting the possibility or probability of a social actor asking the appropriate and relevant questions in order to secure the necessary information and understanding to accomplish his or her goal (i.e., to secure a loan).

This difficulty is further exacerbated by the fact that much (legal, etc.) information is encrypted in a way that renders it incomprehensible to the very people who might most benefit from access to it (in this case, inner-city small business owners). At one level, untangling this kind of encryption problem can be managed if dealt with in a conscientious and systematic way. That it remains a problem in light of the attention afforded it at local, state, and federal levels is an indication that something more pervasive is at work in the situation. One explanation is that changing that situation will result in a direct challenge to the governmental and financial networks that enmesh such programs as those designed to offer support and technical assistance to small businesses, especially ones located in inner cities. However, it is beyond the scope of any single case study to provide sufficient evidence to determine whether a specific code or set of codes is directly implicated here. What can be noted is that such a significant reallocation of resources raises contingencies within several social system domains, and so constitutes an implicit threat to replication.

To shift perspective from communication codes to more general system characteristics, the need for a system to ensure its continuation by means of replication is closely related to a system's tendency toward homeostasis, that is, its tendency to maintain equilibrium. There are two primary means for a system to maintain equilibrium in the face of newly introduced forces. It can either adapt itself to the new condition, or it can reconfigure the new force into a shape which the system can assimilate and/or manipulate. In the first case, the system must make some significant self-adjustment, whereas in the second, it conversely causes a change in the new contingency or force. One can argue that a sufficiently robust system would tend toward the second alternative, which is more conservative, requires fewer changes or manipulations, and does not require the nearly always risky application of the principle of *equifinality*.

An example of this kind of homeostatic response is the taking over of specific symbols, images, and issues by the dominant culture and the telecommunication media of "minority" efforts to shift some aspect of the social value system. This is otherwise recognized by scholars as cooptation. Although social movements arise from within a social system, partly as a result of high levels of differentiation, the mechanisms that cohere the system (those that cut across the differentiation) operate to co-opt such movements in order to manipulate or reconfigure them into forms the system can better direct and control. Trivialization of a social movement effectively co-opts that movement and reduces its potency in two ways. It presents the issues around which efforts to create change are focused as insignificant and frivolous. It also reconfigures those symbols into forms already dominant and meaning-laden, and so the new meaning is overwhelmed by the old, dominant, easily recognized, and commonly embraced meaning. The new message comes to merely reiterate the old.

In the case of the articulation of a minority identity, and the articulation of an identity as a minority, this kind of cooptation appears to characterize the efforts of generations of central city minorities. Although it is true that there is no necessary (e.g., genetic or biological) connection between an underclass status and race—indeed, there are Blacks at virtually all socioeconomic levels, there appears to be an institutionalized form of racism which serves to facilitate social and economic differentiation in broad terms across the system.

It may be the case that racism is one of the key triggers of the suspension of code reciprocity, a means of activating differentiation while deploying a mechanism that otherwise coheres system elements by reducing contingencies to ordered alternatives. In this respect, racism serves to assist in the attainment and maintenance of homeostasis of the system. To the extent that this is the case, cooptation of the efforts by minorities to initiate substantive change in their social status and valuation in the system clearly reflects the conservative and robust nature of the system. The capacity to enact the transformation of new forces to fit standard formats means that replication of existing codes will be favored as a means of ensuring the continuation of the system. In this way, the potential for significant and substantive (social) change is subsumed by the system while being made possible in part by the potency of communication codes and their ability to reduce complexity and order alternatives into mutual expectation.

NINE

Rethinking Organizing/Organizational Research

Our studies of community action research are concerned with the formation of organization, organizing, and interaction between organizations. The issue of social difference or the politics of social difference, as the term *minority* is utilized, makes a difference in the ability to organize and the nature of organization at a community level.

In our efforts to engage community action research, we have had to rethink the organization of organizing and the practice of doing research within this newer context.

LESSONS TO BE CONSIDERED

Weber (1970) refused to attribute to bureaucracy an intrinsic dynamic content. Instead, Weber offered us a list of traits that typify bureaucracy.

Lesson 1: Bureaucratic Character

   a. The duties of functionaries are officially circumscribed by
      laws, rules, or administrative dispositions.
   b. Organizational functions are hierarchical and so integrat-
      ed vertically by a system of command such that at all lev-
      els subordinates are controlled by superimposed authori-
      ties.
   c. Administrative activity is spelled out in written docu-
      ments.
   d. Functionaries require professional apprenticeships.
   e. The work of functionaries demands complete devotion to
      the office.
   f. Access to the profession is synonymous with access to a
      particular technology, jurisprudence, administrative ser-
      vice, and so on.

But Weber did not provide us with an investigation into the bureaucracy's substantive social traits; for instance, how is it rooted in the
social milieu and in the increase of power? Weber's enumeration of
traits is useful, but it matters little if one adds or subtracts a criterion; nothing enables one to decide whether, in the absence of a
particular trait, a social complex is or is not a bureaucracy. A
broader understanding of organizations is necessary.
        Weber's formal criteria are not incorrect in what they
affirm, but rather in what they deny or ignore. Interpretative social
science utilizing the concept of culture can supply at least a partial
corrective to the oversights of classical organizational theory. To
this end, we propose to look at organizations as action systems
integrated through the symbolic reproduction of communicated,
generalized media of motivation. In so doing, we focus on function,
communication, and relationship, rather than on structure, person, or position. The concept of organization we have in mind is
defined in the following manner: Organization consists primarily of
an open-ended context of significant symbols and modes of legiti-
mating social action that enables selective responses to changes in
the communication environment.
        Among other things, this concept of *organization* does not
require *a priori* formal distinctions either between intraorganizational and extraorganizational communication relationships or
between formal and informal relationships within organizations.
The principal theoretical and research orientations suggested by
this concept of organizational culture are found in Lessons 2
through 5.

Lesson 2: Orientation of Bureaucratic Culture

a. Attention must be paid to the rich diversity of organizations rather than swallowing them up as a whole into an image of formal organization that deprives them of intrinsic content. From the cultural perspective, what is interesting is not so much the structural composition of formal organizations as the largely *ad hoc* generation of meaning-networks that bind each of them idiosyncratically.

b. Bureaucratization must be seen as a social function and a system of meaningful behaviors and not only as the formalization of an isolated communication system. This necessitates a historical perspective on organizational bureaucratization that regards it as a purposive human enterprise. This perspective draws organizational goals and ends into the framework established by the interpretative context of organizational meaning—and suggests the variability and indetermination of ends—in the form of a historical dependent variable within the interpretative process.

c. The relational communication functions performed by an organization with respect to external social forms, as well as among the various intraorganizational subgroupings, indicates the importance of the roles of symbolic differentiation and of the legitimation of interest for the comprehension of organizational behavior.

d. Given the symbolic and relational character of organizational sociality, no reliable prediction of the organizational future can be ventured based solely upon knowledge of the organization's historical conditions, which are extensions of established communication structures and events. The temporal structure of organizational culture is not linear, instead it is spiral-like. The explanatory powerfulness of the interpretative context subsists only through continuous interpretation and discretionary selection on the basis of generalized principles of motivation. Organizational tradition guides without governing; if it were otherwise, the least circumstantial novelty in the communication environment would render the tradition vulnerable to institutional irrelevancy.

Lesson 3: Direct Attention to the Interpretive Structure of Commitment

Interest in the mechanisms through which complex action units emerge and sustain themselves over and against their environments, as well as dissatisfaction with the theoretical powerfulness of linear causal analysis, have spurred increased emphasis on the concept of *system*. In some cases, the concept of system remained predominately structural–functional, therefore centering inquiry on how the concept of structure illuminates the complex interactions underlying relatively stable parts/whole integration.

But the concept of system calls attention to something more important for the comprehension of organizations than the principles of pattern-maintaining parts/whole self-differentiation. More than the internal ordering of parts, social organizations presuppose a process of systemic negotiation with the environment by means of selection and generalization. In exchange, the system responds selectively to external influences exercised by factors such as politically mediated limitations upon market and resource exploitation, expectations about minimal working conditions, unions, community standards, competitors, philanthropic pressures, and the like.

The plasticity of the organizational system hinges on the permeability of its *communication* horizons. This permeability, in turn, triggers system response as a whole, producing differentiation along available discretionary dimensions that enable organizationally purposive adjustment to the end of maintaining maximal manipulatory latitude with respect to its environment. In this light, we might understand, for example, how the Marxist critique of corporate capitalism actually promotes the survival of the corporate system by articulating for it—and thereby influencing the system toward accommodating—potentially dysfunctional contingencies in its communication environment. Through responding selectively, the capitalist system has been able to detach the issues of working-class interest from the substantive contradiction of class consciousness. We can grasp in greater detail some of the mechanisms of generalized motivation by means of an abbreviated analysis of the multivocal or polysemic character of symbolism. Ricoeur (1970) conceptualizes symbolic polysemy in terms of duplicated intentionality structures, as well as in terms of lexical double-meaning expressions. For instance, in *Freud and Philosophy*, he writes "Symbols occur when language produces signs of a composite degree in which the meaning, not satisfied with designating some one thing, designates another meaning attainable in and through the first intentionality" (p. 35). First-level meaning bears within itself and invokes a collection of symbolic connotations. We can avoid the linguistic cul-de-sac of patency/latency by playing upon an insight from Geertz (1973): symbols are descriptively thick by virtue of concentrating many layers and nuances of meaning from within the cultural field.

If we approach organizational symbolism on the basis of its suffusing a field of action, then the symbolically generalized action system permeated by multiple meaning potential inscribes orientations that create a range of possible selections that allow organizational actors to particularize experience and action. Organization understood as an interpretative cultural system surpasses any of its possible specifications through the thematic ordering of meanings and acts but does not exist apart from these multiple particularizations. That the organization is a symbolic interpretative system means that the organization is open on its communication environment in such a way that, by interlocking sense and action premises, any locally (in terms of the system) functional combination of sense and action can be articulated and "lived" by a particular organizational subunit. The symbolically suffused action system can be centered from any point within the communication network and then spread (be interpreted) from that point in any interpersonal, temporal, or practical direction. Individuals and groups actualize ("enact") available meaning contingencies, thereby idiosyncratically reproducing generalized communication codes. In doing so, individuals and subunits interpretatively define themselves and organization at large by way of their practical orientations of interest.

Each particular locates itself within the generalized field of action. "Organizational reality" emerges only against something that reflects it, that institutes it, by making it a referent of experience and action. The organizational communication code furnishes the ground for the figure of particularized organizational reality.

Just as holds true for culture, no particular organizational subunit, whether individual or aggregate, can render the organization as a whole the actual object of action or experience. Every organizational interest, however valid, constitutes only a partial reflection of the very symbolically generalized organizational communication structure that sustains it. The outside-in and inside-out perspectives, much like conflict and agreement, or organizational attraction and repulsion, compose extreme selection correlates within the organizational interpretative communication system itself; not only do these require one another in order to have any intrinsic experiential sense, they may actually prove in some cases to be functional equivalents. Thus, for example, no significant influence on a variable like productivity may be unambiguously attributable to specific items like worker satisfaction, reward scales, leadership styles, "climate" variations, and the like. Interactions belonging to this order may depend on broader historical, social, material, and cultural meaning-contingencies informing the interpretative communication system that has emerged historically over and against a particular environment. In any case, the elasticity of the meaning system presupposes some discretionary latitude in processing all such inputs.

Lesson 4: Organizational Motivation is Key

The concept of *motivation* used in this discussion is phenomenological. The phenomenological notion of motivation employs it as a descriptive concept expressing the deployment of situated possibilities for significative coupling. One phenomenon "implies" another not by virtue of an objective or causal relationship, but in light of the meaning orientation the phenomenon exhibits to some human subjects. This is the *raison de etre* given along with every practical circumstance that motivates (guides) the experiential flow of a phenomenon without its explicitly being laid down in any specific aspect of the circumstance. The motivational *telos* resides in the potential for experiential intersubjective validation of the motivational "it makes sense that . . ." and practically in the possible intersubjective performability of the "I can." Together, these social orientations hold open the environment to cognitive and volitional manipulation (Merleau-Ponty, 1981).

Motivation is present in the decision to participate in some project. A motivated project has its original reference in some factual circumstance that furnishes a referential, experiential core in relation to which the reasons for undertaking the task are deployed. A psychological motive is a subjective antecedent that "acts" (or better, is "enacted") only by virtue of its intersubjective significance or meaningfulness. It is the decision that affirms the existence of psychological motives and thereby gives them force of significance under public as well as private scrutiny. Motive and decision are two aspects within a meaning-laden situation. *Motive* is the situation as a reason, and *decision* is the reason as undertaken.

Interest describes motivation perceived as a possibility-undertaken with reference to a future practical circumstance. *Legitimation*, in turn, describes the articulated enactment of interest accomplished by reflectively ordering motivation in terms of previous or inherited symbolic relationships with the organizational communication system. Organizations bind individuals to them by stimulating and structuring interests which, in turn, individuals legitimate reflexively by ordering these interests on the basis of organizational reality codes. The absolute potential diversity of an organization's ability to motivate individuals corresponds to the diversity potential of its communication code. At the same time, the potential diversity of an organization's communication code neither can nor should be nearly as complex as the diversity of all the individual members it employs.

The organizational interpretative system operates by selecting premises for action and providing, thereby, themes or core situations for the idiosyncratic generation of interest and legitimation. In short, it functions by reducing complexity. In so doing, the organizational interpretative system manages "to express" all of its members by simultaneously meaning more than and less than any of its members could ever possibly experience or act upon. Within the limits set by entry and exit rationalizations (themselves already communication horizons), organizations establish a meaning-context for their members in terms of which individuals and groups "make sense" by orienting themselves on the basis of sustainable legitimate interests constructed upon action premises selected by the organizational communication code.

Lesson 5: Getting Contingency Straight

Contingency is a key concept because it underpins the relationship of communication and communication media to social action systems. It offers a possible explanation for how and why the creation of shared meaning enables the formation and functioning of organizations. Such systems presume two areas of contingency: (a) rules for joining or leaving because there exist members and nonmembers, and (b) the role of membership rules determines what behaviors are to be enacted in the organizations.

The level of contingency of each of these two areas is higher than is the level of contingency of the relationship between the two areas. The process of organizing governs this relationship so that "one can characterize the organization mechanism in terms of the systematizing of the relationships between contingencies," because, within the social action system which is the organization, there is a great "need for context . . . to reduce the population of puns and the meaning of puns" (Weick, 1979, p. 183).

For the purpose of communicating this meaning, namely, for guiding choice, the language code is insufficient because, by its very nature, language contains both the possibility of affirmation (compliance) and that of negation (rejection). The more complex the action system, the greater the need for a functional differentiation between the language code in general and special, symbolically generalized communication media, like power, truth, trust, or money, which serve to condition and regulate the motivation for accepting offered selections. These devices greatly increase the efficiency of the system by creating generalized motivational reality constructs.

In part, generalized motivational reality constructs account for what researchers once described as the "climate" of a given organization—the intangible quality of AT&T that distinguishes it from IBM, particularly from the perspective of an organizational member. It accounts for the organization's philosophy, for "the way things are done," for both the typical behavior and the deviations allowed to co-exist. It accounts for the many day-to-day actions that conduct business in a manner unassuming, reliable, and self-perpetuating. It is the stuff that is the organization, the living matter that, like the cells of the body, renews it, containing the patterns which are the blueprints for the entity's structure and functioning, being composed of individual units and yet superseding mere collectivity, enabling growth and adaptation. These constructs also serve as the coding scheme for the text of the organization, as the gatekeepers of ever-present and constantly growing contingency. This task exhausts the utility of language, and so specialized communication media develop to carry out these functions for the system or organization.

A *communication medium* is defined as a mechanism communicating meaning in addition to or as a supplement to language; a code of generalized symbols that guides the transmission of selections. Communication media also have a motivating function, which is to "urge the acceptance of (the other's) selections and make that acceptance the object of expectation" (Luhmann, 1979, p. 232). When the manner of one partner's selection serves simultaneously as a motivating structure for the other, a communication medium can be said to have been formulated. Such formulation is self-reinforcing, drawing the following two assumptions: (a) media-guided communication processes bind partners who complete their own selections and know about this from each other, and (b) the transference of selections means the reproduction of selections in simplified conditions abstracted from initial contexts.

The processes of simplification and abstraction presuppose symbol usage and the formulation of symbolically generalized codes. To take the case in point, power functions as a communication medium by ordering situations which contain double selectivity (yes or no). Power assumes that:

1. Uncertainty exists in relation to the power-holder's selections; in other words, for whatever reason, the power-holder has more than one available alternative. Furthermore, exercising this choice produces in or removes uncertainty from the power-receiver.

2. Alternatives are available to the power-receiver. From this, it follows that power is the influencing of the selection of action or nonaction in the face of multiple possibilities. Power can be said to be greater if it can exert influence in the face of attractive alternatives, and it increases as there is an increase in freedom for the power-receiver.

Therefore, power is a communication medium: the function of a communication medium is to transmit reduced complexity, rather than emphasizing the result(s) of power. Power as a media code regulates contingency by relating it to a possible—and not only an actual—discrepancy between the selection of the power-holder and the power-receiver, and it serves to remove that discrepancy. By extrapolating this, we can say that power secures possible chains of results independently of the will of the power-receiver. Not against the receiver's will, but indifferently or independently of that will; for power is not here a cause but rather a catalyst: it accelerates events, thereby increasing the probability of the ratio of effective connections between the system and the environment. In other words, power is an opportunity to increase the probability of realizing improbable selection combinations.

To recapitulate, power within an organizational (action) system exhibits the capacity to influence the individual's choice among available selections simply by translating preferred selections into expectations. In this way, power contributes to the articulation of the "doing" environment comprised by the organization.

Moreover, by defining power as a communication medium, it becomes possible to avoid conceptualizing power as a possession or as a characteristic of individuals. Rather, to successfully employ power within any organization, the individual must learn to access the power code. Similarly, it is true that theories of power abound in sociological literature, and in that form are often imported by a number of disciplines, including communication, and there most notably in the areas of interpersonal and organizational communication. One characteristic shared by most, if not all, of these theories is the view that power is something that is somehow communicated, and not something that communicates. This is a significant and theoretically useful distinction, for it follows from this that power—as a communication medium—as something that "communicates"—is an articulation of the system (the organization) in the same way that technology in general represents an articulation of its environment (human society), that is, like an iceberg, much of it is actually submerged from the view of its users/participants.

Furthermore, it is now possible to make a distinction between the code and the communication process, so that power is not considered to be the possession either of an individual or a group, that is, not as an inherent attribute or as a characteristic. Rather, the rules for power attribution are themselves contained in the media code. It is this which allows for a separation to be drawn between the "man" and the "office." The implicit and socially embedded nature of communication media make such a reflexive posture possible. This reflexivity greatly increases the efficiency of the system and serves also to aid in guaranteeing its future and continued effectiveness.

This implicit nature of communication media also raises the issue of the identification of the code, in this case, of power. The recognition of power constitutes a special problem, for in order to recognize power there must be a means for measuring power. The preceding description of power makes clear the necessity for a multidimensional measure. Because such a measure does not yet exist, substitutes for exact comparison of power have developed. Briefly, these substitutes are hierarchy, history of the system (i.e., precedents are established, normalized, and then generalized as expectations) and semicontractual arrangements. By these means, direct communicative recourse to power is replaced by these normalizing symbols that also assume a presumed power differential. This is similar to judging the existence and presence of electricity by way of the glow of the light bulb rather than by physically contacting electrical current. And once again, it highlights the embedded nature of communication media.

It is perhaps nowhere more true than within government bureaucracy that "the actual power in organizations depends . . . on influence on careers" (Jasko, 1985, p. 92). To have a successful career, the hopeful candidate must perform all the right organizational moves—including making peer alliances. To do so involves accepting, even anticipating, the implicit motivational imperatives embedded in the organizational text. One needs to make the proper selections, performing the correct actions. In the world of federal employment, few employees of professional standing are ever fired.

These theoretical concepts of generalized motivational reality constructs and generalized symbolic communication media represent an aspect of a genuine communication perspective. This is true because these concepts place communication in a central theoretical position by asserting that such communication processes are more fundamental than any particular form of social organizing, including formal organizing and, therefore, it is reasonable to regard communication as an object of investigation that is the fundamental enabling characteristic of all human social activity.

EPILOGUE

This chapter presents a rethinking of organizing and organizational research within the context of community-based research. Our thinking is not complete nor will it be. But from a practical point of view, we have become engaged in what we may call *community-based marketing*. Community-based marketing is the buying and selling of power to communities, not in the traditional sense of marketing as the "manipulation of needs," but rather of establishing an exchange relationship where there was none, particularly in the service of economic development. It is in this light that the mass media became relevant and should have been utilized more effectively by our consortium.

The goal remains: to develop community-based networks to improve their quality of community. Community-based rethinking is an efficient process that is based on the principle that information and recognition are power. From the community's point of view, power means the community either achieves or is enabled to achieve some goal. The premise of community-based marketing is based on lessons from our studies; persons do not live as solitary, random individuals, but live in and through their membership in community groups or organizations. The rationale for integrating the mass media into community-based marketing is viable because the media require economic return, and communities deal in economic return. Community groups and organizations view mass media, particularly television, as a source of power. It can influence, manipulate, select, and distribute good and bad information. It can make famous, pacify, or disempower someone. Community groups and organizations are formed to become powerful, or increase their power. They will buy into whoever will facilitate their quest for power. As such, the general principle learned from our project is that journalists and reporters could be trained or convinced to be community-based researchers and marketers as they are viewed as powerbrokers anyway by the community. Academics have to demonstrate their ability to be powerbrokers as well. This also requires a rethinking of social science as a deliverer of practical (power) truths.

References

A Citizens' Study of the Franklin County Municipal Court. (1975). Court Watching Project, Inc., 1510 Neil Avenue.

Apel, K. O. (1980). *Towards the transformation of philosophy.* London: Routledge & Kegan Paul.

Battle, S. (1987). *The black adolescent parent.* Binghamton, NY: Haworth Press.

Baxter, E., & Hopper, K. (1980). Pathologies of place and disorders of mind, health. *PAC Bulletin, 11*(4), iff.

Bent, A.E. (1974). *The politics of law enforcement.* Lexington, MA: Lexington Books.

Bott, E. (1957). *Family and social networks.* London: Tavistock.

Burtless, G. (1984). *Public spending for the poor: Trends, prospects and economic limits.* Paper presented at the IRP Conference, University of Wisconsin, Madison.

Cicourel, A. (1964). *Method and measurement in sociology.* New York: Free Press.

Cloward, R., & Ohlin, V. (1960). *Delinquency and opportunity: A theory of delinquent gangs.* Glencoe, IL: Free Press.

Cohen, J. (1967). Chinese mediation on the eve of modernization. *Journal of Asian and African Studies, 2,* 1-14.

Court Watching Project Report, Number 3. (1981). Court Watching Project, Inc., 2674 Westmont Blvd.

Dash, L. (1989). *When children want children.* Fairfield, CT: William Morrow.

Duo, L. (1973). Dispute settlement in Chinese-American communities. *American Journal of Comparative Law, 21,* 10-22.

Economic Report of the President. (1984). Washington, DC: Government Printing Office.

Etzioni, A. (1981, Fall). Refugee resettlement: The infighting in Washington. *The Public Interest.*

Fein, H. (1987). *Congregational sponsors of Indochinese refugees in the U.S., 1979-1981.* Princeton, NJ: Associated University Presses.

Fisher, A. B. (1983). Differential effects of serial composition and hierachical contest on interaction patterns in dyads. *Human Communication Research, 3*(9), 225-238.

Frieden, B. J. (1968). Housing and national urban goals: Old police and new realities. In J. Q. Wilson (Ed.), *The metropolitan enigma* (pp. 21-37). Cambridge, MA: Harvard University Press.

Geertz, C. (1973). *The interpretation of cultures.* New York: Basic Books.

Gottschalk, A. (1984). *Macroeconomic conditions, income transfers and the nonpoor* (IRP Series). Madison: University of Wisconsin.

Habermas, J. (1970a). *Toward a rational society* (J. Shapiro, Trans.). Boston: Beacon Press.

Habermas, J. (1970b). Toward a theory of communicative competence. *Recent Sociology, 2,* 115-148.

hooks, b. (1989). *Talking back: Thinking feminist, thinking black.* Boston: South End Press.

Hyman, H. (1954). *Interviewing in social research.* Chicago: University of Chicago Press.

Ingleby, D. (1980). *Critical psychiatry: The politics of mental health.* New York: Pantheon.

Jasko, S. (1985). *Communication and organization.* Masters thesis. Ohio State University, Columbus, OH.

Kolodny, R. (1979). *Exploring new strategies for improving public housing.* Management Office and Policy Development and Research, U. S. Department of Housing and Urban Development. Washington, DC: GPO.

Lewis, D. A., & Salem, G. (1981). *Community crime prevention: An analysis of a developing strategy.* Beverly Hills, CA: Sage.

Liebow, E. (1967). *Tally's corner: A study of streetcorner men.* Boston: Little Brown.

Lincoln, Y., & Guba, E. (1985). *Naturalistic inquiry.* Newbury Park, CA: Sage.

Lingis, A. (1982). Abject communication. In J. Pilotta (Ed.), *Interpersonal communication: Essays in phenomenology and hermeneutics.* Washington, DC: University Press of America.

Low Income Housing Service. (1985). *The 1986 low income housing budget* (Special memorandum No. 21). Washington, DC: Author.

Lubman, S. (1967). Man and mediation: Politics and dispute resolution in communist China. *California Law Review, 35,* 29-42.

Luhmann, N. (1975). *Macht.* Stuttgart: Ferdinand Eake.

Luhmann, N. (1979). Trust and power (H. Davis, J. Ruftran, & K. Rooney, Trans.). New York: Wiley.

Luhmann, N. (1982). *The differentiation of society.* New York: Columbia University Press.

Luhmann, N. (1995). *Social systems* (J. Bedwarz, & D. Baecker, Trans.). Stanford, CA: Stanford University Press.

Lundmann, R. J. (1980). Routine police practices: A commonwealth perspective. In R. J. Lundmann (Ed.), *Police behavior: A sociological perspective* (pp. 182-200). New York: Oxford Press.

Mattelart, A. (1983). *Technology, culture and communication: Research and policy practices in France.* Philadelphia, PA: Annenberg School Press.

McGillis, D. (1986). *Community dispute resolution programs and public policy.* Washington, DC: U.S. Dept. of Justice, National Institute of Justice, Office of Communications Research Utilization.

McGillis, D., & Mullin, J. (1977). *Neighborhood justice centers: An analysis of potential models.* Washington, DC: U.S. Government Printing Office.

Merleau-Ponty, M. (1968). *Visible and invisible.* Evanston, IL: Northwestern University Press.

Merleau-Ponty, M. (1974). *The phenomenology of perception.* New York: Humanities Press.

Merleau-Ponty, M. (1981). *Phenomenology of perception.* New York: Humanities Press.

Mickunas, A. (1977). Human action and historical time. *Phenomenological Research, 1,* 60-61.

Mickunas, A. (1983). The primacy of interpretive understanding in social research, In J. Murphy & J. Pilotta (Eds.), *Qualitative methodology, theory, and application: A guide for social practitioners.* Dubuque, IA: Kendall/Hunt.

Monterro, D. (1980). The Vietnamese refugees in America: Patterns of socioeconomic adaptation. *International Migration Review, 13,* 1-17.

Moore, K. (1986). *Choice and circumstance: Racial differences in adolescent sexuality and fertility.* New Brunswick, NJ: Transaction Books.

Murphy, J., & Pilotta, J. (1983a). Community-based evaluation for criminal justice planning. *Social Service Review, 57*(3), 465-477.

Murphy, J., & Pilotta J. (1983b). *Qualitative methodology: Theory and application.* Dubuque, IA: Kendall Hunt.

Natanson, M. (1970). *The journeying self: A study in philosophy and social roles.* Reading, MA: Addison-Wesley.

Nonet, P., & Selznick, P. (1978). *Law & society in transition.* New York: Harper & Row.

O'Connor, R. (1981). Law as indigenous social theory: A Siamese-Thai case. *American Ethnologist, 8,* 8-17.

O'Neill, J. (1975). *Making sense together: An introduction to wild sociology.* London: Heinemann.

O'Neill, J. (1982). Can phenomenology be critical? In *For Marx against Althusser.* Washington, DC: Center for Advanced Research in Phenomenology.

Office of Refugee Resettlement (1982). *Report to Congress.* Washington, DC: Author.

Office of Refugee Resettlement (1983). *Report to Congress.* Washington, DC: Author.

Patton, M. (1980). *Qualitative evaluation methods.* Newbury Park, CA: Sage.

Patton, M. (1990). *Qualitative evaluation and research methods.* Newbury Park, CA: Sage.

Piana, G. (1972). History and existence in Husserl. *Telos, 13,* 114.

Pilotta, J. (Ed.). (1982). *Interpersonal communication: Essays in phenomenology and hermeneutics.* Washington, DC: University Press of America.

Pilotta, J., Murphy, J., Jones, T., & Wilson, E. (1981). Trends in community perception of social service planning. *Evaluation News, 5,* 5.

Piven, F., & Cloward, R. (1971). *Regulating the poor: The functions of public welfare.* New York: Vintage Books.

Ricoeur, P. (1970). *Freud and philosophy: An essay on interpretation* (D. Savage, Trans.). New Haven, CT: Yale University Press.

Rose, S. M. (1979). Decophering deinstitutionalization. *Milbank Memorial Fund Quarterly, 57,* 429-460.

Schutz, A. (1964). Equality and the meaning structure of the social world. In T. Luckman (Ed.), *Collected papers II: Studies in social theory* (pp. 226-273). The Hague: Martinus Nijhoff.

Schutz, A. (1967). *The phenomenology of the social world.* Evanston, IL: Northwestern University Press.

Scull, A. (1977). *Decarceration—community treatment and the deviants: A radical view.* Englewood Cliffs, NJ: Prentice-Hall.

Simmel, G. (1964). *The sociology of Georg Simmel* (K. H. Wolff, Trans.). New York: The Free Press.

Simms, M. (1986). *Slipping through the cracks: The status of black women.* New Brunswick, NJ: Transaction Books.

Starr, P., & Roberts, A. (1982). Community structures and Vietnamese refugee adaptation: The significance of context. *International Migration Review, 16,* 15-28.

Stein, B. (1979). Occupational adjustment of refugees: The Vietnamese in the United States. *International Migration Review, 12,* 10-28.

U.S. Bureau of the Census. (1982e). *Statistical abstracts of the United States: 1982-3.* Washington, DC: Government Printing Office.

U.S. Bureau of the Census. (1984f). *Statistical abstracts of the United States: 1984.* Washington, DC: Government Printing Office.

U.S. Congress, Committee on Ways and Means, Subcommittee on Public Assistance. (1986, February). *Pregnancy among black teenagers.* Washington, DC: Author.

Weber, M. (1970). Science as a vocation. In H. H. Gerth & C. W. Mills (Trans.), *From Max Weber: Essays in sociology* (pp. 129-158). New York: Oxford University Press.

Weick, K. (1979). *Social psychology of organization* (2nd ed.). New York: McGraw-Hill.

Widman, T. L. (1982). The philosophical problem of the objective historical sciences. In J. Pilotta (Ed.), *Interpersonal communication: Essays in phenomenology and hermeneutics* (pp. 133-137). Washington, DC: University Press of America.

Wilson, W. (1987). *The truly disadvantaged: The inner city, the underclass, and public policy.* Chicago: University of Chicago Press.

Wing, J. K. (1979). Comments and conclusions. In M. Meacher (Ed.), *New methods of mental health care* (pp. 209-220). London: Pergamon Press.

Zimmerman, D. (1969). Record keeping and the intake process in a public welfare agency. In S. Wheeler (Ed.), *On record; Files and dossiers in American life* (pp. 319-354). New York: Russell Sage Foundation.

Author Index

Subject Index

Please remember that this is a library book,
and that it belongs only temporarily to each
person who uses it. Be considerate. Do
not write in this, or any, library book.